Heidegger

HEIDEGGER

PHENOMENOLOGY, ECOLOGY, POLITICS

MICHAEL MARDER

University of Minnesota Press
Minneapolis
London

An earlier version of chapter 1 was published as "'Higher Than Actuality'—On the Possibility of Phenomenology in Heidegger," *Indo-Pacific Journal of Phenomenology* 5, no. 2 (December 2005): 1–10. An earlier version of chapter 2 was published as "Heidegger's 'Phenomenology of Failure' in *Sein und Zeit*," *Philosophy Today* 51, no. 1 (Spring 2007): 69–78. Chapter 3 was originally published as "The Phenomenology of Ontico-Ontological Difference," *Bulletin d'Analyse Phénoménologique* 8, no. 2 (2012): 1–20. An earlier version of chapter 4 was published as "To Open a Site (with Heidegger): Toward a Phenomenology of Ecological Politics," *Epoché* 21, no. 1 (Fall 2016): 197–217. An earlier version of chapter 5 was originally published as "Devastation," in *Heidegger and the Global Age*, ed. Antonio Cerella and Louiza Odysseos (London: Rowman and Littlefield, International, 2017). An earlier version of chapter 6 was originally published as "The Ecology of Property: On What Is Heidegger's and Bibikhin's Own," in *Heidegger in Russia and Eastern Europe*, ed. Jeff Love, 205–22 (London: Rowman and Littlefield, International, 2017). Earlier versions of chapters 7 and 9 were originally published in Martin Heidegger, *On Hegel's "Philosophy of Right": The 1934–35 Seminar and Interpretative Essays*, ed. Peter Trawny, Marcia Sá Cavalcante-Schuback, and Michael Marder, 37–48 and 83–93 (London and New York: Bloomsbury, 2014). An earlier version of chapter 8 was originally published in *Heidegger's Black Notebooks: Responses to Anti-Semitism*, ed. Andrew J. Mitchell and Peter Trawny; copyright 2017 Columbia University Press; reprinted with permission of Columbia University Press.

Published by the University of Minnesota Press
111 Third Avenue South, Suite 290
Minneapolis, MN 55401-2520
http://www.upress.umn.edu

ISBN 978-1-5179-0502-6 (hc)
ISBN 978-1-5179-0503-3 (pb)

A Cataloging-in-Publication record for this book is available from the Library of Congress.

HEIDEGGER

PHENOMENOLOGY, ECOLOGY, POLITICS

MICHAEL MARDER

University of Minnesota Press
Minneapolis
London

An earlier version of chapter 1 was published as "'Higher Than Actuality'—On the Possibility of Phenomenology in Heidegger," *Indo-Pacific Journal of Phenomenology* 5, no. 2 (December 2005): 1–10. An earlier version of chapter 2 was published as "Heidegger's 'Phenomenology of Failure' in *Sein und Zeit,*" *Philosophy Today* 51, no. 1 (Spring 2007): 69–78. Chapter 3 was originally published as "The Phenomenology of Ontico-Ontological Difference," *Bulletin d'Analyse Phénoménologique* 8, no. 2 (2012): 1–20. An earlier version of chapter 4 was published as "To Open a Site (with Heidegger): Toward a Phenomenology of Ecological Politics," *Epoché* 21, no. 1 (Fall 2016): 197–217. An earlier version of chapter 5 was originally published as "Devastation," in *Heidegger and the Global Age,* ed. Antonio Cerella and Louiza Odysseos (London: Rowman and Littlefield, International, 2017). An earlier version of chapter 6 was originally published as "The Ecology of Property: On What Is Heidegger's and Bibikhin's Own," in *Heidegger in Russia and Eastern Europe,* ed. Jeff Love, 205–22 (London: Rowman and Littlefield, International, 2017). Earlier versions of chapters 7 and 9 were originally published in Martin Heidegger, *On Hegel's "Philosophy of Right": The 1934–35 Seminar and Interpretative Essays,* ed. Peter Trawny, Marcia Sá Cavalcante-Schuback, and Michael Marder, 37–48 and 83–93 (London and New York: Bloomsbury, 2014). An earlier version of chapter 8 was originally published in *Heidegger's Black Notebooks: Responses to Anti-Semitism,* ed. Andrew J. Mitchell and Peter Trawny; copyright 2017 Columbia University Press; reprinted with permission of Columbia University Press.

Published by the University of Minnesota Press
111 Third Avenue South, Suite 290
Minneapolis, MN 55401-2520
http://www.upress.umn.edu

ISBN 978-1-5179-0502-6 (hc)
ISBN 978-1-5179-0503-3 (pb)

A Cataloging-in-Publication record for this book is available from the Library of Congress.

UMP LSI

Für P, mein "Stehen in der Lichtung des Seins"

Contents

Introduction

Heidegger's Eternal Triangle

On July 20, 2014, I published a small article titled "A Fight for the Right to Read Heidegger" in "The Stone" column of the *New York Times*.[1] Predictably enough, given a long buildup of controversies aimed at delegitimizing Heidegger, my argument concerning a profound disconnect between his anti-Semitic prejudice and his philosophy gave rise to hundreds of comments, some of them vitriol-filled. Among these, one stood out for me, its concluding sentences reading: "Not only language but thought takes a holiday when we come to Heidegger. Beware, he still stalks the world."

I asked myself upon scanning through these lines: Where else but on holiday—vacated of or vacationing away from pragmatic, instrumental concerns—does thought truly think and language speak? The holiday in question is not necessarily a beach vacation (and there is nothing reprehensible about taking a beach vacation!) but a more general release to and for the possible and its play, which is only the province of phenomenology insofar as it is an exemplar of thinking.

Then there is the issue of the world. It is ironic, to say the least, to accuse of stalking the world a philosopher who has given us a renewed appreciation of this originally theological term, dissociated it from "global" affairs, and handed it over to secular, existential, and ecological considerations.

Finally, a warning: "Beware, he still stalks the world!" Still—in the twenty-first century, well after his death! Beware: Heidegger is a specter, akin to the specter of communism that has made its bombastic appearance in the first lines of Marx and Engels's *Communist Manifesto*. Which world does he haunt? Or, better, whose world? That of a technocratic stricture, where possibilities are unlimited so long as they are indexed to "technological innovation"? That of unremitting calculation and quantification, insinuating the phenomenology of capital into the fabric of life (and death)? That of the expanding worldlessness, where—devalorized, leveled down, and homogenized—the place becomes a passage on the way to nowhere? (To be sure, *nowhere* is always the final destination, but one can travel there slowly or quickly, taking one's time or squandering it, veering off to unexpected detours or running into it head-on, caring for the beings one encounters along the way or dragging them along indiscriminately as if in a bottom-trawling net toward an end that is not theirs . . .)

Over and above the minor episode my *New York Times* op-ed occasioned, it would not be an exaggeration to say that Martin Heidegger was the most controversial philosopher of the twentieth century. A polarizing figure, he has, beyond a shadow of doubt, influenced generations of intellectuals who have since become canonical in their own right, from Hannah Arendt to Jacques Derrida. Most recently, however, the publication of *Black Notebooks*[2] has spawned further negative reactions to Heidegger's body of work, with some contemporary philosophers, many among them former "Heideggerians," willing to discard his contributions *in toto* on account of his involvement with Nazism and the blatantly anti-Semitic statements peppering these personal-intellectual diaries. The sentiment among the liberal critics of Heidegger is the most uncompromising, as they insist that his practical political stance in the 1930s hopelessly taints his philosophy and blocks any promising ecological potential that may reside in it. They see in *Black Notebooks* the last nail in the coffin of the German philosopher's intellectual legacy, to be shelved, at best, with studies in the intellectual history of twentieth-century totalitarianism.

By now the Heidegger controversy has entered something of a cyclical rhythm, extinguishing and rekindling every ten years or so. Some notable galvanizing moments in its decadal comebacks are Victor Farias's 1987 *Heidegger and Nazism*;[3] the anthology *The Heidegger Controversy* edited in 1992 by Richard Wolin,[4] its publication inciting acrimonious polemics between the editor and Thomas Sheehan, on the one hand, and Jacques Derrida, who withdrew his interview from the book, on the other;[5] and

Emmanuel Faye's 2005 *Heidegger: The Introduction of Nazism into Philosophy*.[6] Released in 2014, the first volumes of Heidegger's *Black Notebooks* added fuel to the fire of scandal, given the philosophical implications of the anti-Semitic remarks they feature. A salient example these new materials contain is the attribution of *Bodenlosigkeit* (lack of soil) to the figure of a Jew, "attached to nothing, making everything serviceable to itself,"[7] in a prefiguration of modern uprooting, which eschews any and all particular belonging. The anti-ecological position Heidegger pins on "Jewry" (*Judentum*) culminates in the unleashing of the deadliest possibility—to make everything serviceable, disregarding the unique possibilities of the beings themselves—and a technocratic politics oblivious to the place of shared existence. While his diagnosis of the prevalent *Weltanschauung* and of the planetary malaise caused by a total (ontic *and* ontological) uprooting is germane to the self-understanding of humanity in late-capitalist modernity, the argument's anti-Semitic trappings threaten to overshadow its critical acumen and embolden the detractors of Heidegger to pronounce his philosophy rotten to the core, with anti-Semitism infecting its very *essence*.

What reawakens each time with the controversy, or what reawakens *it*, is the desire to expel Heidegger and to expunge his contributions from the canon of Western philosophy or from what may be legitimately taught, interpreted, and discussed in self-respecting philosophy departments. But the target of these attacks, personal as they are, is not really Heidegger-the-man, much less Heidegger-the-thinker, seeing that no real effort goes into working through and understanding his texts. Instead, it is everything and everyone he is associated with, not the least posthumously, that is at the receiving end of these proxy wars: in the discipline of philosophy—the "Continental tradition," whose "analytic" detractors delegitimize it by locating its origins in the theoretical position Heidegger took as part of his bitter 1929–31 dispute with Rudolf Carnap; and in the realm of ideology—the opposition to neoliberalism and economic, as well as cultural, globality. The labels "mysticism," "anti-modernism," and "parochialism" stick to his followers (whatever "following" someone in thinking might mean) and to the critics of the currently hegemonic political and economic regimes. And what better way to neutralize a serious threat to the status quo than to saddle it with the weight of past, pre-capitalist, almost feudal oppression, making the "flexibilization" and "mobility" of the workforce look much more alluring than the need for dwelling and learning to live abidingly?

Diffracted through the prism of Heidegger's allegedly inveterate and systemic Nazism, the ecological overtones of his philosophy are received as relics of a close-minded attitude, glorifying German nature *because* it stands for the environing world (*Umwelt*) of the national existence (*Dasein*) proper to the German *Volk*. Attachment to a locale, to a place, and finally to the earth are seen as his reactive, telluric responses to modernization, to cosmopolitanism, to Soviet and American "internationalisms," and, more recently, to globalization. The occasional disparaging remarks Heidegger has made concerning Jewish "rootlessness," akin to the one we've just spotted above, seem to corroborate this hypothesis.

Compelling as the contemptuous readings of Heidegger now in vogue might appear, they overlook a point pertinent both to methodological issues and to matters of substance, namely, that it is impossible to understand his philosophy without understanding his lifelong commitment to phenomenology. As I maintain in the book you are about to read, Heidegger's metaphysical anti-Semitism surfaces in those moments when the phenomenological and fundamental-ontological supports for his thinking, concentrated in the power of the question and in the primacy of possibility over actuality, are at their weakest. If so, then it is futile to reconstruct a "Nazi-leaning" phenomenology of German national existence and its Jewish "negation" in Heidegger's *oeuvre*, since, at the end of such a reconstruction, we will have on our hands nothing more than the formal and crystallized theses that have been spared the impact of deformalization and critique. Regretfully, Heidegger himself failed—and I problematize the notion of failure by resorting to the key tenets of his thinking in chapter 2—to follow through his methodological recommendations with regard to the "Jewish question." This failure, nonetheless, should be seen frankly for what it is: a deviation from his core philosophical commitments and the relaxation of phenomenological vigilance that is only essential to the extent that the possibility of failure is essential to existential actuality.

As is well known, the radical temporalization of thinking in the 1920s and the rejection of transcendental subjectivity, along with its constitutive analysis, distinguish Heidegger's phenomenology from Husserl's. The emphasis on time, born from finite existence itself, is sufficient to throw into doubt the spatially based interpretations of German, as opposed to Jewish, being. Along these lines, chapter 8 argues, in the spirit of Heidegger, that national existence no longer hinges on rootedness in a given territorial domain but in a tradition, that is to say, the historical temporality of *Mitdasein*. Departing from and constantly circling back to the temporal character of Dasein, we must therefore be more—not less—Heideggerian than Heidegger himself in order to right the philosophical wrongs scattered on the margins of his works.

More than that, as we will discover in chapter 5, Heidegger holds the conception of the environing world as a territory to be typically Roman, wrong, and imperialist. Ecology is decisively non- or anti-territorial (or anti-territorialist); its view of the world is that of a dwelling place (*oikos*) where, in an existential a priori, one finds oneself articulated and articulating (*logos*) alongside and with others. In turn, neither Heidegger's politics nor his ecological thinking should be scrutinized in isolation not only from each other but also from the phenomenological framework they are a part of. *Voilà* the "eternal triangle" in the title of this introduction—not, as some might have supposed, the love triangle, in which the thinker was caught up with his wife, Elfride, and his gifted student Hannah Arendt, followed by a number of other women later on. To state it succinctly (and this will be the philosophical leitmotif running through the rest of the book): Heidegger's ecology is eminently phenomenological and political, while his politics are inherently eco-phenomenological, and his phenomenology is "genetically" politico-ecological.

Why is the phenomenological piece of the puzzle, omitted from virtually all standard attacks on Heidegger, decisive for a levelheaded and patient assessment of his works and their philosophical potential? Phenomenology, according to Heidegger, is the realm of the possible unbridled from the actual. A phenomenological procedure, for instance, geared toward political and ecological "realities," is not enthralled with a largely unelaborated and taken-for-granted attachment to the past; rather, it is steered by existential (finite) possibilities, including those emanating from the historical past where they have been left behind. Far from a species of conservatism dressed up in philosophical subtleties and worshipping the fetishes of nation and nature, Heidegger's method seeks orientation from the possibilities for a continued dwelling and thinking. As such, it counters the assorted avatars of modernity (from liberalism and capitalism to socialism and technologicism) that, in the name of absolute possibility and total openness, squander and foreclose singular possibilities, both ecological and political. Hence, phenomenological possibility, like the possibility *of* phenomenology itself, is an opening on a finite horizon, a clearing in the density of what necessarily remains unclarified (the psychologically or psychoanalytically inclined would say *unconscious*; we could also add the *body* and *matter* to the mix), a "thrown" chance where not everything is uniformly possible. In this vein, Part I elaborates the constitutive nature of this delimited possibility in Heidegger's phenomenology.

We should not, for all that, conflate phenomenological possibility with yet another incarnation of a crypto-Kantian transcendentalism, stressing the abstract and ideal conditions of possibility for experience. The argument latent in much of Heidegger's corpus is that the conditioning is itself conditioned by the vicissitudes of political and ecological existence, by the historical shape being-with-other (*Mitsein; Mitdasein*) assumes, and by the ecological milieu within which experiences unfold. Part II of *Heidegger: Phenomenology, Ecology, Politics* explores the ecological enclosure of phenomenological possibility: What is it to open a site ontologically adequate to human dwelling? How does that mode of dwelling suit or not suit the site? In what ways can the immense expansion of that opening inebriated with infinite vastness, transparency, and total clarity become devastating? And what is required for an ecological reappraisal of our relation to things and conceptualization of property?

Despite the fact that none of these issues is independent from political concerns, the latter are dealt with in the third and final part of the book. After revisiting the question regarding the sense of political existence in Heidegger (driven by the possibilities of pre-institutional being-together with others and of dwelling in a place), I examine his incapacity to raise the "Jewish question" phenomenologically, that is, not as a handy answer but as a *question* guarding unrealizable possibilities and refusing the quick fix of a ready-made response. I conclude with a joint reflection with my colleague Marcia Sá Cavalcante-Schuback on how the right to philosophy can be released to existential possibilities and on the political aftershocks of that release.

Phenomenological possibility; the ecology of a site and a habitable—not for much longer, it seems—world; the politics of the possible and of place: Heidegger's eternal triangle makes its eternal return between the lines of all the criticisms and accolades showered on his work. But the triangulation I have just sketched is not exclusive to Heidegger. To a much greater extent than he did, we find ourselves surrounded by its three interlocked sides mapped onto a virtual grid where possibilities, places, and political proceedings shrivel to formalism and abstraction. Although we are dealing with texts by a twentieth-century German thinker, the matter is not a purely academic one, as it pertains to what we refer to as "our contemporary situation," the historical frame (*Gestell*) of being that is "ours," regardless of all the variations in opinions and styles of existence. With periodic flare-ups, the polarization around Heidegger is symptomatic of a sweeping and heated disagreement on how to cope with this frame, how to be and to act within it, if not upon it. So, what if "Heidegger"—not just as a controversial philosopher but, above all, as a *phenomenon*—were the fourth point or corner, bringing the current triangulation of being to visibility? And what if the addition of Heidegger, by throwing our ontological *Gestell* into sharper relief, gave us the chance to reframe this frame, to question its virtual matrix, and to bring down to earth the transcendental forms of possibility, ecological existence, and political life?

Part I
Phenomenology

1. "Higher Than Actuality"

The Possibility of Phenomenology

BEYOND THE MERELY POSSIBLE, OR ON POSSIBILITY THAT IS NOT ITSELF

Paragraph 7 of *Being and Time* famously declares: "Our comments on the preliminary conception of phenomenology have shown that what is essential in it does not lie in its *actuality* as a philosophical 'movement' ["*Richtung*": tendency, direction]. Higher than actuality stands *possibility*. We can understand phenomenology only by seizing it as a possibility [*im Ergreifen ihrer als Möglichkeit*]."[1] But what does phenomenology owe its possibility to? How can we reconstruct the notion of possibility itself on phenomenological grounds? Is possibility something to be "seized," *ergreifen*, on the verge of conceptualization, before passing into a concept, *Begriff*, without remainder? Or is it something one should let be? Do possibilities seized not become opportunities taken from a different, much more pragmatic slant than the one Heidegger has in mind?

To assess the impact of the statement, which has proven programmatic both for Heidegger and for the existentialist philosophy it inspired, I refer to an earlier text, *History of the Concept of Time*, where possibility forms a conceptual bridge between a "radicalized" phenomenology and the existential analytic of Dasein. In a nutshell, possibility makes temporalization (i.e., the very "radicality" of Heidegger's contribution to phenomenology) possible. In contrast to the Scholastic baggage of Brentano's and Husserl's phenomenologies, which view the fulfillment of empty intentionality in intuition on the model of realizing potentiality in actuality, Heidegger toils to exempt the possible from the order that equates it to a deficient, because unfulfilled, actuality. At a distance from the dialectic of the potential and the actual, phenomenological possibility highlights the contours of existence free from the constraints of objective teleology as much as from the modern ideology of unlimited progress.

Since existence is historical through and through, existential possibility is not abstract; it is conditioned by a politically and ecologically inflected finite openness of our world, the world of living together with others and of being within the elemental fold. Theories of intentionality beholden to Scholasticism disregard this double ecopolitical "milieu" of possibility coming to fruition or ending in non-fulfillment. By placing the ecopolitical milieu of the world front and center, Heidegger deformalizes phenomenological possibility, peeling away its abstract qualities, and so revitalizes the possibility of phenomenology itself. Higher than actuality, it turns out to be lower on the ladder of abstraction, or perhaps without any rung on this ladder whatsoever.

Heidegger recasts possibility into a tool for resisting the actuality of phenomenology as a philosophical "movement." Having nothing in common with a dogmatic doctrine, phenomenology guided by the possible is a radical self-critique that undoes its past conclusions and is capable of adapting to, and participating in, the shifting configurations of political and ecological existence. The opportunity it presents breaks out of the cage of pragmatism and opportunism, notably at the levels of thinking, of the history of thought, and of intentionality's embeddedness in the lifeworld that can never be unequivocally assigned the status of a cognitive (or, even, a cognizable) intended object.

Assuming it were possible, then, I panoramically survey the topography of "the possible" in Heidegger. To begin with, "as a modal category of presence-at-hand, possibility signifies what is *not yet* actual and what is *not at any time* necessary. It characterizes the *merely* possible [*das* nur *Mögliche*]" (*SZ* 143). Doesn't Heidegger define possibility simply and unequivocally? "Modal category" undoubtedly refers to Kantian modality, which combines possibility, actuality, and necessity to modify the substratum of the present-at-hand. In relation to the other two modal subcategories, the merely possible is that which is "*not yet* actual," present in the shape of contingency ("what is *not at any time* necessary"). Heidegger's proto-definition, alluding to Kant, confronts us with a contradiction: at variance with the earlier assertion made in paragraph 7, the argument that possibility "signifies what is *not yet* actual" subordinates it to actuality that from a fixed future governs its unfolding. Deficient in comparison to the ideal standard of actuality, possibility is barely distinguished from potentiality awaiting completion and accomplishment. In its mereness, it recoils into a commonplace Heidegger has actually pledged to overturn.

Upon a more careful reading, these sentences reveal nothing more than a negative image of what possibility *is not* or what it *should not* be reduced to. One helpful indication of a greater underlying complexity is the qualification of the remark by "a modal category of presence-at-hand," which is not the only category Heidegger has developed. There is much more to the possible than its present-at-hand mereness; should we reduce it to just *that*, we would let slide both the possibilities of the ready-to-hand and the existential possibilities of Dasein that do not belong in the Kantian table of categories and that, therefore, are not a part of Heidegger's categorial analytic. Another clue lies in how the qualification "merely," *nur*, alludes to deficient actualization. It is not possibility in its full sense but the *merely* possible that is insufficiently actual. Assuming that the definition of possibility in terms of "what is *not yet* actual" and Heidegger's vow to extricate the possible from the lacunae of the actual are valid, we may conclude that the possible is never merely possible, or that, if it is, then it is what it is *not*, exactly when it is (merely) itself.

Now, Heidegger's major preoccupation is not so much with the categorial as with the existential analytic of Dasein, to be retroactively read into everything that goes on in the "tool-analysis." With respect to existence, it is absurd to talk of "what is *not yet* actual," and it is more ludicrous still to invoke "the *merely* possible." The existential possibilities of Dasein and their phenomenological descriptions are never distilled into a pure essence and are never segregated from the impossible; only in and as the impossible does something like the (always impure) possibility of possibility arise and inaugurate futurity and ecstatic temporality itself. Given that, in Heidegger, the impossible is often the index of death,[2] authentic futurity coincides with Dasein's finite existence that "does not have an end at which it just stops" (*SZ* 329). Were it to have an other-than-possible end, finite existence would have been actualized, would have become what it has always already been supposed to be in the moment of death. The irresolvable tension of possibility and impossibility, breaking free from the actual under the cover of death, is best encapsulated in the closing lines of Beckett's *The Unnamable*: "I'll never know, in the silence you don't know, you must go on, I can't go on, I'll go on."[3]

At this point, a brief disclaimer is required so as to appreciate the reverberations of our first step as it bears upon another small chapter in the saga of the knotted intellectual inheritance Derrida received from Heidegger. It is worth noting that "possibility" plays a prominent role in the writings of the French thinker as well—especially in the productivity of aporia, not as poor or "resource-less" as its Greek etymology might suggest. Much of *The Politics of Friendship*, for example, is devoted to a patently Heideggerian discussion of the role possibility plays in temporalization and its implications for political time and for the future. Derrida goes to great lengths to differentiate the halting rhythm of *avenir* (the to-come, which may never come) from the "futureless possible" (*futur*: "life-assured" and guaranteed, a potentiality certain to be actualized) that is not, at least partly, impossible.[4] By way of aporetically enriching the possible with the impossible, he approximates Heidegger's critique of the "merely possible." *Given Time* subverts Kant's transcendental possibility by contending that the conditions of possibility for the gift are the conditions of its impossibility.[5] Even in *Rogues*, the thesis that "democracy to come has always been suicidal"[6] (read: not "life-assured") positions this regime, futural in each of its present iterations, at the forefront of the politics of a self-mutilating existential possibility, possible thanks to the acceptance of its own impossibility.

To return to Heidegger: Dasein's possibilities of being are not contingent or simply "occurrent," *Vorkommen.* Pertaining to a whole range of "possible impossibilities" (such as falling, inauthenticity, and formalization, to mention just a few), they are existentially necessary. This does not imply that existential possibility is antithetical to contingent-occurrent possibility. The former is, indeed, necessary for the latter to occur, to "come to pass," *passieren,* because without Dasein there can be no "world" (*SZ* 64). But the "founding" necessity of existential possibility is not synonymous with the surety of a stable foundation. It is possible *because* it may be not possible, *because* the scarcity of guarantees opens up and simultaneously closes off the futurity of the future, both precluding anything like the actualization of existence *in the last instance* of death and subsuming possibility under the still incomplete actuality. That is why existential possibilities (are any other types of possibility even thinkable without tumbling into the dialectics of potentiality-actuality?) are essentially self-negating, or, as I have put it, self-mutilating.

That which is not "merely possible," that which is other than actuality-in-waiting, is, in violation of formal logic, both possible and impossible. Heidegger wishes to distance himself from an "empty logical possibility" (*SZ* 143) that falls under the principle of noncontradiction and obeys the law of the excluded middle. Although logical possibility is sufficiently detached from actuality, it is too formal and vacuous as a result of swapping logical virtuality for existential futurity. Comprising the indispensable stratum of philosophical traditionalism, formal logic "is grounded in a very definite answer to the question about beings"[7] and, therefore, fails to experience the possibility of that question. It runs aground on the problem of impossible possibility, an oxymoron solely on the terms that are not those of existence. Logically, the contention that, beyond the horizon of its mereness, possibility is possible and impossible is tantamount to arguing that it is both present and absent, or that it is and is not (itself). This deadlock is, nevertheless, irrelevant to existential concerns, tethered as it is to the notion of presence that does not exceed the present-at-hand. The thinking of the tradition will not do there where the possibility of death connotes not absence, ensconced in "not-*X*," but finitude, replete with *positive* ecological and political determinations and entanglements.

Throughout *History of the Concept of Time,* Heidegger tirelessly rearticulates and recycles his anti-traditionalism, the paradoxical building block of *Destruktion*. He chastises those philosophers who, like Kant, have subjectivized the categories, uncritically privileging consciousness in its relation to the object.[8] Methodologically, however, Heidegger's attack on tradition is driven by deeper concerns relevant to the notion of possibility.

The external character of *modern* tradition, demonstrably hostile to everything preceding its "breakthrough" and enamored of subjective interiority through which the outside world is filtered, creates major roadblocks on the path of philosophical investigations. In contrast to "phenomenology radicalized in its ownmost possibility," the "persistently pressing, latently operative and spurious bonds" of tradition hinder the tendency to go back to the things themselves (*HCT* 136). At the risk of diluting Heidegger's uncompromising anti-traditionalism, I propose that what worries him is the spuriousness of traditional bonds, not the existence of the tradition to which they pertain. Traditionalism, understood as the formal imposition of external and spurious constraints on thought, is not the same as tradition conceived in terms of philosophy's "living history." Bearing this distinction in mind, one can envision a tradition divested of its external character, "radicalized in its very possibility," and brought into a greater affinity with radical phenomenology. But the non-exteriority of the tradition that accommodates the ownmost possibility of phenomenology is, in final analysis, that of the things themselves; *ergo*, it does not belong to phenomenology itself, in isolation from them. In other words, when thought is no longer external to the exteriority of the matters themselves, when it dwells ecstatically alongside (in lieu of a dialectical synthesis with, à la Hegel) the matters themselves and in their possibility, the false subject-object and inside-outside dichotomies will be overcome.

More generally, Heidegger alerts his audience to the prejudgments plaguing philosophy in its traditional form and imperceptibly escalating to prejudice: "A question is a prejudgment when it . . . already contains a definite answer to the issue under question, or when it is a blind question aimed at something which cannot be so questioned" (*HCT* 137). So formulated, prejudgment prepares the infrastructure for inauthentic temporality: it manipulates the futurity of the future and forecloses various possibilities—"a fore-having, a fore-sight, and a fore-conception" (*SZ* 150)—that are receptive to interpretation. It chokes possibility off not only *via* a violent imposition of past spurious bonds onto it but also by collapsing the difference between the question and the answer (under the aegis of the potential and the actual, respectively) and, as a result, ensuring that the "correct," the expected, and, in temporal terms, the *pre*ordained answer is given.[9]

Prejudgment should serve as a reminder of "mere possibility" proper to the present-at-hand. Supplanting a richly existential sense of possibility, a question does not survive as such provided it functions as a present-at-hand container for the answer it seeks. Nor is the question nourished in the movement that targets thoughtlessly "something which cannot be so questioned." In the first case, the question is grounded outside itself in the answer it seeks; in the second, it is absolutely ungrounded and unhinged in the manner of "free-floating [*freischwebendem*] thought" (*HCT* 76). Censored, flanked on the one side by what is from the get-go unquestionable and on the other by the final answer, standing out against the invisible double background for everything it intends, the question loses its genetic connection to possibility, which means that it no longer persists in the shape of a question. At least in a single aspect of his approach, Heidegger finds himself on the same page with the critical (Enlightenment) tradition in philosophy: prejudgment thwarts the aspiration of thinking "back to the things themselves" whence possibility may, possibly, derive.

Jean-François Courtine diversifies the sources of Heideggerian possibility, anchored not only to the return to the things themselves but also to the future orientation of Dasein-analysis.[10] The originality of Courtine's conclusion consists in rethinking the relation between phenomenological and existential inquiries, both of them capitalizing on possibility portrayed as a "*thrown possibility*," or else a "thrown *projection*." Heidegger adds: "Dasein is the possibility of Being-free *for* its ownmost potentiality-for-Being [*Das Dasein ist die Möglichkeit des Freiseins* für *das eigenste Seinkönnen*]" (*SZ* 144, 145). Elucidating this possibility allows us to craft a thought-provoking parallel between the thrownness of Dasein in the world and the thrownness of phenomenology in the philosophical tradition:

> A. As thrown, Dasein finds itself always already there in the world, thus in a situation not of its own choosing. But it may also take on its thrownness freely, as something that is "its ownmost," without resorting to the Kantian theoretical fiction of the "as if," *als ob*. Rather than exert a sort of paralyzing influence on Dasein, its immemorial, unchosen thrownness is appropriated in its ownmost potentiality and projected into the future. In spatial terms, reaching back, Dasein stretches forward (*SZ* 371); it transforms its heritage into something chosen, something handed down from oneself to oneself (*SZ* 383). The future orientation of possibility is not and cannot be insulated from the past. Dasein is "the possibility . . . *for* . . . potentiality," a thrown projection where, neither negative nor abstract, freedom involves temporal being. It is in the minimal difference between the possibility of freedom and the potentiality of being that the distinction between projection and thrownness lies: a possible future

project is a throw of past potentialities, uncoupled from their traditionally assured status as actuality-in-waiting. Free because possibly impossible, the projected throw may twist Dasein's "ownmost," *die eigenste*, into that which is perhaps most alien to it.

B. As "thrown," as a way of philosophizing that cannot be built "in mid-air" (*HCT* 138), phenomenology is always already there in the midst of tradition, but radical phenomenology is there in such a way that it can take on its thrownness freely, as its ownmost possibility. That is, phenomenology has all the necessary resources to overcome the externality, the spuriousness, and the prejudicial attitudes of the tradition within tradition itself by reclaiming its "fore-conceived," if blocked, possibilities. Instead of exerting a sort of paralyzing influence on phenomenology, tradition comes back to itself and is freed for "its ownmost potentiality-for-Being," which authorizes it to go back to the things themselves and away from the diversions of "free-floating [*freischwebendem*] thought." Yet, seeing that there are no assurances for the exercise of freedom, the ownmost of phenomenology, if not of philosophy as a whole, may be perverted into what is most foreign to it: formalism, nominalism, and abstract vacuity. Such rendering-impossible of its possibility is part and parcel of the actuality of the phenomenological movement, a distortion that is as existentially necessary as it is structurally vital to the distinction between the possible and the potential.

If what Heidegger wants to repeat when he exhorts us to repeat the tradition are its unkept promises and thwarted possibilities that leave the doors to the futurity of the past ajar, then a strenuously redemptive pursuit of "saving" the tradition underpins, *sotto voce*, his overt anti-traditionalism.[11] The gist of *Destruktion* is this repetition of philosophy's history in "a certain historical conversion,"[12] true to the necessary perversion of the possible in impossibility.

Depending on the perspective one adopts, one may ascribe a narrow or a broad scope to Heidegger's repetition of tradition. At the narrow end, repetition is meant to salvage the "beginning of scientific philosophy" in Plato and Aristotle: "Phenomenology radicalized in its ownmost possibility is nothing but the questioning of Plato and Aristotle brought back to life: *the repetition, the retaking of the beginning of our scientific philosophy* [das Wiederergreifen des Anfangs unserer wissenschaftlichen Philosophie]"

(*HCT* 136). An earlier Husserlian theme of reactivation and a much later Heideggerian problematic of the second (the other) beginning are already palpable in the appeal to retake the beginning—in effect, to rebegin—circling back to the squandered possibilities of the past, by definition set apart from the logic of actualization. A thrown projection of and for thought: it stretches back to send forth whatever one grasps there, regardless of its relation to actuality. Existentially understood, the thread of *Wiederholung* (repetition) in Heidegger entails a repetition of the possible, not of the actual, and, therefore, of what is repeated always for the first time, never having entered actuality and never having been present-at-hand before or after the act of repeating.

Plato and Aristotle represent the promise keepers, the custodians of possibility who are exonerated from the charges of dogmatism Heidegger levels much more unambiguously against post-Aristotelian philosophy. Still, *their* ownmost possibility cannot be discharged to them before a radicalized phenomenology repeats their breakthrough. Heidegger replays the Aristotelian discovery of the categories and the Platonic vision of the *eidos* (as being) in articulating the copula (the "is": being, once again) with categorial intuition (*HCT* 66–68). His retort to Kant draws on the Greeks, who do not require the fiction of the subject, and emphasizes the objectivity of the categories apprehended in the matters themselves. Like any other intuition, that of the categories has its specific objects, chief among them the category of being Kant reduced to a subset of modality in the form of a present-at-hand actuality. Being, as a category one may directly intuit, is linguistically expressed in the copula (*HCT* 59), in which it is as "real" as it has been for Plato and Aristotle. Nonetheless, a detour through the subjectivation of the categories in Kant, who thought of them as pure concepts of *understanding,* thus obviating anything like a categorial *intuition,* is also unavoidable, inasmuch as this detour locates Plato and Aristotle outside philosophical actuality and so taps into the possibilities of their thinking.

Interrogating the copula, asking "What is the 'is'?" phenomenology repeats the inaugural question of philosophy in order to hear[13] it for the first time. Plato and Aristotle begin to live only in the second beginning, in *their* afterlife (alternatively, "*our* scientific philosophy"), which the immanent critique of a radicalized phenomenology conjures up. The questioning *of* Plato and Aristotle repeats the questions they posed, but also questions these foundational texts themselves and their ability to live up to the apertures of the question unto possibility, open above all to its own closure. The act of "seizing" (*Ergreifen*) phenomenology as a possibility (*SZ* 38) is feasible only by dint of a perpetual "retaking," "re-seizing" (*Wiederergreifen*) its (our) post-metaphysical beginning (*HCT* 136), which turns out to be a giving up of its secure foundations.

At a broader end of the spectrum of repetition, Heidegger rewinds the tradition in an ensemble of questioning. "The *genuine repetition* of a traditional question [*Die* echte Wiederholung *einer traditionellen Frage*] lets its external character as a tradition fade away and pulls back from the prejudices" (*HCT* 138). Although the question of being has been raised and has to some extent persisted within the tradition as a "traditional question," it has dissipated in the external character of repetition and in the preemption of the answer it seeks. In response to the question that has traditionalized itself, has delivered (*trāditiō*) itself over to traditional positing, phenomenology beseeches tradition (the very principle of surrender) itself to surrender to the renewed possibility of the question. A repetitive inversion, known in rhetoric as *antistasis* and affecting the pairing possible-impossible, measures the genuineness of repetition in contrast to the sham rehearsals of the question that fades into prejudicial externality. Henceforth, *antistasis* will evince the highest degree of free fidelity to the philosophical heritage.

Repetition grows in intensity as soon as we superimpose the replay of tradition onto all the restarts of phenomenology in a self-critical attempt to avoid the formalization and ossification of its findings. For Heidegger, "it is of the essence of phenomenological investigations that they cannot be reviewed summarily but must in each case be rehearsed and *repeated* anew" (*HCT* 26). The nonlogical, nontranscendental condition of possibility of phenomenology is its condition of eventual impossibility and self-interruption, which is the stipulation Derrida will endorse when it comes to the possibility of the gift. If phenomenology yields any knowledge, that knowledge is, at any rate, neither positive nor cumulative (in a word: positivist). The rediscovery of the matters themselves is possible not in piecing together, summing up, or summarizing bits of information but in attending to the volatile, ever-changing totality of the interpretative situation at hand. Between summarization and totalization, there is a whole world of difference between the external and internal ways of raising the question of being with regard to the possible.

The previously inapparent form of traditional inquiry becomes apparent and undergoes a process of deformalization in "the possibility of assuming history" through repetition. Using terminology that will be integral to his subsequent treatment of historicity, Heidegger observes: "This possibility of assuming history [*die Möglichkeit Geschichte aufzunehmen* (also incorporating or receiving)] can then also show that the assumption of the question of the sense of being is not merely an external repetition [*nicht einfach eine äußerliche Wiederholung*] of the question which the Greeks already raised" (*HCT* 138). The possibility of receiving history is not one possibility among others; it is the very possibility of possibility. The futurity of the past—the historical, detranscendental a priori condition of possibility *for* possibility, clarifying the temporalizing effects of thrown projection—cannot emanate from external repetitions. Heidegger proposes a different kind of repetition: the internal reiteration of history in a *secular redemptive praxis* warranting history and possibility, historical possibility and the possibility of history. The possibility that is "higher" than actuality belongs to a bygone actuality (already neither present-at-hand nor ready-to-hand), which, while no longer actual, retains certain effectiveness as it is projected into the future. To assume history apart from externally repeating it is to exceed the occurrent possibilities of what came to pass and, by the same token, to release the frustrated existential possibilities of past actuality. It is to agree that there is no futurity of the future without a reiteration of the futurity of the past. And it is, finally, to exist.

In view of a secular redemptive praxis that nearly overlaps with existence as such, Heidegger's otherwise opaque sentence lends itself to interpretation: "*Repeating is handing over expressly* [ausdrückliche Überlieferung]—that is to say, going back into the possibilities of the Dasein that has-been-there [*dagewesenen Daseins*]" (*SZ* 385). Besides staging a confrontation between the implicitness of an exterior relation to tradition that hands materials over without their express repetition and the rendering-explicit of interiority that prompts the past possibilities of Dasein to resurface, this sentence stresses another meaning of "handing over" (*Überlieferung*): legacy, bequest, inheritance. Avoiding the imposition of an external form on the matters themselves, rejecting the automatic procedure of handing *down* "occurrent" possibilities, explicit inheritance delivers phenomenology and Dasein *over* to themselves and entrusts existential possibility to the future anterior. Accordingly, phenomenology is what tradition will have been.

POSSIBILITY DEFORMALIZED, OR EXISTENTIAL ENERGY

In line with the existential schema of possibility, it is only fitting to ask what we can do with this notion in the practice of phenomenology and, more interestingly, what it does to such a practice. Near the beginning of the "Main Division" in *History of the Concept of Time,* Heidegger isolates a counter-phenomenological thrust that circuitously brings phenomenology back to itself: "At the very least, it became evident that the development of the phenomenological theme can proceed in a counter-phenomenological direction. This insight does not serve to drive phenomenology outside of itself but really first brings phenomenology right back to itself, to its ownmost and purest possibility [*in ihre eigenste und reinste Möglichkeit zurückgebracht*]" (*HCT* 135).

Heidegger's insight is consistent with the following maxims: (1) the phenomenological condition of possibility is its condition of impossibility and self-interruption; (2) existential possibility does not obey the principle of noncontradiction; and (3) the absolute radicality of phenomenology "does not lie in its *actuality* as a philosophical 'movement' ["*Richtung*"]" (*SZ* 38). The "purest possibility [*reinste Möglichkeit*]" of phenomenology is hardly the "merely possible [*das* nur *Mögliche*]" in the thematic purview of entities that are present-at-hand. Immanently self-critical,[14] phenomenology is purely possible only insofar as it suspends its own conditions of possibility, that is, insofar it thematizes the results of its "actual" investigations (intentionality, the transcendental ego, etc.) without neglecting to dethematize them, trimming the speculative thread that enervates apodictic analyses from within.[15]

In *Otherwise Than Being,* Emmanuel Levinas considers thematization to be "inevitable, so that signification itself show itself."[16] If so, then the energy of thematization is also that of phenomenology "*letting the manifest in itself be seen from itself*" or preparing "*the work of laying open and letting be seen*" (*HCT* 85, 86)—a formulation that will be restated almost word-for-word in *Being and Time*. The possibility of phenomenology as phenomeno-logy, of phenomena manifest in the *logos* that is nothing but their manifestation, makes possible the possibility of the phenomena themselves by *letting* both phenomena and *logos* be, by releasing them to (or un-obstructing) their possibilities. Such letting-be is a strange a priori—the possibility of possibility—that Heidegger refuses to subjectivize, to invest in transcendental subjectivity, to which phenomena would show themselves. That which is seen "*in itself . . . from itself*" in phenomenology regulates the possibilities of the *how* proper to the intentional act of seeing without regard to the seer. In brief, dethematization and desubjectivization are coimplicit in the Heideggerian a priori that dispenses to phenomeno-logy its possibility.

The a priori undergoes a thorough desubjectivization in the trans-subjective givenness of the categorial forms that come to supplant, for example, the subject's transcendental *aesthesis* of space and time.[17] But one does not arrive at the trans-subjective (read: trans-transcendental, i.e., immanent in the matters themselves) givenness without first subtracting being from "the ordered sequence of knowledge" and from "the sequential order of entities" (*HCT* 74), that is, from subjective epistemology and objective ontology. The priority of the a priori becomes a nominal *and* the most concrete feature of the trans-transcendental condition of possibility. This moment in the possibility of phenomenology, in turn, revolutionizes the classical relation of actuality and potentiality, the latter conceived in terms of the *merely* possible: the confrontation of the two is triangulated with the filled-out possibility that is *of* actuality, whether because it relays the futurity of the past or because it seeks refuge in the immanence of the matters themselves. (I explored the intermediate space between the actual and the potential—the space constitutive of the idea of energy in its historical development—in my *Energy Dreams*.[18] Its excess over the merely possible and the teleological ladder of actuality is what is most deserving of the appellation "existential energy.")

Nota bene: in early Heidegger, the possibilities of the *how* do not prescribe the content of what is seen, even if the seen is the *where* from which these possibilities are procured; the *how* is a middle term between the content and the form, between the formal and material conditions of saying-seeing being, just as existential possibility (i.e., the temporalization of time as synonymous with actualization, with the stretch a potentiality must traverse on its way to actual being) stands or falls between pure actuality and potentiality. Heidegger repeatedly stresses that "phenomenology . . . says *nothing about the material content* of the thematic object of this science, but speaks really only—and emphatically—of the *how,* the way in which something is and has to be thematic in this research" (*HCT* 85). That *how* in phenomenology is the -logy part of the word: the *logos* that indicates the way phenomena manifest themselves from themselves, reseizing or repeating *their* beginning for the first time by handing *itself* over to them as their manifestation. The trans-transcendental capacity of *logos* and its spatiotemporal capaciousness are the custodians of phenomenological possibility. Being (*Sein*) is the *how* of beings, the manner in which they are, not an abstraction from their singularity. Similarly, the seeing of the seen is not equivalent to the abstracted form of the seen; it is the being of consciousness as intentionality directing-itself-toward the seen, the directing a priori pre-sented and pre-destined—neither in the order of knowledge nor in the order of entities—to the seen, insofar as it is "*letting the manifest in itself be seen from itself.*"

Even as Heidegger dethematizes and deformalizes phenomenology, he also, and by the same token, de-idealizes it, removing the phenomenological correlations (seeing-seen, thinking-thought, hoping-hoped for) from their logical base in the process of actualization, where a potential *noesis* is fulfilled (a code for "actualized," though, as we will see, Heidegger will drastically reinterpet it) in the *noema* appropriate to it. Crucially, he does so by resorting to possibility that stands higher than actuality to the extent that it regulates the back-and-forth of actuality and potentiality.

In light of Heidegger's insistence on a deformalized (*entformalisiert*) concept of phenomenology (*SZ* 35), the *how* establishes the phenomenological discipline as a practice that doesn't make perfect, but makes more practice. What shows itself from itself, what appears phenomenologically, when phenomenology appears? Not this or that theory neatly contained in a treatise, but an exercise, a performance that refuses to stabilize the results of its investigations. Deformalization is the liberation of the actual to its potentialities in a backflow from actuality that is the birthright of phenomenological possibility. Despite its negative tinges, deformalization supposes and, in a way, accepts the thing it sets out to undo—the form wherein actuality is congealed. Its movement is the movement of deactualization, of a retreat to the potentialities of receiving the given, inexhaustible in any doctrinaire content. But phenomenological possibility, which largely overlaps with existential energy, is more encompassing yet than the tendency toward negating form; it oscillates between the static and the dynamic poles of deformalization, including the reverse (in keeping with the objective teleological perspective) flow from the actual to the potential, or from *noema* back to *noesis*. Positively speaking, deformalization participates in the stirrings of thrown projection, and the de-idealization it undertakes is none other than its return to the roots, to the "radicality" of temporalization.

There is no ideal of indubitable knowledge, such as that Husserl adapted from Descartes, behind the deformalization Heidegger advocates. The radicality of time dwelling in the possibilities of existential energy is an uprooting from stable, a- or extratemporal foundations, upon which such knowledge has been predicated. There is, moreover, no progress in the routines of deformalization, contingent upon a kind of regress, a return to the things themselves. Assuming that deformalization did move forward, the increments of its progress would have been imperceptible and immeasurable without the transcendental divide between the goal it posits and the real state of affairs. That is why phenomenology does not chase after a better, more accurate interpretation that would provide the closest approximation to reality hitherto; it decisively eschews interpretive outcomes in favor of lived hermeneutical acts sheltering the possibility of meaning—of meaning-making as much as of meaning-receiving. At the extreme, phenomenology eschews interpretation, both as an act and as the result of an act, altogether.

As Heidegger writes, the "achieving of phenomenological access to entities which we encounter, consists rather in thrusting aside our interpretative tendencies, which keep thrusting themselves upon us and running along with us" (*SZ* 67). The intricate phraseological web of Heidegger's magnum opus reveals that the technical sense of "thrusting aside our interpretative tendencies," which recall "the actuality of the phenomenological 'movement,'" lies in clearing the ground for the possibility of possibility by breaking through the hermeneutical circle of understanding and the ready-to-hand it invariably deals with: "To say that 'circumspection discovers' means that the 'world' which has already been understood comes to be interpreted. The ready-to-hand comes *explicitly* into the sight which understands" (*SZ* 148). That which the Heideggerian counter-thrust rejects is the interpretation of the world (and, by extension, of phenomenology itself) that merely explicates its preunderstanding, much like the experience that, for Kant, each time avouches the limits of cognitive-categorial schematism. Oddly, resistance to conventional interpretative tendencies strengthens understanding, authorized to understand something other than just itself. The interruption of the hermeneutical circle yields one of the most meaningful conditions of possibility of its continuation.

The message of deformalization, namely, that one cannot gain formulaic access either to phenomenology as such or to its subject matter, dovetails with the thematization of thematization. Both "actual" phenomenology and counter-phenomenological movements are in need of the same palliative of immanent critique proceeding under the heading of the thematization ("the *way* in which") of thematization ("something is and has to be *thematic*"),[19] which, rather than a meta-abstraction, is held in check by and accountable only before the matters themselves. The difference between the two lies in the possibilities consummated in destabilization: intrinsically destabilized, phenomenology is brought "right back to itself, to its ownmost and purest possibility," while counter-phenomenology, or resistance to phenomenological movement in its actuality, is also brought right back to the possibility of phenomenology. But are all counter-phenomenological movements equally productive, auspicious, germinal? And is there a significant incongruence, which Heidegger left unacknowledged, between counter- and non-phenomenological tendencies?

The spread of phenomenological possibility to its other, to what initiates a counter-thrust to phenomenology, rivals the plasticity of Hegelian dialectics. In Heidegger, as in Hegel, the energy of the "movement" (*Richtung*) is indebted to what resists it: first and foremost, the philosophical tradition. Scanning phenomenology in its historical "actuality" (*Wirklichkeit:* itself, one of the words for energy), it is not difficult to recognize in Heidegger's method a staged rehearsal of Husserl's critique of Brentano, who is satisfied with "a rough and ready acquaintance [with] and application" of the structure of intentionality (*HCT* 28). According to Heidegger, it is Husserl who assumes the being of intentionality without articulating it ontologically (*HCT* 113) and pays little attention to the thick fabric of time apart from the retention and protention of perceptual presence. The dual obstinacy at stake here—refusing to relinquish the authoritativeness of tradition and resisting the formalization of phenomenological investigations—invigorates the possibility of phenomenology by suspending, as if from two methodological hooks between which it is stretched, its conditions of possibility. The first suspension is the withholding of the question of being in the externality of tradition; the second is the suspension of suspension (a version of *alētheia*), the undoing of all actual conclusions phenomenology has reached, apparently quenching its possibilities.

Its allegedly unlimited plasticity notwithstanding, Heidegger warns his readers against some undesirable outcomes of the phenomenological endeavor. We have already come across one of these warnings, notably, to avoid "free-floating thought" and refrain from building philosophical castles in "mid-air" (*HCT* 76, 138). Possibilities sink and fall in watery insipidness and in airy indetermination, respectively: in the fluidity of indeterminate potentiality and in vacuous abstraction yoked to the merely possible. But if the possibility of possibility is to find its footing, we will have to look in a direction other than the construction of a system. The key criterion of sound philosophizing, Heidegger notes, "is not the possibility of constructing a system, a construction which is based purely on an arbitrary adaptation of the conceptual material transmitted by history [*der Geschichte überlieferten begrifflichen Materials gründet*]" (*HCT* 18). A system betrays possibility, if not the possibility of possibility, not so much in virtue of subjecting the possible to the imperative of actualization within its totalizing plan but a priori, in virtue of edifying itself on the external transmission of history its very arrangement expresses. In the system, possibility is not grounded but goes to ground, enters concealment.

Faced with the earlier correlation between a free assumption of history and an interior relation to tradition, I take it that Heidegger is aiming his criticism at the "conceptual material transmitted by history" that, when not freely assumed in the internal repetition of tradition, is externally imposed, "arbitrary." By haphazardly adapting the material handed down to us, by acquiescing without further ado to the form in which it comes prepackaged, we squander the possibilities of inheriting tradition in a mode of internal repetition. The arbitrariness of free-floating thought is intimately related to the arbitrary adaptation of this material. Forgetting or perhaps repressing the tradition, free-floating thought unconsciously utilizes the content it desires to repress.

For Heidegger, the grounding possibility of phenomenology is "received" (*gewinnen,* in the sense of reception as a "gain" that is "won over") from its "meaning in the human Dasein" (*HCT* 4). Possibility must be won over, snatched from the destructive and sometimes conflicting demands of systematization, free-floating thought, and the external pressure of tradition. It must be released from this unhealthy torsion into the things themselves, into the world where Dasein is situated in the modes of care and concern. In other words, the grounding possibility of phenomenology must be existential or it will not be at all: it must be handed over from the meaning of existence, itself *fundamentally-ontologically* environmental (ecological and political). While such a possibility verges on the impossible, its ground is objectively groundless, in that it is indexed to thrown projection or finite time dictating the meaning of existence on the hither side of the hermeneutical circle that exclusively preunderstands the ready-to-hand.

However existentially inclined, we cannot conclusively win possibility over from the blocking counter-force. In response to Heidegger's bellicose rhetoric, simply to fight the fight is already to lose before the final announcement of the results (here: the formalized and thematized conclusions of phenomenological research). The release of possibility into its ownmost element is not active; is not an act—either in the colloquial or in the phenomenological-intentional sense—a subject initiates or brings to a head; is not a matter of energy as the act's actuality. It hinges on something else: the practical attitude of letting the matters "revert to themselves" (*HCT* 136) before or after their objectifying thematization. A return to the things themselves is, upon Heidegger's reworking of Husserl, the return *of* the things to themselves. That said, the in-action of letting the reversion happen is not passivity. Not acquiescing with the actuality of phenomenology's formal conclusions, the practical attitude Heidegger puts his finger on nourishes the infinite task phenomenology gives itself, the task of preserving possibility *qua* possibility in "keep[ing] open the tendency toward the matters themselves" (*HCT* 136), which our interpretative endeavors have congested. One can only preserve possibility by letting go of it, jettisoning its identity or self-identity, no longer quarantining it from the impossible, and so risking never to enter its promised land that is otherwise than actuality.

THE EFFICACY OF THE POSSIBLE

The literal meaning of the German *Wirklichkeit* (actuality or energy) is the being-at-work or being-in-the-work of something or someone; in a word, efficacy. Even if possibility stands higher than actuality, it must have what actuality appropriates for itself—the effectiveness that earns it its supreme standing. Yet, the being-at-work of possibility (indeed, possibility's actuality) divorced from the power or the reality of actualization is incommensurate with the ideality of accomplishment, the successful coming to fruition of an empty intention in the objective outcome of an act. Our attitude of letting the matters themselves revert back to themselves, for example, partakes in the efficacy of possibility, its existential energy at odds with the bustling and commandeering activity that, in advance, ahead of its time, ahead of *all* time, holds the final outcome in view.

Jean-Luc Marion touches upon the drawbacks of phenomenological efficacy: "That Being should appear—this ultimate accomplishment befalls phenomenology only in the mode of possibility. But can this possibility be accomplished in fact?"[20] To ask about the factual accomplishment of being is to shift the subject from the form and the method to the material content, about which, as Heidegger has it, phenomenology says nothing. It is to concentrate not on the appearing and its *how* but on *what* appears when being appears. Indisputably important as it is, the question of the accomplishment of being "in fact," *de facto*, or even factically is too impatient in its urge, first, to postulate that there are different "levels of analysis," and second, to leap from one such level to another. With the looming threat of locking phenomenology in the ivory tower of pure theory, it asks of us to locate a passage, for which evidence abounds all around us, from the phenomenological possibility of ontology to ontological actuality. Should we decide to pursue this line of inquiry, we would have to study the phenomenological notion of the accomplishment of possibility from various sides, commencing with intentional fulfillment as a miniature replica of the phenomenological universe with all the possibilities in plain sight. My misgivings about Marion's question aside, I think that the exercise could be worthwhile, since it could lead us, in a somewhat unintended fashion, to core problems of the efficacy of the possible.

In "The Letter on Humanism," Heidegger meditates on the essence of action and brushes aside any judgment of the action's effectiveness measured by the actuality of its effect and "valued according to its utility."[21] He adds: "But the essence of an action is accomplishment. To accomplish means to unfold something into the fullness of its essence, to lead it forth into this fullness—*producere*."[22] It's true that the discussion of possibility has shepherded us beyond action, beyond a rigid opposition between activity and passivity localized in the subject, and beyond the objective outcomes of subjective designs. Nonetheless, the accomplishment that constitutes the essence of action already verges on the structure of Heideggerian possibility.[23] While the essence of action is accomplishment, the essence of accomplishment is "to unfold something into the fullness of its essence," to support the essence of essence, or the possibility of essence, often by means of letting-be, not those of making or actively molding. To be at all possible, essence will forgo actualization. The unfolding of "something into the fullness of its essence" will depend on the notion of fullness over and above active fulfillment (*Erfüllung*) that in European modernity leads the leading-forth (*producere*) down the road of productivism. A preliminary response to Marion would therefore be: The actual or the factual phenomenological accomplishment of the possibilities for being is productive, albeit not productivist; full but not fulfilled as a subjectively posited plan or a goal. In the terms with which chapter 2 operates, whereas phenomenological efficaciousness is a sign of success with respect to the possible, it is a failure in the order of actuality.

Fulfillment operates on every "level" of phenomenology, from intentionality, to the incessant self-rehearsal of the phenomenological investigations, to the appropriative repetition of tradition in "our scientific philosophy." Rereading Husserl, Heidegger writes apropos of the transition from intention to intuition: "Every intention has within it a tendency toward fulfillment. . . . There are specific laws which govern the connections among the possibilities of fulfilling [*Erfüllungsmöglichkeit*] an already given empty intention" (*HCT* 44). In fact, it is not quite right to speak of a transition from one to the other per se; once fulfilled, intention, referring to the structure of all psychic acts that boil down to the dynamics of "directing-toward," *is* intuition—a simple apprehension of that toward which the act has directed itself. Intention is not actualized in intuition; it arrives at the fullness of its essence, thanks to which it becomes more concrete in the sense of concretion that goes along with the self-givenness of being. Thus, phenomenological fulfillment obeys the rules of ontico-ontological efficaciousness, the givenness of being in beings that keeps its (and their) possibilities inexhaustible.

The elementary structure of intentionality emerges in its intuitional concretion as soon as we approach it from another angle, now focusing on that *toward which* it is directed. But, whatever the approach, its "already given" possibility and, with it, the possible impossibility of reaching "that-toward-which" remain intact. The directedness of the psychic act is never exhausted in its possibility; even when it is fulfilled in the object of intuition, it can always set its sights on a deeper, more concrete apprehension of being. Despite its fullness, the essencing of essence does not terminate at a preprogrammed point as does an "empty" intention that, considered under the sign of actualization, arrives at its end in intuition. In its efficacy, intentionality goes back toward the ultimately unobjectifiable beginning (the givenness of being in beings) that invites further advances (or regresses) the more one approximates it. Only ontically does being *in actu* seem to be the concretion of being *in potentia*; ontologically, it is the other way around: efficacious possibility is the self-disrupting concretion of actuality.

Shifting perspectives and telescoping the structure of intentionality out of the range of individual consciousness, we may detect in it a highly condensed version of the drama that unfolds between phenomenology and the tradition. The appropriative repetition of the tradition in "radical" phenomenology brings to fulfillment the tendency already ingrained into past philosophizing in the mode of "an already given empty intention." This fulfillment, however, is not a closure but the very opening of the possible. Whether narrowly or broadly conceived, tradition for Heidegger is directing-itself-toward the question of being, but only phenomenology can disclose, piecemeal, that toward which the tradition has been directed. Phenomenology fulfills the empty and formal intention of traditional philosophy and thereby redeems its possibilities, fleshing them out as possibilities in a vehement refusal to hand them over to actuality and, least of all, to the actuality of a philosophical movement. The talk of a transition from one to the other, from a theoretical intention to intuition, is nonsense, because only in phenomenology can tradition obtain its true concretion. The oft-misconstrued Heideggerian *Destruktion* destroys the external and authoritative imposition of traditionality and of the subject's "privilege" on thinking, simultaneously cultivating the possibilities held and thwarted by the destroyed form.

If phenomenology finds fulfillment only in the matters themselves, then it is never fulfilled when judged against an externally posited set of criteria. Its efficacy, which is also that of the possible, is detectable only below the threshold of actual effects, let alone of ideally posited goals. The definition of phenomenology in terms of the analytic description of intentionality in its a priori has "to be understood from its task [*Aufgabe*], from the positive possibility which it implies, from what guides its efforts and not from what is said about it" (*HCT* 79). The intentionality *of* phenomenology consists in directing-itself-toward the matters themselves, giving rise to the Husserlian slogan "Back to the things themselves!" which, while it can mean "To the actual!" does not abandon possibility, thanks to the emphasis on the "to" that distances us from actuality. Husserl's "battle cry" is not so much a free-standing injunction as a reaction to the historical preponderance of "what is said about" phenomenology over what it lets one say or see, the theoretical or theoreticist discourse-*logos* about phenomenology over the *logos* of the phenomena flowing through phenomeno*logy*. So, the accomplishment of phenomenology "in fact" does not authorize phenomenologists to reach over to and demarcate, in line with naive realism, chunks of actuality or of factuality outside the commerce of phenomena and *logos*.

To be guided by the possible as the compass of one's exertions is to be in tune with the ontico-ontological efficacy of phenomenology's infinite approximation to the givenness of being, accomplished "in fact" and still preserved in its possibility. That efficacy is not a side effect but what is essential to phenomenology, what permits it to accomplish or to fail in its task, what "does not lie in its *actuality* as a philosophical 'movement' [*Richtung*]" (*SZ* 38). Admittedly, the course of phenomenology's actual historical directedness diverges from the task of directing-itself-toward the matters themselves; however, what such apparent shortcomings shed light on is not phenomenology's a priori unattainable mission but, in an analogy to existence, its irreducible and enabling fallenness and inauthenticity. The actuality of phenomenological movement betrays (both expresses and gives up) the possibility of phenomenology, just as in its factical condition Dasein squanders and leans upon its existential possibilities. This is yet another reason for maintaining a conscious (deliberate, discerning, critical) relation to the tradition, which is, for all intents and purposes, the province of Heidegger's *Destruktion.*

The necessary fallenness and inauthenticity of phenomenological investigations intimate that ontological efficaciousness is not synonymous with success; possibility itself is meaningless unless it comprehends a possible failure (as judged by and from actuality) integral to the task, such as the one phenomenology gives itself. It is in this spirit that Paul de Man's remark on Walter Benjamin's essay "The Task of the Translator" may be read: "the translator, per definition, fails. The translator can never do what the original text did. . . . If [Benjamin's] text is called 'Die Aufgabe des Übersetzers,' we have to read this title more or less as a tautology: *Aufgabe,* task, can also mean the one who has to give up."[24]

2. Failure and Nonactualizable Possibility

HEIDEGGER'S FAILURE, OR THE FAILURE *OF* HEIDEGGER?

The existential-phenomenological primacy of possibility over actuality should spur philosophers to rethink many of the practical and axiological categories of human conduct. First among these is failure. What does it mean to fail in a paradigm that has little to do with actualizable potentialities, their accomplishment heralding success? What is failure, understood from the phenomenological-existential perspective? What is the "being" of failure? How does failure fail?

After Heidegger, one can no longer take "failure" for granted, be it in its ordinary-everyday meaning as the privation of success or in its etymological sense (*failen* in Old English denotes "coming to an end," "cessation of functioning or of existence").[1] As such, "failure" furnishes an example of the Heideggerian catachresis, an operation that uses words wrested from their mundane usage as well as their conventional philosophical usage. In thinking and dwelling with human and nonhuman others, failure is the experience that guards over the possibilities constituting and undermining, by continually renewing it, any given order. Paraphrasing Beckett, we might even quip: "Fail politically and ecologically. Fail again. Fail better!" The problem is that for much of its history humanity has failed to recognize its political and environmental failures for what they are and, more gravely still, has divined in them the signs of success within the logic of productivism that leaves no semantic space for the other connotations of the Latin *producere*.

A similar failure of recognition befell Heidegger (who never came to terms with it) as he flirted with National Socialism. The tragedy, here and elsewhere, is not failure per se but the reluctance to accept it, humbly and without resentment, as a key *existentiale.* Learning to live with failure is respecting our finitude with its infinite possibilities. More than success, it is failure—a singular way of failing—that individuates us as single human beings, as groups of individuals, or as humankind engaged with the nonhuman world of the elements, plants, and animals.

I would go so far as to argue that failure is one of the silent keywords that govern the unfolding of the existential analytic of Dasein in particular and the project of fundamental ontology in general: it organizes not only the phenomenality of conscience in a pivotal second chapter of Division II—"Dasein's Attestation of an Authentic Potentiality-for-Being, and Resoluteness"—but also the switch from *Zuhandenheit* to *Vorhandenheit* and the practical-methodological orientation of phenomenology as an impossible praxis standing "above" actuality.

And yet, with respect to Heidegger's "failure," even the most supportive among his commentators cannot resist the temptation to subsume it to the failure or, rather, the failures *of* Heidegger. Actuality irrupts in phenomenology, intruding or obtruding on it in the crassest historico-political instantiation of the thinker's decision. This, to be sure, cannot be otherwise, but the intrusion happens too soon, the fixation on political events depriving phenomenological interpretation of the time it needs to unfold. The failures of Heidegger in the 1930s (and in the subsequent decades, the refusal to take responsibility for his choices) have deflected attention from his original and only partially elaborated notion of failure, transplanted from the soil of pragmatism into that of existential ontology and gifted with a certain degree of positivity. But what if, going through the trouble to track the transformation I have abbreviated as "the Heideggerian catachresis," we were in a better position to look back at the events of the 1930s and their aftermath? What if, instead of hampering phenomenological understanding, political actuality were cast in the light of that understanding?

These questions are too wide-ranging to receive a fair treatment here. I will merely try to hone them in relation to the least nugatory consequences of the Heidegger controversy: the debate between Dominique Janicaud and Philippe Lacoue-Labarthe and the work of David Farrell Krell.

Driving the first debate is the question of the grounds for something like a "moral failing" in Heidegger's case. In *Heidegger, Art and Politics,* Lacoue-Labarthe writes: "To speak of moral failing [*faute*] presupposes that there exists an ethics, or at least an ethics is possible. Now, it is probably the case today that neither of these conditions is fulfilled."[2] He further substantiates his doubts regarding the actual existence and the possibility of an ethics within the Heideggerian problematic of closure, referring to "the general exhaustion of philosophical possibilities" that must affect the ethical, the "delimitation of ethics and humanism," and so forth. Provided that failure abounds with only negative connotations, the discourse of "moral failings" is neutralized: a lacuna *in* morality is meaningless when morality *as such* at long last appears for what it is, or perhaps what it has always been, notably a lack, something missing (sorely or not) both in the order of actuality and in the order of possibility. What is a moral failing in the age of general amorality? And what is a local failure in an utterly failed context? Absent the references and orientational markers in actuality, where are we to seek guidance on the success or failure of a given conduct? Does ethical action fail in the same style as a hammer that does not hit the nail on the head?

Quite understandably, Janicaud finds Lacoue-Labarthe's justification hard to swallow, despite praising his "prudence" and acknowledging the historical "caesura" that governs his theoretical position. For Janicaud, "the only politics liable to unmask Nazism as profoundly criminal is a politics that demands that one 'bend a knee' in front of ethical principles."[3] Should one reject such politics in siding with Heidegger, one would facilitate the closure of metaphysics and augment the thinker's actual moral failure by repeating it at the level of possibility. Conversely, in Janicaud, ethics is the phantom limb of good politics, the prosthetic support that ensures political goodness, or at least its principled superiority over a politics unmasked as "profoundly criminal." Political success depends, in this case, on extrapolitical factors—the ethical precepts behind political failure.

In parallel to Lacoue-Labarthe, Krell undertakes an immanent critique of Heidegger, which is refreshing, Janicaud's rejoinder notwithstanding: "I shall say what I believe would hurt Heidegger most—that his silence concerning the fate of European Jewry between 1933 and 1945 is a failure of thinking, *ein Versagen des Denkens.* . . . I still believe that in Heidegger's texts *there is thinking*, and that when the *thinking* fails an abyss opens right there on the page."[4] His critique is immanent to Heidegger's thought as much as to politics, in that it does not rely upon the *deus ex machina* of ethical principles. At the same time, Krell confronts the "abyss" of failure as a technical absence, as if something in thinking did not attain actuality, did not get actualized as it should. The aftertaste that lingers after reading his diagnosis is that the failure of thinking is a glitch in cognitive equipment, in the interpretation machine that should have processed everything, "the fate of European Jewry" not excepted, in those fateful years. But are the processes and conditions of failure really so mechanical? Although this might appear to be a minor issue, failing to *think* failure is unforgivable, above all if it pertains to thought, as opposed to, say, launching a rocket or baking a cake.

It is in no way trivial to write, as Krell does with reference to Heidegger's texts, that "*there is thinking*" in them. The meaning of the *there is* needs to be explicated: thinking is there neither as a ready-to-hand, easily applicable set of tools nor as a present-at-hand piece of vain intellectual contemplation. That thinking is there indicates that it exists, that it belongs on the plane of existence where there are no lacunae, pure absences, or gaps. On such a plane, does failure open an abyss, the unfillable and unfulfillable hole of lack? An oversight, looking awry is not the absence of sight; it is still a looking, if elsewhere. Within the economy of a single sentence, Krell leaps from the *there is* of thinking to the text ("the page") where its abyssal failure is felt. But a textual failure does not follow the same course as that of thinking: like any crafted, artfully assembled, articulated, technical system, a text can have multiple lacunae, upon which Louis Althusser's "symptomal reading" latches. Not so in the case of the "failure of thinking"!

Krell's ambivalence becomes more pronounced once the failure of thinking is compared to the moral failing that has turned into an apple of discord between Lacoue-Labarthe and Janicaud. On the one hand, an abyss that opens on the page is narrower (less consequential) than that of the moral kind; on the other hand, it is broader than the latter to the extent that it attests to "a failure of life, a *daimonic* failure."[5] Glancing at the situation with a Heideggerian eye, we might come to a realization that at issue is the contrast between morality and ethics—two things that Lacoue-Labarthe treats as interchangeable—that is to say, between a system of rules ready-to-hand for a quasi-mechanical regulation of behavior, on the one hand, and, on the other, a way of life that does not in the least concern the categorial analytic. Existential and categorial failures are, therefore, homonyms: whereas the word is the same, its semantic inflections diverge from one another. Before denouncing Heidegger for his political failures, it would be advisable to decide, on the philosophical register, what is being talked about and how the unspoken classifications of the concept in his work enrich our assessment of his legacy.

In the course of my examination of "the phenomenology of failure" in Heidegger, I will splice authenticity into a recognition of the existentially significant failure to hear the silent call of conscience and distinguish this ethical-existential failure from the failure to follow a norm, a rule, or a law in the public world of the "they." Taking into consideration the distinction between ethics and morality, between an ecology of dwelling and a systemic regulation of conduct, is it plausible to think of failure not as a privation or a dreaded cessation of existence but as one of existential modes, in effect, as the most promising avenue for the involvement in the world that so absorbs and fascinates Dasein? Further, what is the sense of engaging with the fecund notion of failure by "breaking" it? Does "breaking the failure" necessitate breaking *with* it, or is the break bound to repeat that which it purportedly breaks? Then, stepping back from the existential to the categorial analytic, I will read the failure of equipment (*Zeug*), the cessation of its functioning, and the breach it makes in the referential context of involvement on the model of positivity that yields nothing less than the category of presence-at-hand.

THE FECUNDITY OF FAILURE: A PRELIMINARY OUTLINE

Three core motifs crisscrossing *Being and Time* steer the argument that, for Heidegger, failure is something fecund: (1) "the plenitude of existence," (2) "the deflation of actuality," and (3) "the positivity of falling." First, if existence knows no lack, and if failure is to be cataloged together with the other *existentiales*, then failure is part and parcel of fundamental ontology. Second, when the practice of phenomenology and the ecstatic temporality of Dasein are rid of the ideals of actuality and actualization, when they derive their raison d'être from the possible, failure is stripped of its negative undertones. As such, it comes to be associated with possibility, if not with the possibility of possibility. Third, to align failure with the dynamics of falling is to argue that it characterizes not a momentary lapse in the successfulness of existence but the being of Dasein in its everydayness. More often than not, Dasein fails to be what it is, but that failure is inalienable from the specificity of its being.

Let me sharpen the phenomenology of failure by taking a closer look at the three motifs that sustain it. In a familiar refrain, Heidegger will assert that existential plenitude cannot be conceived in terms of everything that is present-at-hand, just as the negation of *Vorhandenheit,* its deficiency or lack (*Nichtvorhandensein*), has no place in the midst of existence: "In this sense, it is essential that in existence there can be nothing lacking, not because it would then be perfect, but because its character of being remains distinct from any presence-at-hand" (*SZ* 283). The not-present-at-hand is both below and above the deficient category it negates: below, it is already or still not-present-at-hand (and, therefore, present-at-hand elsewhere in the succession of the present, the "now"); above, it inches toward existentiality, incongruous with the parameters set by the categorial analytics. In a massive displacement of the presence-absence dualism, the negative modification of the present-at-hand in *Nichtvorhandensein* intensifies the dearth (of usability) ingrained into this category; as emancipation from the categorial domain as such, it works a little like the Hegelian negation of the negation (albeit without the customary synthesis), as the lack of lack that insinuates itself into existence. Why, as Derrida would say, does lack linger in existence "under erasure"? Are existential finitude, imperfection, and failure not so many afterglows of the theological *via negativa* that outlives its provenance in the paucity of human language, inadequate to articulating divine plenitude?

A solution to the riddle of existential failure lies in the amphibology of *Nichtvorhandensein.* There can be, and there is, a nothing that has broken free from lack, and that is both the abyssal foundation of fundamental ontology and the springboard for an alternative theory of failure. Heidegger would encourage philosophical imagination to picture to itself "nonprivative lacunae" in the plenitude of existence, an "existential nullity [*die existenziale Nichtigkeit*] [which] has by no means the character of a privation [*den Charakter einer Privation*], where something is lacking in comparison with an ideal" (*SZ* 285). Such would be the nothing that lacks nothing and that, in its non-identity with itself (it lacks itself and, at the same time, does not lack anything), welcomes anxiety, conscience, thrownness, and projection, as well as, I believe, the existential conception of failure.

All of this passes below the radar in the public world of the "they," the world where Heidegger, too, is periodically taken to court or, more often, judged in absentia. The nullity and silence characterizing, for instance, the discourse of conscience are taken as evidence "held against the conscience on the subterfuge that it is 'dumb' and manifestly not present-at-hand. With this kind of interpretation the 'they' merely covers up its own failure to hear the call [*verdeckt das Man nur das ihm eigene Überhören des Rufes*] and the fact that its 'hearing' does not reach very far" (*SZ* 296). For *das Man*, what is not present-at-hand is absent, negligible, and ineffectual, as a result of drowning in the noise idle talk emits. Thus, the failure to hear the call of conscience covered up by a public interpretation is attributable to the plenitude of our absorption in the world. Ontologically interpreted, *das Man* undermines the premises of its own practice: one can fail most profoundly and spectacularly (for the world of the "they" is a spectacle) solely in the plenitude of existence that manifests itself in idle talk, curiosity, fascination, and other elements of "inauthenticity." The existential conception of failure must depart from and keep returning, tirelessly, to this forgotten plenitude.[6]

Needless to say, the plenum of existence does not stand for the abundance of things, for the Leibnizian infinite subdivisions suturing the intervals readily identifiable things fail to occupy in the world-totality, or for the actualization of Dasein in the "now," akin to Husserl's principle of perceptual presence. To the contrary, while the vector of existence pushes against lack, it is necessarily finite. Existential finitude is not "an end at which it just stops" (*SZ* 329). Were it to have an end interpreted in terms of stoppage, finite existence would be absurdly actualized, would become in the moment of death what it has always already been: a lifeless material thing. The meaning of finite existence without end, of a nothing that lacks nothing, is possibility: "the 'not yet' which belongs to Dasein . . . is not something which is provisionally and occasionally inaccessible to one's own experience or even to that of a stranger; it 'is' not yet 'actual' at all [*es 'ist' überhaupt noch nicht 'wirklich'*]" (*SZ* 243). Thought together with the demand, with which Heidegger saddles phenomenology as an impossible praxis faithful to the existential energy of possibility, his obstinate emphasis on the "possibilization of Dasein" further problematizes the "vulgar" notion of failure.

How to construe failure in a practice of thinking and in an existential comportment that have broken the spell of actual being and the process of actualization encoded in becoming? In actuality, failure appears to be negative because, there, it is a token for our projects' non-fruition and our desires' non-satisfaction. Failure is attached to negativity with a conceptual umbilical cord if and only if it befalls something that has been prevented from being actualized on an interrupted itinerary of becoming. But within the purview of the possible, failure loses its negative character and participates, quasi-transcendentally, in becoming, as the possibility of possibility. The deflation of actuality in Heidegger's reflections on phenomenology was the subject of chapter 1 in the present study; what is of interest here is his reworking of the Kantian transcendental conditions of possibility for experience into existential-ontological conditions of possibility, such as "being-guilty."

Apropos of guilt, Heidegger advises his readers that "not only can entities whose being is care load themselves with factical guilt, but they *are* guilty in the very basis of their being; and this being-guilty is what provides, above all, the ontological condition for Dasein's ability to come to *owe* anything in factically existing" (*SZ* 286). Existential guilt is the ontological condition of possibility for the everyday conception of guilt, equated with Dasein's debt to others. It impels the translation of ontological "being-guilty" (existing; being as being-guilty) into a formal definition of guilt *and* accounts for the failure of that translation, to the extent that it binds guilty feelings to a given individual action (in Christianity: intention or desire) rather than to being. The founded is based on the founding in a breathtakingly unfounded, tenuous way, rendering it possible and impossible. In such mistranslation interwoven with the task of translation, I detect the second theoretical locus for a revised notion of failure.

In the third place, in its fecundity, failure individuates a definite kind of Dasein's being. Still dealing with the paradigmatic example of conscience, Heidegger reasons: "If in each case the caller and he to whom the appeal is made are *at the same time* one's own Dasein *themselves*, then in any failure to hear the call or any incorrect hearing of *oneself*, there lies *a definite kind* of Dasein's *being* [*dann liegt in jedem Überhören des Rufes, in jedem* Sich*verhören eine* bestimmte Seinsart *des Daseins*]. . . . With regard to Dasein, 'that nothing ensues' [*'daß nichts erfolgt'*] signifies something positive" (*SZ* 279). Technically speaking, the mode of being that crystallizes in the failure to hear the silent call is one of falling or everydayness, our concernful engagement in the world in the spirit of inauthenticity. The primal scene of miscommunication is miscommunication with myself across the temporal divide that grants me existence. Given the futurity, the non-presence, and the non-givenness to intuition of the caller (who is none other than myself), the possibility of miscommunication is not just an unfortunate error, not a failure that deviates from a well-trodden progress toward success, but the predicament of existence, in which I cannot help but fail to hear myself. More than that, failure to receive the message from myself is generative and generous: thanks to it—thanks, as well, to a positive "non-happening" where "nothing ensues" and where the unyielding machinery of productivism comes to a grinding halt—I enter a "definite kind of being." It is the state of being dispensed to me by existential-ontological failure.

Heidegger repeats, on the subject of conscience, what he has already conveyed in paragraph 38 of *Being and Time*: "Not-Being-its-self [*das Nicht-es-selbst-sein*] functions as a *positive* possibility of that entity which, in its essential concern, is absorbed in the world" (*SZ* 176). Ontological failure in a matter as decisive as being myself (standing face-to-face or time-to-time with the impending event of my death) empowers me to act, to be concernfully dispersed in the world. Yet, as the caller and the one called, Dasein is "not-being-its-self" (as the latter) and "being-its-self" (as the former), authentic in its inauthenticity and inauthentic in authenticity. It takes an instant or two to take stock of this modification: we are in the thickets of the main idea of the book—Dasein is temporally ecstatic; ecstasis is its "definite kind of being" and its phenomenal unity—and it is this idea that informs, and is informed by, Heidegger's understanding of failure. The failure to be oneself spawns ecstatic temporality; the ecstatic constitution of Dasein makes failure ecstatic. Failure fails ecstatically. Existence, which is another word for ecstatic temporality, exists failingly. So does existential thinking (the truth of phenomenology), which in Heidegger's self-analysis has been and, true to its own postulates, had to be an utter failure: "*The failure*—the other writings and *Being and Time* have not in the least succeeded even only to nudge in the direction of questioning, let alone produce an understanding of the question, an understanding which would lead to a retrieved questioning."[7]

And what about the cryptic "With regard to Dasein, 'that nothing ensues [or succeeds]' signifies something positive"? Does "that nothing ensues or succeeds" presage a failure in the coming about of the event, in its advent? An event uncoupled from the order of actuality? A break in the causal attribution of something that may ensue or issue from something else and a thorn in the side of productivism? All three interpretations carry hermeneutical weight. Look at the failure of the event's advent. That no outcomes are eventually produced, that nothing comes out of it—above all, the nothing of plenitude—is the very thing that makes an event possible. The failure of something to ensue "signifies something positive" for an event that stubbornly sticks to the imperative of possibility, letting actuality and actualization fall by the wayside. Consequently (but, lest we forget, it is the logic of consequences that is in question here), that from which something ensues and that which ensues from it no longer obey the hierarchical difference folded into the cause-effect relation. The order of causality suffers an upset.[8] Wedged between the cause and its effects is nothing: nothing ensues there, nothing happens, and the failure of actual happening is fecund. Existential failure is the germ of *Gelassenheit*, letting-be.

DEAFENING TALK, SILENT TALK: THE BREAK

An intricate web of failure permeates the ontology of conscience as much as the existential ontology it is a part of. And, since conscience attests to the "authentic potentiality-for-being" of Dasein, authenticity is the modalization (and the modulation) of failure.

In *Reduction and Givenness*, Marion verges on avowing the structural necessity of failure to how we access being: "if being makes itself accessible only through the claim it exerts, if that claim can demand a response only by exposing itself to a deaf denial of 'gratitude,' then the ontological hermeneutic of the nothing *can* fail, since in order to be carried out, it *must* be able to fail."[9] Within the medium of conscience, the expression of being is taciturn, its silence signaling not the privation of speech but the existential condition of possibility for discourse. The "voice" of conscience is the fecund failure of *logos*. The hubbub of idle talk is possible thanks to—but without "gratitude," as Marion observes—Dasein's silent appeal to itself, the appeal that drowns in the phenomenon to which it gives rise. "Losing itself in the publicness and the idle talk of the 'they,'" Heidegger writes, "it [Dasein] *fails to hear* [*überhört*] its own self in listening to the they-self. . . . [I]t *listens away* to the 'they' [*und überhört im* Hinhören *auf das Man*]" (*SZ* 271). Dasein fails to hear itself because it hears too much, because it overhears everything in the deafening plenitude of a fascinated listening to the "they" first attuned to the silent hearing of oneself. Carried out to its end, listening to oneself *must* fail, in that there is really—actually—nothing or no one present to listen to there; in so failing, one will listen away from oneself, to the "they-self," which is not the other but, also like my futural self, no one in particular.

In a textbook case of failure's fecundity, by listening away from myself I listen to the they-self. Existing publicly, phenomenally, "one's way of being is that of inauthenticity and failure to stand by one's self" (*SZ* 128). But how does failure bear fruit? In what way does the failure "to stand by one's self" maintain its fecundity if, betrothed to the possible, it rebels against the rules of actuality's game, first among them cause-effect relations? If its positivity cannot be an outcome, even less something failure produces, it must be attributable to the internal transformation, the metamorphosis, in that which fails.

"Listening away" (*Hinhören*) presupposes a "turning away," a departure from the "listening to." In phenomenology, the failure to hear that which (or the one who) was meant to be heard is a modification in the intentionality of Dasein, in how Dasein directs itself toward something, someone, or itself. In rhetoric we may recall the figures of *aversio* or *apostrophe,* those breaks in discourse hailing someone else, either present or absent. Discontinuity does not signal the collapse of listening or speaking altogether, but a modulation in the spoken or the heard that, compared to the first noematic target, is experienced as a failure of hearing or speaking. The positivity of failure resides in this modulation that, contra Husserl, Heidegger seems to have granted to the nonideal, worldly workings of intentionality. For the latter, intentionality (i.e., directedness-toward) is never direct, affected as it is by the originary sociality of Dasein as Mitsein. The failure of Dasein to hear itself is not an accident, but the result of its necessary dispersion and factical predicament of falling, with which it starts as with a given. Factical Dasein *must* start from *aversio*, from a convolution of sociality, directing its speaking and hearing elsewhere.

The call of conscience is a special permutation of intentional directedness, modulating the straight line of intentionality and, *in extremis*, bending it into a circle: "the 'whence' of the calling is the 'whither' to which we are called back [*Das Woher des Rufens im Vorrufen auf . . . ist das Wohin des Zurückrufens*]" (*SZ* 280). Failure materializes here in the guise of a difference between the "point" of departure and the "point" of destination, where the "whence" and the "whither" do not coincide. But this difference, this non-coincidence of departure and destination, is what opens up the space-time for projection and thrownness—the space-time in which Dasein *can* exist as a stretch or as a temporalizing stretching out. As it often happens, everything rides on the status of the copula. How close must one "stand by one's self" in order to avoid failing? Is it possible to diminish the distance *ad infinitum* by repeatedly emitting and receiving the call in the closed circuit of transmission from oneself to oneself? Is there something like the "optimal ecstatic constitution of Dasein" for Heidegger? Even accepting that it is I, myself, who addresses me from the future (in Hollywood movies such as *The Terminator* franchise, time travel initiated to save oneself or one's relatives is, therefore, a profoundly existential matter), this missive will not be relayed without a detour of the difference between the caller and the called, the split "between" Dasein and itself embodying inauthenticity "in the mode of its genuineness [*uneigentlichen Verstehen . . . im Modus seiner Echtheit*]" (*SZ* 148). The "failure" to be authentic and to stand by oneself flows out of and into the temporality of existence.

That is to say: authenticity cannot be tantamount to a recovery of the "original" direction and directedness—or, in the episode of the call of conscience, the self-directedness—of Dasein. In order for it to work at all, authenticity is obliged to work *with* failure as a given. Breaking with the habit of listening away to the "they," which for its part is a primordial interruption in the listening to oneself, Dasein must listen away from listening away and resort to the *aversio* of *aversio*, the break of the break, repeating the existential negation of the negation in *Nichtvorhandensein*: "If Dasein is to be able to get brought back from this lostness of failing to hear itself, and if this is to be done through itself, then it must first be able to find itself—to find itself as something which has failed to hear itself" (*SZ* 271).

Is the cognizance of failure (Dasein's understanding of failure as such and its self-interpretation as a *failed existent*) a necessary and sufficient condition for overcoming it? Doesn't failure linger as what is acknowledged and, indeed, what must be acknowledged recurrently, if Dasein is to attempt standing by its self? Where does reading the "*aversio* of *aversio*" as a strange negation of the negation leave the chances for a clean break with Dasein's failure and inauthenticity? And would an authentic attitude be ever able to dodge the need to negotiate with and "modalize" failure, immanently transforming it from within?

Going against the grain of his own thinking, Heidegger wishes for a clean break with—not a sublation of—Dasein's failure of Dasein: "this listening-away must be broken off [*Dieses Hinhören muß gebrochen*]; in other words, the possibility of another kind of hearing which will interrupt it must be given by Dasein itself. The possibility of its thus getting broken off lies in its being appealed to without mediation" (*SZ* 271). The apparatus that breaks failure off is anything but mysterious. Because conscience issues its call without curiosity or fascination, its silent appeal arouses another kind of hearing, from which the wave of worldly plenitude has receded, exposing the seabed of lucid anxiety. In the existential nullity that replaces the plenum, Dasein faces itself naked, without mediations either by the things in the world or by others. After failure, another kind of hearing comes into being in another world (which is still, to be sure, this world here-below) reduced to its worldhood.

Heidegger's desperate anti-dialectical footwork aside, several problems with the "break" linger on. First, what is the fate of the "unity of the phenomenon" Heidegger endeavors to reestablish throughout his thinking of existence? It seems that "after the break" the qualitative difference between authenticity and inauthenticity would be so great that no unity could be restored. Moreover, no phenomenon could appear there where *logos* keeps silent. The silence of the break matches the world emptied of phenomena, diminished to its worldhood, and no longer fit for living or dying in. The call of conscience is the limit of language: enabling in the everyday inauthenticity of Dasein and prohibitive vis-à-vis the existential expression of authenticity. Second, and more fundamentally, Dasein's appeal to itself "without mediation" disregards the minimal spatiotemporal distance-lag of its ecstatic constitution and the parameters within which any decision is made. This distance and this lag themselves are mediations, the media through which the message from oneself to oneself travels. And mediations, as well as the media, always retain the possibility of failure.

The clean cut of the break is, in Heidegger's eyes, a decision, if not a meta-decision: a choice to make a choice "from one's own self" in order to "'make up' for not choosing" and for getting carried away by the Nobody (*SZ* 268). The object of the choice has to do with intentionality itself, with the modulation of its directedness, the direction in which Dasein will turn or turn away. Does "choosing to choose" break with failure decisively? I do not mean that the existential decision, let alone the decision to decide, is a onetime occurrence; to be in effect, it must be made repeatedly. I am thinking, alternatively, of Heidegger's provocative singling out of freedom "only in the choice of one possibility—that is, in tolerating one's not having chosen the others and one's not being able to choose them" (*SZ* 285). Freedom leads Dasein past the acceptance of the original and ineluctable failure to make the choice for or against sociality. Mirroring Nietzsche's eternal recurrence, it retrospectively chooses "not having chosen the others," choosing thereby the *ur*-failure to choose.

FAILURE AND "LAWBREAKING"

Consistently with Heidegger's philosophy, the "vulgar," negative, nonproductive notion of failure is not to be brushed off as erroneous, for it contributes to a fuller sense of the phenomenon *failure*. That is why phenomenologists are obliged to juggle two kinds of failure: (1) the failure to hear the silent call of conscience, to stand by oneself, and to be or to remain resolute; and (2) the failure to follow the norms, the laws, and the rules woven out of the prefabricated threads of commonsensical meaning. In the context of normativity, failure is set up, measured, and judged over and against the haphazard constructs of the "they" with the attendant conclusion that Dasein does not have the wherewithal to live up to this publicly concocted ideal image. It is thus transposed onto the existential arena from the thingly world of reckoning and manipulability, of concern and machination.

As Heidegger concentrates on "vulgar" failure, his language grows richer and more nuanced. Here, one comes across *Verfehlungen*—failures denoting that something is missing—and *Unterlassungen*—the omissions and defaults of acting: "Does it [conscience] not rather speak definitely and concretely in relation to failures and omissions [*Verfehlungen und Unterlassungen*] which have already befallen or which we still have before us?" (*SZ* 279). But the empirical definiteness and concretion of conscience, dictating how one must act and making it known when one has acted badly, bespeaks a vulgar approach to the voice of silence as an innate mental faculty. To curtail it to functionality is to "stick to what '*they*' know as conscience, and how 'they' follow or fail to follow it" (*SZ* 289).

The vulgar framing of conscience straitjackets it in what we formally receive from others and what we follow without making the first metachoice, without the retrospectively embraced intention to follow and without submitting preunderstanding to interpretation. Relevant to this framing is Derrida's reading, in *Of Spirit,* of the problematic of "guidance" and "following" in Heidegger's "Rectorship Address" and *Being and Time.* While, authentically, conscience guides us just like a question demands and commands "without being followed, obeyed, or listened to in any way,"[10] inauthentically, we follow it without any explicitly assumed guidance, be it as meager as the choice of the original absence of choice. Between and within each of these possibilities, failure makes itself known in the negative: successful guidance is coupled with the failure of following, and successful following with a failure of guidance. The objective and mechanical security of rules and norms that invite mindless obedience is predicated on the existentially insecure foundation of the "they."

The other manifestation of vulgar conscience presides over the transformation of its principles into a set of "manipulable rules" and its derivation from the world of concern. Those who construe conscience as "having debts" (those who, so to speak, economize it) make it conditional upon Dasein's concernful dealings with others. Henceforth, the voice of conscience monotonously declares one's "failing to satisfy [*nicht genügen*], in some way or another, the claims which others have made as to their possession. This kind of being-guilty is related to *that with which one can concern oneself*" (*SZ* 281–82). What sort of dissatisfaction does the judgment of conscience lean upon? "The common sense of the 'they' knows only the satisfying of manipulable rules [*handlichen Regel*] and public norms and the failure to satisfy them" (*SZ* 288). A "manipulable rule," *handlichen Regel,* is ready-to-hand, *Zuhanden,* in a regularized, technical, or technicist manner. Shunning this mechanized version of morality and conscience, which percolated even into Kant's non-utilitarian philosophy, Heidegger again exhibits a desire for what Derrida calls the "rigorous non-contamination . . . of the thought of essence by technology."[11] To the extent that he challenges this reading, Bernard Stiegler notes that the late Heidegger is no longer averse to "the questions that technics addresses to us,"[12] including with regard to conscience. But for the early Heidegger, in any event, the failure to satisfy this or that public rule or norm is secondary to the failure of thought (of which he stands accused by Krell), where thinking recrudesces to "common sense" that *regularizes* and *technologizes* the criteria for success and for failure.

The vulgar grasp of conscience feeds into a legalistic conception of thinking and human behavior that is anathema to Heidegger. The law, described as a conjunction of definite manipulable rules that are followed "without guidance" and that protect the property of others in the mode of concern, exports chunks of the categorial analytic to that of existence. More than a collection of statutes, it is the principle behind a systematic and escalating transgression of boundaries, contaminating the purity of the two analytics, between Dasein's comportment toward things and its comportment toward itself and others. Determined to secure the imperiled distinction, Heidegger recommends that "the idea of guilt must not only be raised above the domain of that concern in which we reckon things up, but it must also be detached from relationship to any law and "ought" [*ein Sollen und Gesetz*] such that by failing to comply with it [*wogegen sich verfehlend*] one loads himself with guilt" (*SZ* 283). So much so that the difference between the ontic and the ontological conceptions of guilt, as well as between the failure to hear the silent call of conscience and the failure to comply with the legally posited "ought," will adumbrate the scope of authenticity.

Attending to conscience, Heidegger in effect blends its vulgar failure with lawbreaking: "Yet, the requirement which one fails to satisfy need not necessarily be related to anyone's possessions; it can regulate the very manner in which we are with one another publicly. . . . This does not happen merely through law-breaking as such, but rather through my having the responsibility for the other's becoming endangered in his existence, led astray, or even ruined" (*SZ* 282). Whereas, structurally, lawbreaking is the analog of the existential "break," in its effects, illegal behavior upholds the system it purportedly breaks: the transgressors of a law are locked within the world of concern in a privative mode, whether they meddle in some of its mechanisms or try to work around them. Lawbreaking is not enough to effectuate a break with the law not so much as an institution but as the mechanized principle for one's transactions with others. One must be allowed to fail otherwise, on terms and conditions incomprehensible to a legal, legalistic mind-set—or without any terms or conditions whatsoever.

Levinas usually receives credit for developing the notion of responsibility for the other that, preconscious or preintentional, operates outside an explanatory net of alibis and criminal motives. The unchosen ethical "responsibility for the other's becoming endangered in his existence" is, however, prepared in the bowels of what constitutes sociality for Heidegger. Beyond the causal and axiological attributions of one's being for or against the other, and beyond, also, an objective measure of sufficiency, the assumption of hyperbolic responsibility can only culminate in a failure, stirring one to further ethical action *ad infinitum*, as Levinas rightly surmises. This failure is not, emphatically, a mechanical malfunction in the law-machine, a glitch within the mechanisms of legality, but a break *with* that mechanism and, Heidegger hopes, with the *Gestell* of technicity, in which the humanity of late modernity is trapped.

Hereafter, we run into a score of aporias pertaining to the mechanics of a non-mechanistic break with the legal mechanism of assigning responsibility. For instance, Heideggerian sociality germinates on the grounds of radical individuation: "What is it that so radically deprives Dasein of the possibility of misunderstanding itself by any sort of alibi and failing to recognize itself, if not the forsakenness [*Verlassenheit*] with which it has been abandoned [*Überlassenheit*] to itself?" (*SZ* 277). Being forsaken and abandoned to oneself rectifies the failure of self-recognition and self-understanding, for which sensible alibis are plentiful. Face-to-face with my mortality, in the lucid transparency of worldhood, I turn away from the turning away, am deprived of the failings that co-occur with my total absorption in the world of everyday concern. But Dasein's tumult does not end there: I must turn away again, returning to the other otherwise as, over and above what's mandated by my legal responsibility, I pledge (in which voice and with what words?) neither to forsake nor to abandon her in light of our shared (albeit, unshareable) condition of being forsaken and abandoned to ourselves.

For all his railing against machination and manipulation, Heidegger's discontent with the law diverges from Hegel's critique of the Kantian formal and abstract idea of legality. In Heidegger's view, the problem with the law is that it is *inadequately formal,* in that it yields nothing but definite, concrete, and technical criteria for guilt. The "idea of 'Guilty!' must be sufficiently *formalized* so that those ordinary phenomena of 'guilt,' which are related to our concernful being with others, would *drop out*" (*SZ* 283). How does this demand of formalization sit with his earlier dogged insistence on a deformalized (*entformalisiert*) concept of phenomenology (*SZ* 35)?[13] Where does the failure of formalization begin, and where does it end? And, to paraphrase John Sallis, where does phenomenology begin and end in *Being and Time*?

WHEN EQUIPMENT FAILS

The philosophical nexus of failure and concernful engagements, where the "technological theme" receives its earliest consideration from Heidegger, exceeds the limits of *Being and Time.* Roughly in the same period when Heidegger gave a course on Plato's *Sophist* in Marburg, he discussed the possibility of failure as "constitutive for the development of *technē*" and postulated that *technē* "will move securely" only "if it risks producing a failed attempt": "*Die τέχνη wird um so sicherer gehen, wenn sie einen Fehlversuch riskiert*" (*GA* 19:54). The sweep of technological innovation is contingent upon countless failed experimental travails that jointly carry the wave of "progress." But what happens when equipment fails to function in everyday life? Presumably, another sort of techno-failure materializes here.

A broken tool is no longer silently and unobtrusively present, nor is it proximate to us: "when, for instance a tool definitely refuses to work, it can be conspicuous only in and for dealings in which something is manipulated" (*SZ* 354). A conspicuous tool "merely drops out [*nur affallen*]" of the technical milieu, whereas an ontologically guilty conscience exits the logic of technicity; hence, the former does not shake up the technicist *Gestell* as thoroughly as the latter. Alongside the other, already documented instances of breakage, such as breaking the failure and lawbreaking, a conspicuous tool creates a break, *ein Bruch,* in the referential context of circumspection (*SZ* 75). In the gap of the unusable, from which a previously functional thing has been wrested, a present-at-hand object appears.

When equipment fails, failure borders on lack; yet even here it is twice brought back into the fold of positivity. The first time, in circumspective use. There, failure denotes the unsuitability of equipment to the task at hand, as Heidegger illustrates: "when we are using a tool circumspectively, we can say . . . that the hammer is too heavy or too light" (*SZ* 360). The stress on unsuitability sends thought back to the noematic variations objectified in equipment: a particular directing-toward turns out to be inappropriate to the toward-which of its directedness, which does not, however, preclude its suitability for something else. Despite being too heavy for driving a nail into the wall, a hammer might be just right for breaking the wall, even if that was not the original intention in using it. The hammer's momentary failure does not cancel out the chance of its readiness-to-hand in a different context of circumspective concern.

The second time, in the present-at-hand. Say a piece of equipment fails such that it ends up being absolutely unusable: under these circumstances, instead of signifying pure lack, it is illuminated "in itself" as something present-at-hand. The malfunction of a thing does not produce a vacuum in the world of Dasein, much less so in the world of things. Rather than causing the malfunctioning thing to drop out of the world, it leads to a glitch in understanding, "when we merely stare at something, our just-having-it-before-us lies before us *as a failure to understand it anymore*" (*SZ* 149). The fecundity of the hermeneutical glitch is that of the philosophical attitude in general: failing to understand a thing by relating through it to the world it helps us modify, we pay attention to what it is in itself. Non-understanding invites thought, in particular theoretical thinking. The philosopher is the one who fails to understand and, not knowing how the world works, is aware of not-understanding as something essential, making a life (and, at times, eking out a living) out of it. To sum up, the positive aspect of the double failure of the thing, when it comes to using and understanding it, consists in the categorial swing from the ready-to-hand to the present-at-hand.

A watered-down variation on Dasein's forsakenness and abandonment is discernible in equipmental failure: "That with which one's concernful dealings fail to cope . . . reveals itself in its insurmountability [*in seiner Unüberwindlichkeit*]" (*SZ* 355). The concernful resignation Dasein experiences in "understand[ing] itself in its abandonment to a 'world' of which it never becomes master" (*SZ* 356) mirrors the forsakenness of Dasein to itself in care and its individualization by the impending mortality that precludes any possibilities of misunderstanding (as well as of understanding). Besides the fact that they belong to the categorial and the existential analytics, respectively, the differences between the states of resignation and forsakenness boil down to the fate of the world: is the world reaffirmed through an occasional break in one of its parts, or does it evanesce in the anxiety of a forlorn Dasein reduced to itself? The world of failed concernful dealings communicates pockets of its noncommunicability, its material resistance to our projects. Ruptures in parts of the world only serve to increase the pressure it exerts on us; the world's disappearance as a whole from Dasein's horizon hands it over to total mastery and, pivoting back to concernful dispersion within the schema of worldlessness, manipulation.

In the regime of actuality, where the world of practical dealings takes place, "everyday concern understands itself in terms of that potentiality-for-being which confronts it as coming from its possible success or failure [*möglichem Erfolg und Mißerfolg*] with regard to whatever its object of concern may be" (*SZ* 337). To stick to the letter of the text, Heidegger omits failure and leads readers to believe that the default state of a pragmatically interpreted world is that of success. Concern, after all, admits only one modalized possibility of success and un-success, *Erfolg und Mißerfolg*, weighed against the material fulfillment or nonfulfillment of intentions in their outcomes. Strictly speaking, equipment cannot fail; it can only be unsuccessfully actualized or improperly employed. But we can contemplate *failure* under those exceptional circumstances, extraneous to the categorial analytic, when Dasein's "object" is Dasein itself, that is to say, when Dasein is the "object" of care and when it understands itself or fails to understand itself in terms of its own potentiality-for-being, that is to say, in terms of its possibilities. When equipment fails, all that is left for us is to hope that unsuccess will turn into success: that the break in the totality-of-significations will be filled, its promise actualized. That is why *failure* is to be reserved for existential descriptions that keep possibility intact, without sacrificing it to the ontology of actualizable potentialities.

3. The Phenomenology of Ontico-Ontological Difference

BETWEEN TWO PHENOMENOLOGIES

Of phenomenology, can there be more than one? Is such a thing possible? How many actualities can there be for a phenomenology focused on possibility?

There are, undoubtedly, countless phenomenologies that refer to, intend, and are *of* something: perception or religious experience, the social world, or landscape and place. There are, likewise, those most intimately associated with certain proper names (e.g., Max Scheler or Maurice Merleau-Ponty), around which philosophical movements and professional organizations accrete. But the phenomenological focus on regions of being and its scattering into "schools of thought" cannot put into question the oneness and unity of phenomenology. The regionalization, compartmentalization, and disciplinary shaping of phenomenology bespeak its formalization and the institutionalized division of intellectual labor, manufacturing the "actuality" of phenomenological movement (see chapter 1).

It is against these deleterious trends that, in 1927, Heidegger advanced a different kind of multiplicity: "There is no such thing as *the one* phenomenology, and if there could be such a thing it would never become anything like a philosophical technique. For implicit in the essential nature of all genuine method as a path toward the disclosure of objects is a tendency to order itself always toward that which it discloses."[1]

The conclusion that when it comes to phenomenology there *must* be more than one would have been incontrovertible were it not for Heidegger's own writings from the 1920s, especially *History of the Concept of Time, Being and Time,* and *The Basic Problems of Phenomenology.* His main concern in that period is to uncover the ontological bases of phenomenology and, indeed, to interpret phenomenology as "the *method of ontology*" (*BPP* 328). The ontological interpretation of phenomenology ranges from the elevation of possibility over actuality and the reflections on intentionality as the being of consciousness[2] to an investigation of how the being of entities shows itself in the self-presentation of phenomena (*SZ* 35), not to mention setting reduction to the work of transitioning from ontic reality to ontology, from the apprehension of beings to the understanding of their being (*BPP* 21). But what does it mean that phenomenology is or ought to be executed as an ontology? Do Heidegger's ontological principles not compel us to practice phenomenology in the difference between beings and being and, therefore, to locate it in the space or the spacing of ontico-ontological difference? Returning to the opening question of this chapter, we can now conjecture that, so understood, phenomenology will be both one and more than one, irreducible either to the beings that show themselves or to their being (*logos*) that gives itself and withdraws from the self-showing of phenomena.

Already in the early 1920s, Heidegger was not convinced that Husserl's phenomenology held the ontological resources he had sought in it. This, in my view, is the subtext of the harsh remark Heidegger made in a letter to Karl Löwith on February 20, 1923: "Husserl was never a philosopher, not even for a second of his life."[3] If to be a philosopher is to think ontologically with respect to the being of beings, then, in Heidegger's estimation, Husserl, who had not attained the heights of ontology, is not a philosopher. Unfair as the epistolary assessment may be, it explains why, at the height of the confrontation with Husserl, in a 1930–31 course at the University of Freiburg, Heidegger turned to another phenomenology—which could well be *the other* of Husserl's phenomenology—that of Hegel, previously deemed a sworn enemy of the "authentic fundamental tendency of phenomenology": "When today the attempt is made to connect the authentic fundamental tendency of phenomenology with the dialectic, it is as if one wanted to mix fire and water."[4]

Thus, my working hypotheses are as follows. First, everything Heidegger notes concerning the Hegelian phenomenology of spirit (and, particularly, concerning its absolutizing stance) is meant as an anachronistically marshaled refutation of Husserlian phenomenology. And second, "Husserl" and "Hegel" are, above all for Heidegger himself, incalculably more than names associated with two schools of thought or currents in or of phenomenology; they correspond to the encryptions of "ontic" and "ontological" phenomenologies, of consciousness and of spirit. Whereas Hegel sublates consciousness in spirit, Heidegger will dwell on the impossible, unsynthesizable, groundless position in the middle without mediations, from which to take stock of the spacing of ontico-ontological difference proper to phenomenology, at once singular and plural, both one and more than one. In the words of *Ontology: The Hermeneutics of Facticity*, he will ally without alloying, gather together without mixing them, dialectical fire and phenomenological water.

Tacit or explicit, Heidegger's rejoinders to Husserl are not outright dismissals; they are the obverse of the reproach addressed to Hegel's philosophy, where "everything ontic is dissolved into the ontological, . . . without insight into the ground of possibility of ontology itself" (*BPP* 327) and, therefore, without safeguarding the possibility—miraculously preserved in Husserl—of phenomenologically reducing the ontic to the ontological. It is not enough to opt either for a reconstructive construction of the world on the foundations of absolute knowledge or for the transcendental constitution of the object by pure consciousness. Between the two phenomenologies, suspended in the no-man's land of ontico-ontological difference, thinking will experience unrest well in excess of the dialectical "restlessness of the negative" and the negativity of phenomenological reduction. From this unrest, phenomenology *qua* phenomenologies will glean its possibility.

Complicating the bid to think between the two phenomenologies is Heidegger's contention that the one bears no relation to the other. "The *Phenomenology* [*of Spirit*]," he writes, "has nothing to do with [*hat nichts zu tun . . . mit*] a phenomenology of consciousness as currently understood in Husserl's sense. . . . A clear differentiation [*klare Scheidung*] is necessary in the interest of a real understanding of both [the Hegelian and Husserlian] phenomenologies—particularly today, when everything is called 'phenomenology.'"[5] (I must observe, *en passant,* that negation is itself highly suspicious, if only because, according to psychoanalysis, it is one of the most potent defense mechanisms of the ego. "This is not my mother," in Freud's influential essay on the subject, says the exact opposite of what it declares: the woman in the dream *is* my mother, but it would be too traumatic for me to admit it. The same goes for the statements that concern us here: "This is not phenomenology" and "Husserl is not a philosopher.") The need for a "clear differentiation" does not impel those who are moved by it toward a meticulous and dry, scholarly comparison with its earnest recommendation to advance "understanding," a form of consciousness confined to the relatively early stages of Hegelian phenomenology and to pragmatic dealings with the world of concern in Heidegger's own project. A "real understanding" of both phenomenologies signifies something else altogether: a critical rehashing of the ontico-ontological difference in and through the "clear differentiation," with the undertones of *krinein* (to divide, separate, discern, or judge) Heidegger has just evoked. This difference and this differentiation are so intense that they thwart the relation between the two phenomenologies, which have "nothing to do with" one another. Between them there is only a non-relation, as Husserl hinted in a handwritten note on the margins of his copy of *Being and Time.* In the sole remark penned in the section of the book on Hegel's conception of time, he confessed, "I am able to learn nothing here, and seriously, is there anything here to learn at all?"[6]

Having reached the conclusion that he has nothing to learn from Hegel, from Heidegger's treatment of Hegel, or (most likely) from both, Husserl has disengaged his thinking from that other phenomenology, excusing and absolving himself from a dialogue with it. That no dialogue will bring the two phenomenologies together is partly due to their articulation in different conceptual languages, even when the same words (e.g., intention) enter their vocabularies. But, more crucially, it is due to the conflicting claims each lays on the *logos* of phenomena and on the becoming-phenomenal of *logos.* Instead of splitting (the one) *logos,* the two phenomenologies conjure up irreconcilable *logoi* that cannot hear, let alone understand or learn from, each other, for instance through a Gadamerian "merging of horizons." Vain are the hopes for a philosophical meta-language capable of gathering together the *logoi* that fall on the hither side of the dialectic of the one and the many. Their grafting onto Heidegger's ontico-ontological difference forecloses this gathering-together. Supposing that the relation between the two phenomenologies is at all conceivable, it will be a "relation without relation," similar to the ethical bond of the I and the other in the philosophy of Levinas, where at least one of the terms (the other who stands in for the absolute) is absolutely absolved, free from relational ties. An infinity stretches between the two—the infinity to be thought.

THE BEING OF CONSCIOUSNESS

As Heidegger clandestinely stages it, the relation or the non-relation between Husserl and Hegel is an apposition of the relative phenomenology of beings and the absolute phenomenology of being: the philosophy of beings without being and of being without beings. A fleeting glance at this apposition will suffice to realize that it is nothing like a simple contrast or a neat alignment. Although Hegel, too, presents his readers with the phenomenology of "relative" consciousness, this relativity is—Heidegger keeps reminding his listeners or readers—already reconstructed from the standpoint of the absolute. The phenomenology of spirit envelops that of consciousness, inasmuch as Hegel begins absolutely with the absolute, which "is other and so is *not absolute*, but relative. The not-absolute *is* not yet absolute" (*HPS* 33).[7] In dialectics, consciousness yields the most relative kind of knowledge (*HPS* 34), one where the absolute is at the furthest remove from itself and where it subsists in a negative modality of the "not-absolute," while remaining itself in its otherness. At the same time, consciousness, purified by means of phenomenological reduction, is the horizon (the absolute horizon, perhaps) of Husserl's phenomenology. Its being, status, or standing is the site where the relation without relation of Husserl and Hegel will be enacted.

Before reviewing the two phenomenological ontologies of consciousness, a word on the absolutizing tendencies of Husserlian phenomenology is in order. All such tendencies converge on the practice of phenomenological reduction, Husserl's admission ticket to the realm of pure consciousness as that which is irreducible, that which survives bracketing, parenthesizing, setting aside. The outcome of reduction is absolute, insofar as absolutely irreducible. Reduction is the absolvent movement of separation from the world of natural attitude, from everything transcendent and given through adumbrations; it suspends natural consciousness that, with its limited ontic perspective, "finds everywhere and always only beings, only phenomena, and judges all that meets it in accordance with the results of its findings" ("HCE" 118). Nonetheless, there is one thing reduction cannot suspend: consciousness. That is why *Destruktion* must step in and step behind the modern philosophy of consciousness so as to develop "a critique of all ontology hitherto, with its roots in Greek philosophy, especially in Aristotle, whose ontology . . . lives as strongly in Kant and Hegel as in any medieval scholastic."[8] Without any reliance on the absolute, the critique Heidegger denominates *Destruktion* is eminently phenomenological and historical; it reawakens "a principal understanding of the thematic problems of the Greeks from the motives and the attitude of their way of access to the world"[9] by repeating the possibilities that organized their historical experience at the closure of metaphysics.[10]

The absolutizing tendencies of reduction are, for their part, truncated. As soon as it chooses sides, eidetically and exclusively looking at the non-adumbrated reality, Husserlian *epochē* falls short of the absolute that does not belong on one side only or, indeed, on any side: "Yet what is an absolute that stands on one side? What kind of absolute stands on any side at all? Whatever it is, it is not absolute" ("HCE" 101). Husserl orchestrates little more than an upturn of the natural attitude; having arrived at the non-phenomenal, non-adumbrated being of consciousness, he takes the side of this being, by which he is transfixed, ignoring the relation between the intended as intended (*noema*) and beings *simpliciter*. (Marion labeled this neglected relation the ontological "accomplishment" of phenomenology "in fact.") The bracketing of adumbrated reality dispenses with what is given relatively and incompletely, from one perspective or another, in favor of the absolute givenness of pure consciousness. But, in so doing, it takes the side of what has no sides, eschews the labor of mediation, aborts the "dialogue between natural and real knowledge" and the critical "comparison between ontic/pre-ontological knowledge and ontological knowledge" that, in Heidegger's reading of Hegel, constitutes consciousness *qua* consciousness ("HCE" 138). Ontically absolute, pure consciousness is ontologically relative owing to its very "purity," the purified one-sidedness distilled and sequestered from the world of the natural attitude.

On the heels of phenomenological reduction, the being of consciousness is intentionality, the directedness of consciousness toward something, its being, in each case, *of* something. Intentional consciousness is relative knowledge (and relative being) par excellence. Inherently relational, it is circumscribed by that of which it is conscious and rests on the intended, despite having been insulated from adumbrated reality as such. In this respect, it diverges from absolute knowledge that is no longer or not yet *of* something: "Is not knowledge as such a knowledge of something? This is precisely what Hegel denies and must deny when he claims that there is a knowledge which is qualitatively *not* relative, but absolute" (*HPS* 14). Prior to its fulfillment in intuition where noetic acts and their noematic targets join each other in quasi-tautological *correlations*, intentionality (i.e., the being of consciousness, or, simply, being) is essentially a *relatum*.

The ontic orientation of intentionality is its directedness toward the perceived, the remembered, the anticipated, and so forth; the ontological trajectory of absolute knowledge is that it "must not remain bound but must liberate and ab-solve itself [*sich losmacht, sich ab-löst*] from what it knows and yet as so ab-solved, as absolute [*als ab-gelöstes—absolute*], still be a knowledge" (*HPS* 15/21). The absolution of absolute knowledge from the known explodes noetic-nomatic correlations, freeing cognition, at long last, from the "correspondence theory of truth"—truth as *adequatio,* not of *rei et intellectus* but of the intuiting and the intuited—that dominates the entire field of pure consciousness. The true is not the fulfillment of empty intentionality in intuition or in the ontic presence of the intended. Dialectical truth is the whole, that is, being or absolute knowledge itself, and, moreover, it is the whole that delimits itself by receiving the other within.

The dialectical self-determining whole raises dilemmas of its own. For one, the ec-static character of existence prohibits the integration of Dasein into a whole until the instant of its death. For another, the grievance Heidegger voiced only several years before his first sustained engagement with Hegel against absolute knowledge was that such knowledge disbanded beings themselves and ignored "the original belonging together of comportment toward beings and understanding of being" (*BPP* 327). In a similar manner, Heidegger subtly rebukes Husserl, who, in contrast to Hegel, favored the intentional comportment toward beings over the understanding of being. Relative *phenomeno*logy is dedicated to the appearing of phenomena in a knowing bound to the known in intentionality; absolute phenomeno*logy* is concerned with the phenomenal appearance *logos* gives itself by negating and sublating its other. Therefore, "phenomenology is the *absolute self-presentation of reason (ratio*—Λόγος), whose essence and actuality Hegel finds in *absolute spirit*" (*HPS* 30). Only in the difference between, not in the synthesis of, the two phenomenologies, where at least as much disappears as appears, will the "original belonging together" of the ontic and the ontological, of phenomena and of *logos*, come through.

Does the denunciation of Hegel for his forgetting of beings apply to Heidegger's reading of *Phenomenology of Spirit*? In the reconstructive construction of the world from the vantage of absolute knowledge, we—those who know absolutely—care for the truth of being and for the truth of beings, for knowing itself and for that which is known: "we have in our knowledge *two* objects, or one object twice. This is the case necessarily and throughout the entire *Phenomenology*, because *for us* the object is basically and always *knowing*, which in itself and according to its formal essence already in its turn has its object, which it brings along with it" (*HPS* 48). So long as absolute knowledge is more or less other to itself—so long as it is conditioned by the known—its intentionality is split, the noematic target doubled into the knowing and the object of this knowing. Our attention is divided between two objects or, alternatively, fissured in straining toward a double, spectral object ("one object twice"). In the double bind of its being bound to two objects, in this hyper-delimitation, absolute knowing is delimited, released from its objective and subjective limits alike.

It is high time to call these two objects or the double object, the one counted twice, by their names: the ontological and the ontic, the being of beings comprehended as self-consciousness or, in a later text on Hegel, "experience" ("HCE" 139), and the known experienced beings as they are known and experienced. The absolute is only absolute if it spans these two modalities without necessarily reconciling them, that is, if it holds them together in a tension approximating the intensity of ontico-ontological difference. Touched by the absolute, the object turns into more than itself, overflows the limits of its identity, splits into two *or* becomes one and the same . . . twice (the dialectical and the ontological inflections of this "or" should be distinctly audible). And being? Isn't it more *or* less than itself, arrived at through ontico-ontological difference, in which alone it appears and from which it withdraws (as nothing *in* being)? In light of this analogy—the *ana-logos* thronging with redoublings (*an-*)—we can better appreciate the remark Janicaud made in passing in a text on the Hegel-Heidegger dialogue: "the most secret proximity [of Heidegger] to Hegel . . . perhaps lies hidden in the friction with regard to phenomenology."[11]

The dialectical splitting of the object of knowledge into the knowing and that which is known is the centerpiece of what, for Hegel, constitutes the being of consciousness. Heidegger encapsulates Husserl's ontology of consciousness in the statement "The being of consciousness is intentionality"; Hegel's speculative definition is: "The being of consciousness is self-consciousness." What in Husserl's phenomenology would have been the height of impoverished theoreticism, of a reflection on reflection that treats noetic acts as new noematic objects, is in Hegel's dialectics the sign of richness and negatively mediated concreteness, of absolute knowledge that fleshes itself out by determining itself. The ontic orientation of consciousness toward phenomena is, from the standpoint of this knowledge, inseparable from its ontological directedness toward itself in a movement of re-flection that, far from a wistful afterthought, shadows the reconstructive construction of experience from its absolute beginning.

As a result, to know absolutely means "not to be absorbed in what is known, but to transmit it *as such*, as *what is known* to where it belongs as known and from where it stems" (*HPS* 47). It means, *contra* Husserl, that the life of consciousness does not have to be extinguished in the presence of the intuited, and that a living intentionality, the *dunamis* of striving toward . . . , or possibility, need not reach its end (is not depleted or exhausted) in the actuality of that toward which it strives.[12] In a scenario where intentionality attains fulfillment, quelling the unrest of consciousness, Husserl flagrantly conflates the being of Dasein with the being of its intended targets, and, in the acts of consciousness, "knowing . . . forgets *itself* and is lost exclusively in the object" (*HPS* 129). Once knowing forgets itself, Dasein automatically comprehends itself (without really knowing its knowing and being) as something present-at-hand, such that its being "lost exclusively in the object" nullifies ontico-ontological difference. The relativity of relative phenomenology comprehends existence on the basis of the present-at-hand; the absoluteness of absolute phenomenology holds out the positive possibility of being lost in the object, the possibility of consciousness being lost in itself as its own object and of re-finding itself in itself.

In defense of Husserl's phenomenology, reduction has shown that consciousness itself does not appear and that, moreover, what defines the being-conscious of consciousness is this nonappearance, the nonadumbrated givenness setting it apart from transcendent reality, or, in Heidegger's language, from everything that is not-Dasein. Evidently, the ontology of pure consciousness parts ways with that of the present-at-hand. But in dialectics the "appearing of phenomenal knowledge is the truth of knowledge" ("HCE" 108) not at all insulated from adumbrated reality. Hegel rejects the immediate conflation of consciousness and "the outside world" only to accompany consciousness in its becoming as a phenomenon that appears in this world, which has now shed its semblance of exteriority and of something utterly transcendent. Ultimately, the thrust of Husserl's reduction is analytical, and, hence, partial compared to the synthesis of analysis and synthesis that is the bread and butter of the Hegelian absolute.

Much depends on the modes of objectivation or phenomenalization distinguishing the two phenomenologies. When *logos* itself appears in relative knowledge, it does so as the alienation and deadening of the subject, whose psychic life undergoes objectification in self-evidence; however, when it makes its phenomenal appearance in the realm of the absolute, *logos* comes into its own and gains a new lease on life. In Hegel, the consciousness of consciousness and the intentionality of intentionality bear no trace of the derivative and abstract character Husserl's phenomenology has charged them with. They owe allegiance to the being of the absolute, which, in its separation and absolvent absolution from everything relative, is absolutely inseparable (inalienable) from us: "the absolute is from the start in and for itself with us and intends to be with us. This being-with-us (*Παρουσία*) is in itself already the mode in which the light of truth, the absolute itself, beams [*anstrahlt*] upon us. To know the absolute is to stand in the ray [*Strahl*] of light, to give it back, to radiate [*strahlt*] it back, and thus to be itself in its essence the ray, not a mere medium through which the ray must first find its way" ("HCE" 98).

The being-with-us of the absolute is *its* becoming-phenomenal, the becoming that is as superfluous as it is necessary in that it runs its course *after* the absolute has already become everything it is, as seen from its contingent beginning. The shining of the absolute upon us does not put us in a spotlight beaming from the outside, as a luminous object over and against us. It radiates from within, with reflected or refracted light ("to give it back, to radiate it back"), with the ontological luminosity of consciousness as self-consciousness and, in the last as well as the first instances, as absolute spirit. Of course, our being-with the absolute deserves a patient deconstructive analysis. If the absolute is one *with* us, then it lets go of its identity (its absoluteness) and, no longer one, is minimally separated from us as much as from itself in the shape of a simple unity, by the nearness (the absolute nearness) of its presence. The separation of the absolute from itself is the apotheosis of the ontico-ontological difference Hegel allegedly forgot in his phenomenology.

The intentional ray of the transcendental ego in Husserl's phenomenology emits subjective light that shines upon its objects' noematic surfaces. When it is with us, this ray is already outside us, coordinating the self-transcendence of consciousness as the consciousness of. . . . Its arrow is unidirectional: consciousness intends something other—albeit not absolutely other, the transcendent. But the absolute, as Heidegger puts it, "intends to be with us" and, therefore, *intends us* whenever we ourselves intend anything whatsoever. The relinquishment of this other intentionality drastically undermines the phenomenological idea of constitution. In truth, to attribute pure activity to Husserl's constitutive subjectivity is to miss the point of his philosophy: besides relying on the passive synthesis of temporality, this subjectivity lives off what it constitutes in the hylomorphic production of meaning. But Husserl himself is only vaguely aware of these theoretical difficulties. If in the relative phenomenology of consciousness the constituting is in part ontically constituted by the constituted, in the absolute phenomenology of spirit the constituting is ontologically constituted by the absolute that intends it. In much of his thought, Heidegger will reflect upon the inversion of intentionality, detectable in Hegel's dialectics and imbued with ontological connotations. The "call of being" in *Being and Time* and, in a different sense, in "The Letter on Humanism," as well as the call of thinking that flips around the question "What is called thinking?" are the most prominent examples of this ontological inversion that turns us into the objects of another regard (of the absolute, which Levinas translates into the absolutely Other).[13]

The ontological reversibility of intentionality is the reason why, in censuring "current phenomenology" as contrasted to the phenomenology of spirit, Heidegger writes: "it is crucial that once again we determine correctly what the genitive means in the expression 'phenomenology of spirit.' The genitive must not be interpreted as a *genitivus objectivus*. Easily misled by current phenomenology, one might take this genitive to be object-related, as though here we are dealing with the phenomenological investigation of spirit that is somehow distinguished from a phenomenology of nature or that of economics" (*HPS* 23–24). Spirit is not—at least not exclusively—the object of phenomenology but also its subject; "phenomenology is . . . *the* manner in which spirit itself exists. The phenomenology of spirit is the genuine and total coming-out of spirit" (*HPS* 24). Enunciated in the language we are already abreast of, phenomenology is the *how* of spirit.

There is no semantic equivalence between the seemingly parallel expressions "phenomenology of consciousness" and "phenomenology of spirit," save for the understanding of the former as the mode of appearance of the latter. In the contemporary phenomenology of consciousness, *logos* fades into the "study" of phenomena, craving the honorable designation "discipline." This phenomenology is not *of* consciousness (subjective genitive), since consciousness itself does not appear or is not allowed to appear in it; phenomenology is *not* the manner whereby consciousness itself exists. So much so that, to extrapolate from Heidegger's conclusions, consciousness, as the object of phenomenological study, ceases to exist, loses its existential undertones, and receives the same status as the ontic domains of nature or economics. The razor-thin line of demarcation, cleaving the genitive in "phenomenology of . . . ," is drawn so as to restore the ontico-ontological difference Husserl erased. Of phenomenology, there is more than one in the one, not the least because the genitive form in "phenomenology of . . ." is inherently equivocal.

THE BEING OF EXPERIENCE AND TRUTH

The transcendental objectification of consciousness in Husserl's phenomenology, as the phenomenology *of* consciousness but not one *proper to* consciousness, shapes the concepts of experience and truth. The ontic truth of experience is the veracity of the present-at-hand, the fulfillment and the confirmation of empty intentionality in intuition (*HPS* 20). The fulcral function assigned to consciousness is that of verifying the appropriateness of the fit and the soundness of the relation between the experiencing and the experienced. The truth of such consciousness pivots on judging the accuracy and measuring the degrees of proximity between the "merely" intended and the "really" intuited in a sort of pre- or nonpredicative judgment built into the acts of perception and undergirding all so-called abstract judgments.[14]

Experience, for Husserl, *is* judgment or—this amounts roughly to the same thing—ontic critique. Consciousness feels the ontic disquiet of shuttling between the poles of comparison, but it is insensitive to the ontological turbulence one experiences when one dwells without abiding in the split between the ontic and the ontological, in the spacing of the ontico-ontological difference. Any residual unrest is subject to immediate pacification through a more stringent and exacting, if not necessarily exact, application of the rules of comparing, weighing, and judging. What has thus vanished from the relative and naive phenomenology of consciousness is the experience of experience, which is not the apogee of theoretical consciousness but the being of experience that "means *being* this distinction" ("between the ontically true and the ontological truth") ("HCE" 133). And what evaporates from every correlation of consciousness, regardless of how scrupulously one has judged the co-belonging of its two elements, is the absolute ontological-existential truth of experience.

When in the seminars of the 1930s and 1940s Heidegger mines Hegel's texts, he is searching for this very truth so demonstrably wanting in Husserlian phenomenology. Truth as the truth of the absolute is neither pure objectivity nor pure subjectivity; it is experience itself in the ontological-existential register of the term: "The will of the absolute to be with us, i.e., to appear for us as phenomena, prevails as experience" ("HCE" 143). In truth, the will of the absolute, which wills "to be with us," absolute knowers, achieves the above-mentioned reversal of intentionality, so that we are both the experiencing subjects and the experienced objects of that will. From a dimensionless perspective of the absolute, the ontic experience of given phenomena—indeed, of phenomenal givenness as the self-giving of the absolute—presents itself in a new light. Neither a proto-mathematical comparison nor a dispassionate judgment of the fit between intentionality and intuition, experience is the *pathos* of undergoing with . . . , consciousness's being-transformed with the experienced, with itself, and with the absolute.

Consequently, Heidegger proposes an interpretation of "experience as denoting, both negatively and positively, *undergoing an experience with* something" (*HPS* 21). The "with" of experience is propitious to the subtle inflections of existentiality: the being-with, *Mitdasein,* of consciousness comes to refer to the facticity of its unfolding alongside its objects, to its reflexive return to itself as self-consciousness, and to its being in absolute proximity (*Παρουσία*) to the absolute. The small preposition "with" assembles the positive and the negative, the ontic and the ontological, the existential and the categorial, for ontico-ontological difference to take its nonplace. The first of the three meanings of "experience with" is the only one that makes sense in the phenomenology of relative consciousness. The rich existentiality of the "with" wears off in the judged appropriateness and the co-belonging of the experiencing and the experienced.

To experience with . . . is to suffer with . . . and to be mutually transfigured by that with which one experiences or suffers. Rather than precluding dialectical alteration, the truth of the absolute and the absoluteness of the absolute necessitate it. Speculative verification, shuttling between the experiencing consciousness and the experienced content, verifies and authenticates the truth of both in and through their becoming otherwise than they were: on the side of the experiencing, "consciousness *verifies* to itself what it really is," so that "in this verification" it "loses its initial truth, what it at first thought of itself" (*HPS* 22); on the side of the experienced, "*something is verified* . . . as not being what it first seemed to be, but being truly otherwise [*sondern in Wahrheit anders*]" (*HPS* 21/30). Verification does not only take time to be carried out. It also takes time into account and, more boldly put, it *is* time.

Experiencing with . . . and suffering with . . . signify that one has forfeited the self-identity of consciousness, which has changed along with that of which it was conscious—something that remains unthinkable in the fixing of noetic acts (the intentional aiming at . . . that either successfully hits or, in a failed attempt, misses its target). In Husserl's terms, this forfeiture will have been explained with reference to a deficiency in phenomenological attitude, a lapse in judgment, a lacuna within experience itself that has not yet brought the experienced firmly into its grasp. After all, ensconced in the structure of noetic-noematic correlations, phenomenological time implies a provisional emptiness of intentionality not yet or already not fulfilled and, therefore, unfurls in a *temporary deferral* of the thing's presence to intuition. Provided that time is absorbed in potentiality to the detriment of possibility, nothing fundamentally changes in the intending and in the intended once the directedness-toward of consciousness is actualized in that toward which it has been oriented *ab initio*.

Much different is the dialectical truth of experience that takes time to emerge from the alteration of consciousness and of its double object, itself and its other. While the beginning is already absolute, the absolute, standing or falling furthest from itself in or at the beginning, is other to itself, with its otherness indicating the relativity of consciousness. In order to get in touch with the truth of the absolute, verification must render this otherness truly other, *in Wahrheit anders*, without thereby negating the truth of the beginning and without repeating the mistake of ontic judgments that, in a gesture of facile criticism, pour their scorn on the erroneousness of "what . . . first seemed to be."

Although, just as he has done in the early 1920s, Heidegger accuses Hegel of contributing to the metaphysical neglect of time's temporalization[15] and aligns this feature of dialectics with Husserl's own insistence on the scientificity of phenomenology (*HPS* 11), other aspects of the 1930–31 lecture course dealing with the temporal character of truth in the phenomenology of the absolute contest these criticisms. By and large, Heidegger's onslaught on Hegelian temporality is well known: the time of the dialectic passes over and covers over the ecstatic-existential temporality of Dasein, for which it substitutes the mediated "fall" of spirit into time (*SZ* 436). And yet, the thesis regarding truth as an alteration, mutually undergone by the experiencing and the experienced, discredits the argument that Hegel has excluded temporality from his thinking of being. Accepting that "experience" is synonymous with "the being of beings" ("HCE" 135), one must admit that the essence of the being of beings is time, the time of experience and the experience of time. The crucible of experience is the crossing of the ontic and the ontological right in the midst of the phenomenology of spirit. *Logos* is time itself: the phenomena that "dissolve" in it disappear into their innermost finite ontological matrix.

Consistent with my working hypothesis that the specter of Husserl haunts and is at the same time conjured away from Heidegger's readings of Hegel, the truth of sense-certainty and of perception (hence, of what has not yet been ontologically verified and, in being verified, altered) is the only truth contemporary phenomenology is acquainted with. In sense-*certainty*, conceptual weight bears down upon "certainty," which "means the entirety of the relation, in knowing, of a knower to what is known" (*HPS* 54), at the expense of "sense" and its hylomorphic arrangement, so decisive for the practitioners of twentieth-century phenomenology.[16] The certainty of sense-certainty is a moment of repose, when consciousness delights in the sensed plenitude of experience, when it no longer or not yet questions what is known, its relation to what is known, and itself. The richness of sense-certainty is a symptom for the overstimulation and oversaturation of consciousness, trounced by the infinite empty variety of what appears before it and satisfied with not thinking through the mode, the *how*, of knowing that ties it to the known. Existential possibility is the sole protection from such oversaturation and mindless satisfaction in the phenomenological notion of truth as the fulfillment of empty intentionality in flesh and blood, in the presence (at hand) of that toward which it has tended.

In the ontic domain, where the manifold of sense-certainty predominates, does intentionality know fulfillment? There, sense-certainty collapses due to its intrinsic non-fulfillment: "When we generally intend the thing, we find that 'this' *sends* our intention *away* [*von sich wegschickt*]. It sends our intention away, not generally, but rather in a definite direction of something which has the character of *a* being *this*" (*HPS* 58/82). The internal breakdown of sense-certainty is another illustration for the pulverization of intentionality reflected by, rather than absorbed into, the intended. The intentional comportment splitting and branching off into multiple directions is the conceptual forerunner of Dasein's practical and concernful dispersion that corresponds to the definite modes of its being-in-the-world. The intention is not fulfilled in the "this," but only referred to another "this," connected to it with the webs of a signification-weaving world. The infinite deferral of fulfillment in the presence of the intuited, the elusiveness of that which is intended, frustrates some of the axiomatic moments in Husserlian philosophy.

Aside from "hyletic phenomenology" that, at the limits of sense, recommends the study of sense data before the hylomorphic production of meaning,[17] Husserl's project focuses not so much on the pure "this" as on the perceived as perceived, the remembered as remembered, or, more generally, on noematic unities, where sense data are already (a priori) synthesized. Among noematic objects, Husserl singles out and absolutizes the perceived, given that the present of perception is the ground from which experience, memory, and expectation burgeon and in which they are fixed and consummated. All ontic critique of consciousness is to be undertaken from the perspective of the experiential present, molding both past and future horizons.

Mindful of temporal retention and protention, Husserl does not infer that the place of perception is in the middle and that, as Heidegger reminds us, "through the mediation of perception, sense-certainty first reaches understanding and therein gets to its own ground as the true mode of consciousness" (*HPS* 83). Perception is not the absolute; it is a path toward the absolute, itself nothing other than a path. Fusing it with the final destination, Husserl forgoes mediations, neglects the middle term, and paints a black-and-white, either/or canvass of psychic life: either intentionality is empty, when it merely intends and represents the intended for itself, or it is full, when representations receive the desired corroboration in perceptual presence. That perceiving is a hermeneutical act of the perceiver who nonthematically interprets (or else, nonpredicatively criticizes) the perceived X *as* X—that it is an act of preunderstanding on its way to explicit interpretation—is a verdict Heidegger reaches thanks to the Hegelian placement of perception in the middle, in the transitional form of consciousness, which could not have been any more dissimilar to the exaltation of perception to the status of the ground and the end of psychic life in Husserl. Between the two phenomenologies, there are no mediations and no middle ground, if holding them together requires, for example, mediating the same object as, at the same time, the middle and the end.

The middle place of perception matches the speculative concept of appearance that "must be grasped *as* appearance, as a middle" between appearing and disappearing. "It is important to remember again," Heidegger adds, "that Hegel does not take the essence of appearing only as self-showing, as becoming manifest, as manifestation. Rather, appearing also means a *mere*-showing and vanishing. There is in appearance a moment of negativity" (*HPS* 109, 117). The moment of negativity and of an immanent critique of appearance is nowhere to be found in Husserl's phenomenology of perception, for which phenomenal presence is tantamount to pure positivity. Adumbrated givenness admittedly means that in the appearing of phenomena something (not the least the appearing itself) does not appear and that several dimensions of the thing remain occluded, however temporarily, behind those that have just given themselves to sight. Yet the givenness of the noema, of the perceived as perceived, is complete and absolute, so much so that it is translucent for the act of perceiving. There are no traces of "vanishing" in the appearing noema and, consequently, there is no need to resort to signification, so as to "fill in the blanks" by interposing the sign in the place of the absent thing or parts of a thing.

While, for Hegel, "'to appear' or 'to be a phenomenon'" is "to become other in remaining self-identical [*sich-anders-werden in der Selbstgleichheit*]" (*HPS* 75/107), for Husserl, to appear is to testify to an identity between the perceiving and the perceived in the present of intuition. But Hegel, too, is not beyond reproach: the absoluteness of the absolute, the identity of knowledge and will, the becoming-rational of the actual, and the becoming-actual of the rational subsume the otherness of phenomena, as appearance and essence become (mediately) the same. It is the role of the phenomenology of the in-between, the phenomenology of ontico-ontological difference, to respect the promise of appearances that give themselves, even as something withdraws from their givenness. Heidegger's own concept of truth as *alētheia,* or the giving withdrawal of being, should be construed in the context of this phenomenology of the in-between.

A close and often exceptionally sympathetic reconstruction of Hegel's thinking in Heidegger's texts and seminars of the 1930s and 1940s[18] nevertheless gives their readers and participants to understand that, taken separately, the two phenomenologies do not have the requisite resources to address the intertwined questions of beings and of being. The symmetry of this accusation clashes with the conclusions of the 1923 course on ontology and hermeneutics, where Heidegger pegged the saving grace of

Husserl's philosophy onto the kind of critique that cuts through the "sophistries" of dialectical play with the form/content, finitude/infinity, and other distinctions. "It is," as Heidegger summed up his argument then, "what the critical stance of phenomenology ultimately struggles against."[19] A decade later, the "critical stance" migrates to the relation (without relation) between the philosophies of Husserl and Hegel. Neither is deemed adequate to the critical mission it set for itself: the phenomenology of spirit makes phenomena dissipate in *logos,* and the phenomenology of consciousness causes *logos* to melt into phenomena. Hegel is indicted for betraying the question of beings (*die Frage nach dem Seienden*) as a catalyst for their sublation (*Aufhebung*) (*HPS* 41/60). Husserl stands accused of neglecting the question of being, bracketed or set aside in the course of phenomenological reduction that disengages pure consciousness from everything transcendent, all the while ontically relativizing the being of that consciousness.

In the role Heidegger allotted to it, phenomenology is an ontological (i.e., ontico-ontological) enterprise, and it wastes its essential possibilities in the exclusive privileging of phenomena or of *logos*. When *logos* is absolutized, "there is no introduction to phenomenology, because there can be no introduction to phenomenology" ("HCE" 154); when phenomena are prioritized, there is nothing but an introduction to phenomenology, a "preliminary conception" or a *Vorbegriff.* Only in the suspended middle between the two (but are there only two?), in the space or spacing between the dearth of introduction and a relentless introduction, between *logos* and phenomena, between the one and the others, will the most basic question of ontology resound.

Part II
Ecology

4. To Open a Site

A Political Phenomenology of Dwelling

THE LIGHTNING ROD OF ECOLOGICAL POLITICS

From the beginning of metaphysics in the West to its end, philosophers have sought to do away with the divide between ethics and politics. Typically, their proposals revolved around the need to diffuse the political in the ethical: from the idea of the good (Plato) or the final end (Aristotle) guiding the organization of public life, through the state viewed as the highest stage of realized *Sittlichkeit* (Hegel), to the stateless, anarchist communities reliant on decentralized networks of personal interactions and attuned to the needs of each. Within this line of thought, Heidegger is not an exception. In his own style, he, too, bridges ethics and politics. Predictably, he takes another distinction to be more fundamental, namely, the distinction between being and beings at the core of the phenomenology of ontico-ontological difference. But we should rid ourselves of the illusion that, in a kind of mechanization or standardization of his method, Heidegger *indifferently applies* ontological difference to diverse areas of human life. Bearing on politics and ethics, this difference is filtered through the contrast between economy and ecology as manners of dwelling, of organizing an abode or letting it be. For Heidegger, then, the fault line passes not between ethical and political relations but between ecological ethics and politics, on the one hand, and their economic renditions, on the other.

To get a feel for the ecological underpinnings of ethical and political life as opposed to its economic arrangement, we must turn to the summer

1942 lecture course on Hölderlin's hymn "The Ister" and the winter 1942–43 course *Parmenides*, delivered at the University of Freiburg. At the time of war, in that politically terrible period, Heidegger puts forth a somewhat unorthodox reading of "politics" *via* an interpretation of the Greek *polis*. On both occasions, he stresses the primacy of the *polis* over the political, most likely as part of his ongoing and largely veiled critique of Carl Schmitt. "If 'the political' is that which belongs to the polis," he says in the Hölderlin seminar, "and therefore is essentially dependent upon the polis, then the essence of the polis can never be determined in terms of the political, just as the ground can never be explained or derived from the consequence."[1] Another formula with which the scholars and readers of Heidegger are conversant is discernible in these lines: the essence of *polis* is nothing political, just as the essence of technology is nothing technological. What, then, *is* its essence?

For all its clarity, such a formulation of the question might not be the most felicitous, because it anticipates a self-assured answer. But the *polis* engenders nothing other than the question: What is question-worthy and what, in ceaseless questioning, shelters the being of human beings (*HHI* 85)? It is for this reason that, in both seminars, Heidegger works with the pair of Aristotelian definitions of the human as *zoōn lógon echon* and *zoōn politikon*, each of them representing, simultaneously, a vital facet (i.e., a portion of) and the whole of humanness. The first explicitly mentions *logos*, the second involves *oikos*, and the composite amounts to the unity of eco-logy. (As a hint, the confusion reigning between parts and wholes here is not accidental; it has to do with the close relation—to the point of substitution—of "house" and "language," *oikos* and *logos*, to being.)

The ecological groundwork for the *polis*, affecting the human dwelling, is apparent in the linguistic lineage that ties it to the word *polos*, "the pole, the swirl [*Wirbel*] in which and around which everything turns" (*HHI* 81). Returning to this connection in the Parmenides seminar, Heidegger notes that "*polis* is the *polos*, the pole, the place around which everything appearing to the Greeks as a being turns in a peculiar way. . . . The pole, as this place, lets beings appear in their Being and show the totality of their condition."[2] The pole is the uninhabitable center of habitation, the marker of a place that lends it coherence and identity. At the same time, it is a polarizing factor, potentially set over and against other such poles-*poleis*.

Strife, *polemos*, or, simply polarization can (and does) result from politics, to which, in a circular fashion, it gives birth. But it does not exhaust the meaning of the political. Before clashing with the other, one must learn to dwell—with oneself and with others.

The geometrical elements of Heidegger's foray into the *polis*[3] set up the semantic perimeter of this shared dwelling place and accentuate the limitations of a purely political abode. A pole is a vertical thing that marks the difference between what is above and what is below. Probably, the verticality of political and theological hierarchies obscurely commemorates this basic political geometry. The rest of beings turn around the pole, or with it, provided it is thought of as a liquid swirl, such that the curvature of their movement delineates the circumference of the world as their environment, *Umwelt*. In this roundness, beings are "gathered" (*HHI* 86), joining the circle of what is homely. They are not assembled into their political environment by force or by the decree of a law or a protolaw (*nomos*); the pole "lets beings appear in their Being," which can only happen through the articulations of *logos*. That is why I qualify Heidegger's ontological politics as "ecological."

Lest it appear to be totalizing, the *polis* is an incomplete, unfinished dwelling, uniting the negative and positive aspects of incompletion (and, by implication, of existential failure). First, positively and continually failing, its circle cannot be closed off, in that the questioning it provokes lacks a final answer. It "must remain what is *worthy* of question for the Greeks" (*HHI* 86)—that is its enabling openness *and* a feature that makes being at home itself unhomely, uncanny, uninhabitable.[4] Second (and with this we are inching toward the negative failure of polarization), a place, a site, cannot be laid out only with regard to the vertical axis of ontological politics; to be a dwelling, it needs to afford the dwellers access to the horizontal axis, as well. The horizontality of a dwelling place inheres with the *ēthos* of ethics—that, together with ontological politics, completes Heideggerian ecology—and what ecological *logos* articulates are these complementary axes of "above" and "below," "left" and "right."

Equally incomplete is Heidegger's notion of being, united with the *polis* in "a primordial relation": "This word *polis* is, in its root, identical with the ancient Greek word for 'to be,' *pelein*: 'to emerge, to rise up into the unconcealed.' . . . The *polis* is the abode, gathered into itself, of the unconcealedness of beings" (*P* 90). To emerge, to rise up—these are also the activities of *phusis*, which Heidegger reads as yet another Greek word for being. In the rising emergence of the one and of the other, verticality prevails, very much in harmony with what Derrida lambastes as *phallogocentrism*. Upward and downward growth in what is cultivated and edified eclipses a lateral extension, despite illuminating the relation between being and beings.

The measure for the in-between of human dwelling is the interval between sky and earth, figuratively mapped onto the *polos* of the *polis* and further alluding to the excluded middle of ontico-ontological difference. So, in ". . . Poetically Man Dwells . . ." Heidegger writes: "The upward glance passes aloft toward the sky, and yet it remains below on the earth. The upward glance spans the between of sky and earth. This between is measured out for the dwelling of man."[5] Not quite transcendence, dwelling requires taking a stance, positioning oneself, if only by virtue of a glance, on the vertical line (Plato, of course, comes to mind) that supposedly repeats, recalls, or recollects the rising emergence of *phusis* and *polis*. The facticity of the human bodily position—walking upright—is a cipher of this ontological comportment, as it was symbolic of ethical uprightness in Plato and Aristotle, or, on a less charitable reading, of a phallogocentric worldview. The ontic human stance is, nonetheless, not arbitrary, in that we assume it on the grounds of "the abode, gathered into itself," and so internally interrelated by *logos*. Political and physical (or, better, *phusical*) ecologies infinitely reflect each other, like two immense self-articulated vertical mirrors.

Still before World War II, in the mid-1930s lecture course *Introduction to Metaphysics*, Heidegger chided the modern misunderstanding of *polis* as "state" for having repressed its ecological stance. There he goes so far as to suggest that politics properly understood is the foundation of fundamental ontology ("the ground and place of human Dasein itself"). A historical dwelling of Dasein, it maps out the "here" of existence and schematizes a possible vertical position in its midst, while "state," *Staat*, fossilizes this stance into an institution and makes it scarcely perceptible: "One translates *polis* as state (*Staat*) and city-state (*Stadsstaat*); this does not capture the entire sense. Rather, *polis* is the name for the site (*Stätte*), the Here, within which and as which Being-here is historically. The *polis* is the site of history."[6] Besides the unmistakable ecological overtones of the word "site," Heidegger tips his audience off to how the "here" of *polis* is shaped into a coherent place when we let its internal articulations—its *logos*—shine through. This sense is the one that the current translation of the Greek, much like our own word "state," obscures.

To bring to a close the discussion of the vertical pole embodying the political, it is worth consulting yet another seminar from roughly the same period as *Introduction to Metaphysics*: I mean *On Hegel's "Philosophy of Right."* When analyzing the meaning of the law, *Gesetz*, in terms of what is posited, Heidegger offers these sources for reflection: *Satz* (proposition), *Stange* (rod), *Gestänge* (rod assembly).[7] Propositions are the modified (and watered-down) versions of *logoi*, while a rod assembly is a mechanical system of articulations. What these sundry semantic suggestions unearth is the tension between the ecological and the economic elucidations of law. Propositions, retaining a faint memory of *logos*, are to be juxtaposed to the rod assembly, which is an entirely artificial construction. If the rod, *Stange*, is a semantic plank between these extremes, that is because it spans the *polos* of political habitation and a mechanical apparatus (say, the Hobbesian "artificial animal") that aggregates political actors.

Figuratively, the Heideggerian *polos* of the *polis* is a lightning rod, *Fangstange*, a vertical contraption mounted over a house or another inhabited place it protects from lightning strikes. Though fraught with risk, it shelters the dwelling itself; though not apt for habitation, it allows for inhabiting. Its verticality is ontic as much as it is ontological. The most question-worthy—the highest possibility of being—is embroiled with the least question-worthy and the lowest, which, as I argue in chapter 8, coincides for Heidegger with the distended figure of the Jew. The highest question of fundamental ontology, thoroughly political according to the original signification of *polis*, is imbricated with the lowest, the barely questioned, despite having been known for a long time in Europe as "the Jewish question." It is, nevertheless, grossly inaccurate to assert that there is here a kind of conceptual antagonism or a logical incompatibility between the political site of Greek or German being and the essential placelessness (and non-being) of the Jew.

Heidegger's engagement with *Antigone*, spanning various seminars and even decades, presents the negation of the *polis*—being high above it (*hupsipolis*) or without it (*apolis*)—as the most extreme political eventuality. *Introduction to Metaphysics* defends a Nietzschean vision of those who are *hupsipolis apolis*: they are the uncanny and violent creators, incapable of dwelling and, in their non-abidance, which subtracts them from the general rule, upholding what they themselves cannot do for others. "Rising high in the site of history, they also become *apolis,* without city and site, lonesome, un-canny, with no way out amidst beings as a whole, and at the same time without ordinance and limit, without structure and fittingness [*Fug*], because they *as* creators must first ground all this in each case" (*IM* 163). So, the political ecology Heidegger fosters does not revel in the parochial or bucolic harmony of *oikos* and *logos,* the one virtually identical to the other; it requires rupture, non-belonging, overstepping the limit, substituting for a geographical site the site of history. This is not surprising, seeing that fundamental ontology locates Dasein in the world, among beings, but without an appropriate place allocated to it in this order, with which it is not of a piece.

Seven years later, the Hölderlin seminar will displace hermeneutical weight from the excessive "rising above the site" of the *hupsipolis* to the "downfall" of the *apolis,* while still maintaining that these movements of existential spatiality are constitutive of the human: "it is the essence of the *polis* to thrust one into excess and to tear one into downfall, and in such a way that the human being is *destined and fitted into* both these counter-turning possibilities and thus must be these two possibilities themselves" (*HHI* 86). I emphasize the words "destined and fitted" in this passage, since they take over the functions of *logos* within this strange ecology of the un-homely. In their heart of hearts, the "here" harbors a "nowhere," a site contains placelessness, *logos* embraces the *alogon,* the dwelling is uncanny or un-homely, and the world is worldless. The homelessness the economic (presumably, anti-ecological) paradigm introduces into politics, ethics, and other spheres of human life—the ontological homelessness Heidegger associates with the Jews (*GA* 95:97)—exhibits the inner truth of the human. The disaster modernity has let loose is one where the placelessness proper to the place has been hypostatized and, in its uncontrollable expansion, has gone on to devour every single place without exception.

THE OPENEDNESS OF ECOLOGICAL ETHICS

As I have delineated it thus far, the ontological or the ecological scope of ethics overlaps, *prima facie,* with that of politics. On the occasion of reading

Heraclitus's Fragment 119, *ēthos anthrōpōi daimōn,* Heidegger clarifies: "*Ēthos* means abode, dwelling place. The word names the open region in which man dwells. The open region of his abode allows what pertains to man's essence, and what in thus arriving resides in the nearness to him, to appear."[8] *Ēthos* is, therefore, akin to the *polis,* which at bottom speaks of a site. But that is only the first impression. The articulation of ethics and politics I've cited earlier precludes their conflation. Approached with care and rigor, the discussion of *ēthos* broaches a different dimension to that of *polis.* The turning of beings happens not only around the vertical pole of politics but also in the open horizontal region of ethics. There is no *oikos* without either of these dimensions. Dwelling, or being a Dasein, is standing at the "zero-point" where the vertical-political and the horizontal-ethical axes intersect.

Why is *ēthos* horizontal? Continuing his elaboration of Heraclitus, Heidegger appends the adjective "familiar," *geheuer,* to the abode, whence ethics derives. When the thinker himself is in his homely place, by the stove, shivering of cold, he pronounces, *Einai gar kai entautha theous,* or, as Heidegger hears this phrase, "Here too the gods come to presence" (*BW* 257). The phrase, he adds, "places the abode (*ēthos*) of the thinker and his deed in another light. . . . *Kai entautha,* 'even here,' at the stove, in that ordinary place where every thing and every condition, each deed and thought is intimate and commonplace, that is familiar [*geheuer*], 'even there' in the sphere of the familiar, *einai theous,* it is the case that 'the gods come to presence'" (*BW* 257–58). The familiarity of one's surroundings is the stage for the appearance of the unfamiliar, of what or who descends or ascends the pole in the midst of all beings. The ordinary, the intimate, and the commonplace belong and contribute to the flatness of a place, within which the extraordinary and the uncommon (which would have otherwise passed imperceptibly, absolutely unacknowledged) may irrupt. In this very moment, the "even here" will turn into the "even there," disrupting the horizontal immanence of life with the vertical movement of quasi-transcendence. Dwelling "between earth and sky" is being suspended between ontological or ecological ethics and politics.

(Most languages do not have a word for saying what is neither here nor there, and both here and there. In Spanish and Portuguese, such a word corresponds, approximately, to *ahí* or *aí,* which conveys "your here with regard to mine, which, for you, is over there," "there where you are, as far as I can tell from my here." *Ahí* or *aí* identifies the unfamiliar within the spatially familiar and expresses the ordinary-extraordinary quality of dwelling. It is not by chance that the respective Spanish and Portuguese translations of Dasein are *ser-ahí* and *ser-aí,* "being here-there." As such, they reveal the ethical ground of fundamental ontology and the axiom that Dasein is, in and of itself, a *Mitsein,* being-with, in the gap between here and there.)

Having revisited the episode at Heraclitus's stove, Heidegger can restate *ēthos anthrōpōi daimōn*: "The (familiar) abode for man is the open region for the presencing of god (the unfamiliar one)" (*BW* 248). Or, in other words, the circular closure of the dwelling is open in its closedness, insofar as it admits (and, indeed, exists in order to admit, to welcome better) the unfamiliar. At the same time, in a display of its full ecological character, *ēthos* surpasses the dwelling: it requires the neither active nor passive preparation of "the open region for presencing" by *logos,* which—Heidegger observes in 1969—"much more originally than 'to speak'" means "*to let* presencing [*Anwesen* lassen]."[9] The ecology of ethics combines the horizontal rounding of the dwelling with a stand within it, such that this stand corresponds to the stance or status of politics, later on perverted into the state or the *status quo*. But what about ethical flatness? How does it jibe with the articulation of a vertical stance with a horizontal rounding off? It is not that throughout his writings and seminars Heidegger provided disparate definitions of ethics, but that he alternated between concentrating on the *oikos*-aspect and on the *logos*-aspect of *ēthos.*

And this is the gist of the course on *Basic Concepts of Aristotelian Philosophy*: ethics and politics converge around their shared orientation and commitment to *logos.* "This standing-out of the human being, this 'comporting-oneself' in the world, this 'comportment,' is *to ēthos.* Therefore, politics as knowing-the-way-around the being of human beings in its genuineness is ethics."[10] Again: "*Ēthos* means the 'comportment' of human beings, how the human being is there, how he offers himself as a human being, how he appears in being-with-one-another."[11] Despite its horizontality (e.g., in how one appears in "being-with-one-another"), ontological or ecological ethics demands, as politics also does, that one take a stance (*Haltung*: hence, a vertical position) among beings and comport oneself (*sich-halten*) pursuant to the stance taken. Now, "comportment" is something quite different from "behavior," in that the "how" of comportment, highlighting the various aspects of Dasein, is a modality of *logos*. As Heidegger explains: "For us to get *logos* in view, it is important that this fundamental division of human being-possibilities, among orientations to *logos*, is seen in its basic possibility of *logos*."[12] Ontological or ecological politics and ethics are the orientations to and the basic possibilities of *logos*, both arising from and giving rise to human dwelling.

Yet, in a highly problematic way, in what seems to be a minor slippage, Heidegger converts the dwelling into home. We have seen how the dwelling yokes together the homely and the unhomely, the familiar and the unfamiliar, the closed and the open. We also know that the anti-ecological, economic attitude disrupts this tense balance and promotes the horror of planet-wide homelessness. Heidegger, too, contributes to the disruption of the dwelling's articulations, when, in the 1944 public lecture *Introduction to Philosophy—Thinking and Poetizing*, he violently endorses the homely, the closed, the familiar: "We call the circumference that is historically enclosed [*umhegten*] and nourishing [*hegenden*], that fuels all courage and releases all capacities, that surrounds the place where humans belong in the essential meaning of a claimed listening: the *home* [*die* Heimat]."[13] Barring listening (itself, claimed in advance), nothing and no one can penetrate the blockade of the enclosed circumference that is the home. Gone is the pole of quasi-transcendence suspended between the here and the there. Hardly anything remains of the openedness of *ēthos* within the freshly erected circular walls. Has it escaped Heidegger that the total familiarity of home, as much as the worst instantiation of homelessness, rules out the possibility of dwelling?

So pervasive is the 1944 retreat to the enclosure of the home on Germany's philosophical home front that it affects the sense of dwelling. "Dwelling [*Wohnen*]," Heidegger says at the outset of the lecture, "is what we call the native sojourning in the realms in which the human belongs."[14] "The human" does not pinpoint just any human being or grouping but what makes humans human, what dispenses to them their humanity—for instance, the aptitude for dwelling. This much is evident from the subsequent sentence, which confronts the more or less abstract definition of humanity with "historical humans." It follows that to be incapable of native sojourning, of belonging to the ontological realm of the human (e.g., in the difference between earth and world) is to be subject to exclusion, a ban or an exile that is, by and large, self-imposed. The human will be ecological, or it will not be at all, which is to say that those who, in Heidegger's assessment, do not or cannot dwell—the Jews, the Cartesian subject, "the historyless" (*GA* 95:96–97), the uprooted, the agents of calculation and economic-technological machination, and so forth—are sidelined from the "realms in which the human belongs." They are worldless, and so un-human.

The distorted *ethical* determination of humanity we have just witnessed diverges from the *political*, where *hupsipolis apolis* was the foremost condition of being human. More concretely, today, more than seventy years later, we are caught up between two closures or foreclosures of dwelling: its involution into a parochial, nativist, exclusionary, at times anti-Semitic home (in Heidegger and in contemporary right-wing politics) and its devolution into the homeless and indifferent homogeneity of a globalized technicism (which the German thinker ruthlessly criticized). Heidegger's blunders notwithstanding, his diagnosis of the fate of being in modernity is correct, and the challenge is to develop it to its ecological conclusions without lapsing into parochialism, redolent of a reactionary antimodernism.

THE FALL OF *NOMOS*—FROM ONTOLOGICAL RANK TO ECONOMISM AND NIHILISM

In contrast to political and ethical ecology, modernity has inaugurated a political and ethical economy. With an eye to Heidegger rather than Ricardo, Marx, or Mill, I use this phrase with reference to the widespread machination, accounting, calculation, and quantitative valuation that are our default attitudes outside the economic scope. But, above all, I would like to single out the rare tributes to *nomos* in Heidegger's writings, in a bid to reconstruct his take on economy in light of Western metaphysics and its culmination in nihilism.

Prior to its formalization in the idea of the "law, rule in the sense of mores," *nomos* rests "on the commitment of freedom and assignment of tradition; it is that which concerns a free comportment and attitude, the shaping of the historical Being of humanity, *ēthos*, which under the influence of morality was then degraded to the ethical" (*IM* 17–18). A "free comportment and attitude," *nomos* was a factor of ethics, an orientation that freely received the assignment of being itself and that evaluated human conduct against this assignment. Heidegger will hone this insight in his "Letter on Humanism," recalling that "in Greek, to assign is *nemein*. *Nomos* is not only law but more originally the assignment contained in the dispensation of Being. Only the assignment is capable of dispatching man into Being. Only such dispatching is capable of supporting and obligating. Otherwise all law remains merely something fabricated by human reason" (*BW* 262).

The work of "mere fabrication" of the law by human reason corresponds to the degradation of *ēthos* to the ethical with the help of morality, or, more to the point, through the invention of *moral economy*. The technicization of the law (of *nomos*), which begins as early as the philosophy of Plato and Aristotle, flags the detachment of the order it institutes from the original ontological assignment, now executed in the ontic apportioning of territories, properties, and eco-nomic effects. The etymological connection of *nomos* to pasturage underwrites this transformation. When the law conforms to *logos* (the self-showing *and* self-encryption of being in beings), then it verges on ethical and political ecology; when it stems from logical or logistical concerns, it becomes almost entirely economic.[15]

It is finally to Heraclitus that Heidegger turns for the ecological view of *nomos*. Launching his argument from the springboard that is the pre-Socratic's Fragment 124 ("the most beautiful world [*kosmos*] is like a dungheap [*sarma*], cast down in shambles"), Heidegger suggests that what being assigns in its free dispensation to human beings is something like an ontological rank: "Being as logos is originary gathering, not a heap or pile where everything counts just as much and just as little—and for this reason, rank and dominance belong to Being. If Being is to open itself up, it itself must have rank and maintain it" (*IM* 141–42). In the ethical openedness of being, *nomos* figures as a rank, assigned and kept by being itself. Dwelling, according to this assignment, is letting one's abode be organized by *logos*, as mediated through *nomos*. Conversely, the Heraclitean "heap" (*sarma*) anticipates the ranking of values and statistical differentials unmoored from being and *logos*. As soon as an exclusively quantitative measure rises to the dignity of the "objective" criterion of rank, buttressed by the "subjective" notion of value, everything "counts just as much and just as little" as everything else that is potentially reconcilable in a numerical equation or in the worldview of a valuing person. That economy in which *nomos* ceases to receive its directives from being inhibits our capacity to dwell among statistical data or in amorphous worldviews. It is this inhibition that precipitates nihilism.

An intermediary conclusion: the problem for Heidegger is not economy per se but the defacement of *nomos*, evident in the economic activities properly so called (the production and circulation of goods and money) and in the contemporary forms of morality, history, politics, and thought. What is the nature of this defacement? I have already mentioned the "unmooring" of *nomos* from being and *logos*, but, to be more nuanced, it should be added that this separation is a tear *within logos*. The double gesture of *logos* is a gathering gatheredness, and "both [moments] must happen 'for the sake of Being.' Here gathering means seizing oneself when one is dispersed . . . [b]ut this gathering, which is still a turning away, can be carried out only by virtue of the gathering that, as a turning toward, pulls beings together into the gatheredness of their Being" (*IM* 180). From an ecological standpoint, gathering and being gathered are the attitudes indispensable to dwelling: receiving and being received into the abode. When we neglect one of the moments at the expense of the other, the possibility of dwelling evanesces. Historically (and most of all in the history of being), gatheredness has been sacrificed to gathering, compelling *logos* to fade into logic and *nomos* to dwindle to a principle behind a system of laws. This turning away from the passive element of *logos* has made us believe that we could organize our planetary, linguistic, psychic, and other kinds of dwelling without being organized or ordered by the demands of these same dwellings. No longer counterbalanced by the other moment of *logos*, the active gathering flipped into its opposite, non-abidance and dispersion.

The "economy" that evolved from the purely active and domineering *nomos* is an effect of the lopsidedness of *logos*. Calculation and accounting (i.e., some of the most emblematic economic activities) are, rather than its root causes, the late ramifications in this evolution. They are the centerpieces of nihilistic modernity in politics, ethics, economics, and everything that goes under the name (or the paleonym) *culture*. The lopsidedness of *logos* is not at all abstract: it curbs our existence itself and we move exclusively "within the horizon of 'balances,' 'taxations,' 'shares,' and 'costs.' . . . Even Nietzsche thinks in terms of this schema of the nineteenth century. Nietzsche turns the 'calculating of values,' i.e., the accounting into the final form of Western metaphysical thinking" (*P* 55). Not by chance "value" has become a key category in modern ethics and economics: the former is a not-so-easily-recognizable version of the latter. Both operate with the ranking of values, regardless of the ranking of being (objective *and* subjective genitive), which is not the same as conjecturing the respective positions of beings in the Great Chain of Being. Their "calculation" works with value differentials that, on the plus side, translate into benefits, and, on the minus side, into costs. That is what the betweenness of human dwelling, the interval between earth and sky, has been reduced to—a cost-benefit analysis and, ultimately, arithmetic differences.

Valuation is a form of assignment spanning the grounds and ends of an action. So long as it informs a given *e*valuation, such an assignment is a reckoning (counting *on* and *with* something), which "first makes planning and reckoning in a purely 'calculative' sense both possible and necessary."[16] The metaphysics of value transitions to economism after reckoning comprises nothing but quantities, thus undermining the thinking of the grounds and ends of an action. As a totalizing quantification gets under way, nihilism grows in strength, which it then channels into the destruction of *any and all* grounds and ends. In faulting Nietzsche for the nihilistic overtones of the will to power (i.e., the differentials of force submitted to a philosophical valuation and transvaluation), Heidegger groups Nietzsche's thought he otherwise admires with the general economization of existence that has dispensed with both dwelling and *logos* as the anachronistic remnants of the past: "Earlier we showed that . . . [the] will to power is of itself a value estimating. Now, from the essence of estimating as absolute reckoning, its essential affinity to will to power has emerged."[17]

At times, Heidegger confounds the economic attitude with accounting and calculation, assuming that the law, the *nomos,* of economy is the law of numbers. But it would be foolish to imagine an economy without the production and circulation of commodities and money, let alone to suppress the need for a patient examination of how it burdens with *nomos* the dwelling (*oikos*) that participates in this composite word.

In Heidegger's last seminars (Le Thor, 1969, and Zähringen, 1973), production emerges in the shape of the human *self*-production glorified in Marxism. Here, too, Heidegger detects the utmost nihilism that develops in tandem with economism: "The most extreme danger is that man, insofar as he produces himself, no longer feels any other necessities than the demands of his self-production" (*FS* 56). "Marxism is indeed the thought of today, where the self-production of man and society plainly prevails. . . . [T]he self-production of man raises the danger of self-destruction" (*FS* 73). The danger Heidegger alerts us to has to do with the old split between the two aspects of *logos,* the gathering and the gathered, such that the former gradually gains ground over the latter until receptivity, or "letting presence," recedes from the human horizon. In self-production, the human refashions itself into its own ground and end, oblivious to its ontological assignment and couched in technological, mechanistic terms. The *nomos* of this economy begins with the split within *logos* that, once aggravated, cements the reign of nihilism ("the danger of self-destruction"). For Heidegger, then, Marx presides over the unholy marriage of the Feuerbach-inspired self-referential valuation of the human (bringing divinity down to earth) and the value of production for production's sake (making this divinity machine-like).

Circulation is, more noticeably still, affected by the lethal *nomos* of economy that, as the last seminars advance, paves the way for "the epoch of orderability": "in such an epoch, which is now ours, everything and every means of calculation are constantly at the disposal of an ordering. . . . Everything (beings as a whole) from the outset arranges itself in the horizon of utility, the dominance, or better yet, the *orderability* of what is to be seized" (*FS* 74, 61). "Ordering" and "orderability" are the semantic offshoots of *nomos,* full of active, commanding, if not commandeering, connotations that bar dwelling to the human beings who have unlearned how to let themselves be received in whatever orders the world beyond their command. "Orderability," a possibility that spells out the end of the possible, governs in advance the insertion of any being, including those not yet in existence, into the arrangement Heidegger describes. And even those presumably firmly in command are also ordered by this ordering into the same line as all other beings made available for manipulation and use. Expelled from the possibility of dwelling, we are accounted for in the inexorable logistics of a hyperactive *nomos.* The dwelling crumbles not when it is disorganized but when it is too tightly controlled, its components dominated and seized "at will." Henceforth, Dasein circulates together with the elements of its world—"beings as a whole"—on the uniform surface of manipulability.

THE SECRET SOURCES OF POLITICAL ECONOMY

By the time Marx gave it a dialectical makeover, "political economy" became an object of critique, as the title of *Das Kapital* openly states. Peering into the yet untapped economic depths of capital, Marx hoped to discover the power imbalance between the workers and the owners of the means of production in its objective form, that is, in surplus value that had not been restituted to the immediate productive agents. He dubbed these depths "the hidden abode of value," without questioning the strangeness of this abode—a dwelling for what does not and cannot dwell. His oversight is not accidental: political economy is not the deepest layer of human activity, where the violations of political ecology occur. More radical than that is the economization of politics, which, on Heidegger's interpretation, coincides with cardinal developments in the history of being, that is, in our relation to being.

In the colossal translation of Greek categories into Latin—the translation Heidegger takes issue with everywhere in his *oeuvre*—the meaning of "politics" undergoes a dramatic sea change: "The political, which as *politikón* arose formerly out of the existence of the Greek *polis*, has come to be understood in the Roman way. Since the time of the *Imperium*, the Greek word 'political' has meant something Roman" (*P* 45). Whereas the Greek *polis* was predicated on the *polos* around which beings rotated (coming into un-concealment in this rotation) and the space for dwelling opened up, the Roman *imperium* commanded beings to hand themselves over to sight and oversight on the territory it occupied: "the basic comportment of the Romans toward beings in general is governed by the rule of the *imperium*. *Imperium* says *im-parare*, to establish, to make arrangements: *prae-cipere*, to occupy something in advance, and by this occupation to hold command over it, and so to have the occupied as territory" (*P* 44). Instead of opening a site and letting beings be gathering and gathered through *logos*, the empire lays the foundations for and claims whatever transpires on its pre-occupied territories for itself. Its commanding voice authorizes a *nomos* already partly deaf to *logos* and fixated on gathering beings to the detriment of gatheredness into being. Whatever its political realities, *imperium* is always and necessarily economic.

Besides changing the human comportment toward beings, imperial command alters the ontological style of dwelling, as it economizes politics. To "occupy something in advance" one is not required to dwell on, in, or with it; seizing the occupied for oneself and assimilating it to the imperial framework suffices to relate to it as a being. *Imperium* interferes with the dwelling in all its materiality, seeing that we can no longer treat the earth as the bearer of human activities and our elemental abode. Parallel to the becoming-imperial of politics, the earth, *terra,* is overlaid with *territory,* and, therefore, with plots of land, property, real estate, and so forth.

In a signature move, Heidegger rehashes the respective Greek and Roman conceptions of the earth in such a way that the geographical situations of Greece and Rome burst at the seams with ontological *gravitas*. The collective experience of the earth the Greeks pieced together from their navigation among the islands scattered in the Aegean Sea was that of the land "in-between"; "for the Romans, on the contrary the earth, *tellus, terra,* is the dry, the land as distinct from the sea" (*P* 60). The Schmittian standoff between land and sea turns out to be, on this view, squarely Roman. More than that, it is the Greek, not the Roman, grasp of the earth that has favored dwelling, which belongs in the in-between that does not belong anywhere, in an open closedness of archipelagic existence, neither fully here nor entirely there. The roots of the competing paradigms of being and dwelling extend all the way to the contrast between the geopolitics of Hellenic islands and the massive land blocks of the Roman Empire. And our contemporary question is: Which political ecology will the Europe of the EU adopt—Greek geopolitics or Roman territorial expansion?

To add insult to injury, the Roman codification of the earth as *terra* underwent a second formalization in the notion of territory. With the *oikos* (our elemental dwelling) already badly disfigured, the new *nomos* of the earth intervened by preordaining and ordering it for settlement that will a priori obey imperial command: "*Terra* becomes *territorium,* land of settlement as realm of command. In the Roman *terra* can be heard an imperial accent, completely foreign to the Greek *gaia* and *gē*" (*P* 60). To settle is, by any stretch of the imagination, not the same thing as to dwell: in its wearisome struggle against the un-homely and the uninhabitable, against the earlier inhabitants whether or not they are human, and against the elements themselves, the act of settling does not open a site but actively founds or re-founds *itself,* causing the receptivity demanded by and for dwelling to become more elusive than ever. The territory engulfs the earth, on which it stands. Its imperial command charts an ideal map of the terrain, losing sight of the elemental materiality that undergirds territorialization. The empire is ineluctably economic, in virtue of blanketing with its territorial *nomos* a world increasingly unglued from the earth and from places of dwelling. Globalization, beholden to yet another representation of *terra* in the form of a globe where no one can dwell, exacerbates this tendency of dissolving even territories in the medium of pure abstraction.

Such an economy is unsustainable on its own, both because it requires an alien (ecologic) substratum it overwrites and because, in it, in this economy, the imperial *nomos* obliterates the *oikos*, garnering the total and unconditional power of devastation. In *Black Notebooks* Heidegger frequently berates this "unconditional machinal economy [*unbedingten machinalen Oekonomie*]," which augurs the vanishing of limits, *Grenzen*, that could still constrain power (*GA* 96:185). In an eco-nomy divested of limits and conditions, the power of *nomos* is no longer restricted by the *oikos* it had to serve or to prepare, and, for this reason, power and the economy wax unwieldy (in any event, who can dwell in the unconditional?). Modern politics is born from the still growing chasm between the dwelling and the principle of its active organization, in contrast to *polis,* which, as the provenance of the political, pursued the ecological unity of the dwelling and of the *how* of its appearance (i.e., *logos*). If, in modernity, "politics has nothing to do with *polis* anymore [*Politik hat nichts mehr mit der* polis]," that is because it now operates as "the authentic executor of machinations with beings [*die eigentliche Vollstreckerin der Machenschaft des Seienden*]" (*GA* 96:43). The total character of political machination, economic in the restricted and in the "general" senses of *economy,* is the culmination of a long process that has seen *nomos* drift away from the dwelling, from the earth, and from the territory. What Lenin lambasted as the "politics of small tricks" is a minuscule portion of this overall political machination or economization, our default comportment to all beings.

"Unconditional machination" is the economic common denominator, reconciling the ethical and political conduct of modern subjects. It is responsible for the transformation of modern politics into "power politics," *Macht-politik* (*GA* 96:260), the unrestrained *nomos* reigning supreme over a world no longer apt for dwelling. Hence, "'ethics' and the [moral] 'stance' are merely the economic means for the unconditionality of power [*'Sittlichkeit' und 'Haltung' sind alles nur noch oekonomische Mittel für die Unbedingtheit der Macht*]" (*GA* 96:186). The assemblage of machinational ethics and politics in modernity is a degenerate replica of the constellation of *polos* and *ēthos* in the ecological disclosure of dwelling. Power, like the pole of the *polis*, persists at the center, albeit no longer as a vertical axis or a vortex around which a dwelling could light up. Again like this pole, it orchestrates a procession of beings, without, however, providing a sheltering circumference as their abode, but only a series of reserves readied for use. Ethics, for its part, continues to convey something of the horizontality of *ēthos*. But, while the ethical medium (literally: the middle, *Mittel*) draws its authority from the dwelling, from being-in-between, it sweeps through the middle, purging it of everything still unaffected by the commanding grasp of power. This time around, the media ethics furnishes are the means for facilitating the smooth dynamics of power and ensuring that it is a truly unconditional affair. *Logos* survives here in the guise of instrumental rationality, the logic of means and ends.

Indeed, the unconditional—that which is absolutely separate, separated, withdrawn, untouchable and consecrated—is the negation of in-betweenness, thus of being and of dwelling: "*Zwischen ist das Seyn sebst.*"[18] At the same time, it causes whatever it conditions to be purely present, available for use, for counting, accounting, and manipulation. The cleft between *nomos* and *oikos*, or between the gathering and gathered dimensions of *logos*, annihilates all other relative gaps, all in-betweens. It reeks of nihilism. Little wonder that the political expression of the unconditional *nomos* spinning the wheels of machinational economy is a "despotism of no one," *Despotie des Niemand* (*GA* 96:132), that is, the complete displacement and veiling over of power on a globe wiped clean of dwelling places, opened closures, and existential possibilities.

THE NEED FOR HOUSING AND THE DESIRE FOR DWELLING

Back to the metaphysical tradition of thinking about economy! Since Aristotle, philosophers have comprehended the economic domain as one of necessity. For them, freedom has connoted liberation from economic preoccupations, from every concern with money or with food on the table and a roof over one's head. Economy has been condemned for its proximity to the ever-renewed needs of the body and for its interference with theoretical contemplation, which could blossom only in the plenitude of free time (of *scholion/otium* or leisure). Only with Marx is economic freedom thinkable in the desideratum that producers take charge of the means of production and the product itself, or that they freely decide on how to dispose of the surplus value they generate.

Heidegger's plea not to mistake dwelling for housing belongs within the tradition that links the ensemble of economy with the privation of freedom. In terms that are not entirely his own, we might say that housing is an economic necessity governed by need; dwelling is an ecological mission responsive to desire. Housing is the ontic sheltering of the body; dwelling is the ontological manner of being. "Buildings house man. He inhabits them and yet does not dwell in them, when to dwell means merely that we take shelter in them. In today's housing shortage even this much is reassuring and to the good; residential buildings do indeed provide shelter; today's houses may even be well planned, easy to keep, attractively cheap, open to air, light, and sun, but—do the houses themselves hold any guarantee that *dwelling* occurs in them?" (*PLT* 144). The difference between housing and dwelling reiterates the one between being and existence, or between being and beings. If Heidegger's flora and fauna *are* but, unlike the human, do not exist, then plants and animals can be housed but can never dwell. Housing "shortage," "planning," "cheapness," and "upkeep"—these are all economic considerations that fall on the ontic side, wedded to the animal dimension of human biology. They shore up or weaken an economy, where a house is an object for manipulation like any other and *nomos* is "the directing need,"[19] rather than ecology, where a dwelling largely orders our own existence in advance and *logos* is a "giver" beyond necessity and the capacity to receive.[20] The house is an artifact wholly determined by need; dwelling is an *existentiale* responsive to desire, for which nothing is lacking, and which is enshrined in the essential failure to dwell.

Nevertheless, the distance between ontic housing and ontological dwelling—the distance *ecologically modulating* ontico-ontological difference—is historically variable. In the epoch of a global and impersonal despotism, the economy of housing is at the furthest remove from the ecology of dwelling: "Now is there still, in these times, something like 'at home,' a dwelling, an abode? No, there are 'dwelling machines,' urban population centers, in short: the industrialized product, but no longer a *home*" (*FS* 74). Unconditional machination does not spare the house, which resembles today more a complex machine than a dwelling place. There isn't an intimate place of being—a hearth whence we venture into a larger world in order to practice the economy of seizing, controlling, and commanding beings, the place that would ignite the process of appropriation, all the while being exempt from this very process. Which is to say that there isn't an ethical or ecological refuge from the cold calculative-appropriative rationality. The horizon of orderability, usability, and manipulability encircles us and the locales we inhabit with absolute closure masquerading as the openness of infinite possibility. Riveted to the technicist *Gestell*, architectural imagination (e.g., that of Le Corbusier) sees in houses a conjunction of efficient mechanisms that can help refuel their inhabitants for the next day's economic tasks. Immersed into the universe of need, this imagination is unaware of desire's existence (above all, the existence of the existential desire for dwelling).

It is as though need and its fulfillment or frustration were not only all there is but also all there could ever be. "One is content with beings, and renounces being so decisively that one does not allow this renunciation to count as such. . . . Perhaps this complacency about the experience and cultivation of beings stems from the fact that man, in the midst of beings, thinks only about what he needs. Why should he need a discussion of the meaning of the word 'is'? Indeed—it is of no use."[21] The renunciation of being does not count, unaccountable as it is within the economy of beings, unaware of the ecology of being. The absence of desire is not of the same order, nor does it belong to the same genus, as the absence of an object of need, since desire is aroused where nothing is lacking. Our need for housing satisfied, the desire for a dwelling fails to disconcert us. Proficient in the rules and codes of a language that works as a naming game, content to find useful and easily decipherable labels for things, we do not yearn for a language apt for dwelling, the language that is a "house of being." Who needs anything other than this nominalist *nomos*, particularly in a cultural milieu where *logos*—besides not satisfying any needs—stands for something mystifying and totalizing-totalitarian, parochial and nationalist-chauvinist, outdated and irrelevant?

True: *we do not need logos,* but it is this not-needing that makes it so essential. "Man attends either to what he needs or to what he can do without,"[22] yet the either/or of need and desire has fallen into silence in the hubbub of satisfied and dissatisfied needs. So much so that in our ethical, political, and environmental courses of action we do not hesitate for a second between this *either* and this *or.* Ecological theory and practice must justify themselves on economic grounds, accounting for the entire planet on the basis of the need to procure (planetary) housing for members of the human species and others that are useful to us. Contemporary economicist ecology is, understandably, reactive, given the severity of the environmental crisis. In addition, the ontological explanation for the reaction governing our conception of ecology is that need overrides all other considerations, first and foremost, those of desire. What would politics, ethics, and ecology be like if they did not have to put out fires (set alight by the widespread and indifferent economization of the world) with materials procured from the very incendiary economic rationality that has degraded our planetary dwelling to its present condition (of a house on fire)? How would the desire for dwelling, surpassing any need that typically presumes the non-negotiable exigencies of survival, shape and be shaped by that other ecology?

THINGS: THE LAST REPOSITORIES OF ECOLOGY?

Given Heidegger's predilection for the categories of existence, it would seem inconsistent that things could lend a hand (whose hand would they be *to*? or would they have to be completely out of hand to live up to this task?) to an ecological revival. There are, for all that, compelling reasons to shift the emphasis onto things in the age of impersonal economic despotism.[23] First, the massive withdrawal of existence under the pressure of unconditional manipulation makes any appeal to existential concerns, thought to offer resistance to widespread manipulability, ineffective. Second, "thing" is not an economic concept, contrary to "object" and "commodity," their being exhausted in production-consumption. Third, things share with *logos* the quality of being gathered gatherers, which is why a voiceless *logos,* harking back to Heraclitus, may first irradiate from things. Fourth, in contradistinction to economic entities, things are beneficial to dwelling, inasmuch as they invest lived space and time with meaning, or, more radically yet, are the seeds of time and space. Taken together, in another kind of "fourfold," these reasons chart quite an unexpected way out of the technological framing of being, without underestimating the dark depths of contemporary nihilism.

Formulaically stated, Heidegger's things are *logoi* not (yet) expressed in speech. For one, his early phenomenological notion of the world as a "totality-of-significations" implied that the spatial articulations of things with one another anticipated their discursive articulation, and that the pre-interpretation of the world relied upon the unthematized, haptic familiarity with thingly interconnections. By the time Heidegger composes "The Origin of the Work of Art," with its example of a Greek temple assembling the elements above, below, and around it, as well as "Building, Dwelling, Thinking," featuring a bridge that "*gathers* to itself in *its own* way earth and sky, divinities and mortals" (*PLT* 151), the model of thingly articulations undergoes further refinement. Analogous to *logos*, things gather the world; "gathering or assembly, and an ancient word of our language is called 'thing'" (*PLT* 151). But they are also gathered into the ensemble they help articulate. Gathered gatherers, they physically pre-delineate the way of and to language.

In another essay, Heidegger explains that "the Old High German word *thing* means a gathering, and specifically a gathering to deliberate on a matter under discussion, a contested matter. . . . The Romans called a matter for discourse *res*. . . . *Res publica* means, not the state, but that which, known to everyone, concerns everybody and is therefore deliberated in public" (*PLT* 172). The assembly nonverbally called by the thing itself is, thus, inherently political and material, dependent on spatial jointures and on preserving the interval (of being and dwelling) that distinguishes each thing from the others. Among Germanic, Latin, and Greek precedents for the language of things, Heidegger does not cite the Hebrew root *d.b.r.*, which articulates both modes of articulation, that of speaking and that of the things (in Hebrew, the word for discourses and for things is the same: *d'varim*). The thing speaks, the speech things, and we dwell within and between the kaleidoscopic instantiations of these *d'varim*.

Likewise, in *Being and Time*, Heidegger conceives of existence as "fallen," a word he wants to inherit from Judeo-Christian theology in a way akin to failure, without the negative connotations that surround it in the original context of its enunciation. A fallen existence is tarrying *alongside* things, which means that a dwelling cannot utilize them *for* the creation of its material infrastructure. Were it to do so, it would have been exclusively economic, not ecological. We dwell between things and in their meanwhile, *in medias res*. Things open the sites they occupy, making room for space (*Raum*) itself and for the time it takes to linger in or with them: "Thus the bridge does not first come to a location to stand in it; rather, a location comes into existence only by virtue of the bridge. . . . Only things that are locations in this manner allow for spaces. What the word for space, *Raum*, *Rum*, designates is said by its ancient meaning. *Raum* means a place cleared or freed for settlement and lodging" (*PLT* 152). The finite clearing for being in *logos* finds its material equivalent in lived space, "a place cleared or freed for settlement," prepared to receive the dwelling that will gather and receive us within itself.

Assuming that dwelling happens nowhere but in the clearing of the "there" of existence, of the *Da* of Dasein (*BW* 241), and granting, further, that this "there" is never entirely empty, pre-occupied as it is by things, the ontological experience of homelessness is also that of thinglessness. The relation between "thing" and "world" is contestable, above all in Heidegger: whereas in 1928 he advances that a thing (such as a stone) is "worldless," in his postwar writings he places things at the origin of the world, or, as I have just shown, close to the source of *logos*, time, and space. The world cannot come about nor can it last without things; it disintegrates the moment we exchange them for consumable objects. That "homelessness is coming to be the destiny of the world" (*BW* 243) is due, to a certain extent, to the evacuation of things from its midst. The "there" of existence, like the difference between housing and dwelling, is neither immutable across human history nor immune to how it is historically rearranged, enlarged or narrowed down. There are limits to its economization and territorializing colonization that, when transgressed, close off the clearing of the *Da* and proscribe being and dwelling.

What I mean by "economization" is the encumbrance of the things and the world they co-create with the time, spatiality, and language (*nomos*) that are alien to them. To our modern sensibility, it is a given that to replace the time, space, and language of things with the metaphysical "framework for our calculative domination and ordering of the 'world' as nature and history" (*HHI* 48) is to domesticate existence, rid it of its unfamiliarity and uncanniness. In doing so we eliminate from the world its openedness, habitability, worldliness. At this late hour on the metaphysical clock, we have no other choice but to learn, or to relearn, how to dwell from the thing, from what does not dwell yet shelters the material possibility of dwelling in its time, space, and speechless *logos*. There can be only an ecology of things, for an economy is more fitting to a commerce with objects; where there are no things, there is no hope for ecology. Never tiring of Husserl's "Back to the things themselves!" we should hear this slogan in a Heideggerian tonality, as a plea to return to the last, thingly repositories of an ecological comportment in our homeless, worldless, devastated world.

5. Devastation

THE ONTOLOGICAL DEVASTATION—OF ONTOLOGY

What do we do when we devastate the world? What does devastation do? What has it done and what does it keep doing to "us" and through "us," the devastated devastators? And is there still anything untouched outside the reach of its implacable force, its acts, the actuality of its deactualizing effects?

It is exceptionally difficult to raise, let alone to address, these questions because their referent is so vast as to be nearly unthinkable. They overlap with the question concerning the meaning of being adjusted to the historical ontology of the twenty-first century when beings are devastated and, more crucially still, *being is devastation*. In a dialogue that bears a blazing signature-date, May 8, 1945, Heidegger registers a kindred insight: "The being of an age of devastation would . . . consist precisely in the abandonment of being [*Das Sein eines Zeitalters der Verwüstung bestünde . . . gerade in der Seinsverlassenheit*]."[1] We will undoubtedly return to the "abandonment of being," *Seinsverlassenheit* (which comprises the being we abandon and the being that leaves us behind), seeing that an effective response to devastation depends on how its meaning, entwined with the meaning of being, resonates with us. But, all the twists and turns of abandonment notwithstanding, contemporary being—and its "contemporaneity" is nothing new; it "has not existed just since yesterday" (*CPC* 133), and might be as old as Western metaphysics—is the devastation of being, rather than being's withdrawal.

In everyday speech, devastation is interchangeable with destruction, yet, Heidegger asserts, it is "more than destruction. Devastation is more uncanny than negation [*Verwüstung ist mehr als Zerstörung. Verwüstung ist unheimlicher als Vernichtung*]. Destruction only sweeps aside all that has grown up or been built up so far; but devastation blocks all future growth and prevents all building. Devastation is more unearthly than mere destruction. Mere destruction sweeps aside all things including even nothingness, while devastation on the contrary establishes and spreads [*bestellet und ausbreitet*] everything that blocks and prevents."[2] The *more* of devastation, setting it apart from destruction and negation, is the surplus ingrained into its ability to establish and spread its worldlessness on the face of the earth, to create a reality of its own, however derealizing. It is this, its surplus over destruction and negation, that empowers devastation to step into the shoes of being and to enter its viral code into the matrix of fundamental ontology.

As its upsurge begins to affect dwelling, which consists in building and cultivation, devastation signals a growing impossibility of growing and a buildup of homelessness. Staying with the logic and the vernacular of the preceding chapter, I am tempted to say: destruction destroys housing, while devastation devastates dwelling, striking not at the actual but at the possible, at the possibility of actuality. Devastation, *Verwüstung*, is a growing force, a tumor-like growth, the spread of a desert, *Wüste*, where nothing grows. Which means that being is desertification, the pressing advance of the desert—vast, unoccupied, desolate, vacant, vacated of beings. Being "as such and as a whole" is en route to becoming a wasteland.

Let us take a deep breath and a step back. Have we not just now defined the ontological by the ontic, being as such by a phenomenon from the ambit of physical geography, committing thereby a cardinal sin against Heidegger's philosophical position? We have, and in this we are justified: together with the difference between earth and world, which the spreading worldlessness has expunged, ontico-ontological difference (pregnant with the in-between, i.e., with the placeness of place) has already collapsed due to the workings of devastation. "'Devastation' ['*Verwüstung*'] means for us, after all, that everything—the world, the human, and the earth—will be transformed into a desert [*Wüste*]" (*CPC* 136/211). Another manner of saying this is that everything will be made so vast that the contours of things will be ontically blurred and differences will be ontologically erased on the windswept surfaces of the wasteland, the wasteworld, and the human waste we are tirelessly producing and we have ourselves become. Globalization (cultural, economic, political) is but a sideshow to this devastating vastness.

From the Late Latin *devastatio*, "devastation" is more expressive than *Verwüstung* as far as the implosion of ontico-ontological difference is concerned. A speculative word par excellence, de-vastation negates the vast all the while affirming and propagating vastness. It can act and counteract itself, to the extent that its uncanny force parasitically binds itself to the site of existence (is there—can there be—any other kind of site?), which is Dasein, marking the difference between being and beings. Installed there, in the place of existence, devastation widens ontico-ontological difference up to the point where its distended outlines morph into indifference, the ensuing vastness overflowing every limit. That devastation can be "established" or "installed" shows how it occupies the turf that used to be reserved for *fundamental* ontology.

Heidegger desperately looks for exceptions to this terrifying ontological regime. With the younger interlocutor for his mouthpiece, he intimates in "The Evening Conversation" in the compilation *Feldweg-Gespräche 1944–5* that something escapes the force of devastation in the forest, in "the capacious, which prevails in the expanse [*das Geräumige, das in der Weite waltot*]" (*CPC* 132/205). The capacious makes room for existence, whereas the vast pertains to space, an uninhabited and uninhabitable abstraction. The former receives beings, and yet refrains from violating their singularity; the latter is hermetically closed off in its enormous extension, which is nonetheless congenial to the way the desert, akin to a black hole, "draws in" and "integrates" (*einbeziehen*) everything even as it spreads outward (*CPC* 136/211). What is opportune for existence is not the vastness of the desert that suffocates with its very infinity, but the "open, yet veiled expanse [*offenen und doch verhüllten Weite*]" (*CPC* 132/205) of the forest. Another ontic geographical reality, the forest regulates ontico-ontological difference, this time not hollowing it out but potentiating and endowing it with meaning. And, on the contrary, deforestation, participating in a spiraling cause-and-effect of desertification, is the harbinger of the ontic loss of habitat and the ontological erosion of dwelling.

The open closure or the enclosed opening of the forest invites existence into itself by virtue of a de-limitation that turns out to be devastation in reverse. The limits it sets have nothing to do with the transcendental conditions of possibility for experience, and everything to do with the phenomenality of finite beings that give and withhold themselves in their self-presentation. Embodying the vastness of devastation, the desert eliminates the ecological-experiential limits within which the appearing of what appears is possible. Hence, its absolutely open expanse coincides with absolute closure.

There needs to be just the right mix of the open and the veiled for beings to thrive in and to "have" their worlds. Heidegger's word for this mix, for this precarious proportion, is *Lichtung*, clearing. An arena for being and understanding, the clearing is an opening in the forest: a rarified site among the trees surrounded by the density of matter, of wood or the woods, that is, of what the Greeks called *hulē*. The strategy of deforestation, desertification, or devastation that in the end amounts to the same is to clear the clearing by removing the opacity around its veiled opening. None of the three processes finds respite until the dense vegetal-material, wooden frame of the clearing—the frame that stands for the being-limit of every limit—has been undone. To paraphrase Heidegger, destruction destroys that which is framed; devastation strikes at the frame. As the frame vanishes from sight, the framed disappears *and* is present everywhere. The desert is this unframed unframing, the historical culmination of aspirations toward total translucence, shared by the Gnostic fight against the evilness of matter and the (pre-critical, pre-Kantian) Enlightenment dream of inaugurating an unbounded reign of reason.

Devastation, as the younger interlocutor in the dialogue spells it out, "is driven unconditionally [*unbedingt zu betreiben*]" (*CPC* 136/211). It unfolds in the name of the unconditional, demolishing all delimitations that crop up as so many obstacles on its path. Unconditionally, devastation de- or unconditions what could still demonstrate itself in the clearing, not to mention the existential-phenomenological conditions for demonstrating anything. Besides the frame, or along with it, devastation devastates the in-between where every dwelling is situated, *das Inzwischen*, before its formalization into a difference. To be precise, devastation adjusts the in-between for the epoch of global errancy, when the earth becomes "an errant star," or else "a mad star," *Irrstern*, "which, straying between planetary devastation and the concealment of the beginning, bears the inbetween, which is the abyss [*die zwischen der planetarischen Verwüstung und der Verbergung des Anfangs irrend das Inzwischen trägt, das der Abgrund ist*]" (*TE* 72/85).

A ray of hope shines in these lines, even if the light itself emanates from the black sun of melancholia. Although there is no more place for the in-between on the vast plains that devastation exposes and leaves behind—although there is no more place for place—a difference gapes between everything thrust open, exposed, unsheltered by devastation and the concealed beginning, the event of another growth. Having definitively exited the veiled expanse of the forest, we are at the mercy of an intensifying polarization between the translucent openness of the devastated, desertified planet, on the one hand, and the complete withdrawal, the self-veiling of the beginning, on the other. Complicating this schism is the fact that much of Heidegger's thinking around devastation responds to a line from Nietzsche's Zarathustra: "The desert grows: woe to the one who harbors deserts! [*Die Wüste wächst: weh Dem, der Wüsten birgt!*]"[3] The concealment (*Verbergung*) of the beginning is the desert harbored (*birgt*) within Dasein in the aftermath of devastating ontico-ontological difference. In the closure of metaphysics, the event of another growth culminates in the deserts growing within and outside us.

We thus cross the other threshold of ontological devastation, namely, its affinity to the emergence out of itself and overall growth of the Greek *phusis,* rendered in Latin as *natura.* The first threshold was visible in how the vastness of devastation parasitically occupied the site of existence and ontico-ontological difference, distending them to the point of making their finitude implode and empty out into the limitless. Having let devastation into Dasein, having allowed that which does not let anything into itself inhabit the place of existence, the human is expelled outside itself (truth be told, Dasein has never been *in itself,* self-contained) and shape-shifts into "the satellite [*Trabant*] of the devastation" (*TE* 69). That is the moment of devastation's *Bestellung,* its establishment within the in-between of fundamental ontology. The instauration of devastation is not static. It spreads (*ausbreitet*) in a surplus over mere destruction and negation, and its spreading out is also parasitic, considering that it usurps the tendency of *phusis,* in which Heidegger discerns the ancient Greek word for being. Thus, being is a *growing* devastation, which is to say, the expansion of deserts, of placeless space, of desolate vastness.

"The desert grows": Heidegger hears Nietzsche's expression with an ear tuned to the literal. A thing "in" *phusis*, the desert takes upon itself the activity of *phusis* as a whole: to grow, to emerge out of itself. Supplanting the plant that has served as the time-honored synecdoche for self-emergent growth, the desert, clear of vegetal traces, now blossoms into the flower of devastating nihilism. The "abandonment of life" in devastation "allows for nothing that emerges [*aufgeht*] of itself, in its emergence unfolds itself, and in unfolding calls others into a co-emerging [*Mitaufgehen*]" (*CPC* 137/212). Still, devastation does not prohibit emergence and unfolding; it is not, to reiterate, a negative "event [*Ereignis*] through which any and all possibilities for something essential to arise and to bloom [*aufgehe und erblühe*] in its dominion are suffocated at the root" (*CPC* 136/211). The event of devastation arises and blooms from the suffocated root of blooming and arising, which is why the desert can grow and why that event itself may be described as "far-reaching" or "extending its grasp," *vorausgreifende* (*CPC* 136/211). The bifurcated root it suffocates, growing out of and thanks to that very suffocation, is (1) the fertile earth, representing the fourfold of the entire elemental ensemble conducive to life, and (2) the finite opening of Dasein, the clearing, the space-time of ontico-ontological difference. All that remains are growing piles of sand, yet to be thought through philosophically.

DEVASTATION AND DISARTICULATION

As he muses about the meaning of the desert, the older interlocutor in "The Evening Conversation" points to sand in passing only to renounce the notion that a "waterless sandy plain" exhausts the meaning sought after. A profound sense of the desert, he intimates, lies in (or on) "the immeasurable surface as a plain of lifelessness [*unabsehbare Oberfläche als die Ebene des Leblosen*]" (*CPC* 137/212). Once we swap the double root of *phusis* and Dasein's existential ontology for the suffocation of and at the root in devastation, a monstrous surface (exposed but resistant to demonstration) unfurls, spreads out, and spreads lifelessness as so many seeds or grains of sand. Devastation and desertification are rooted in uprooting, above all in "the complete uprooting of beings from beyng [*vollzogenen Entwurzelung des Seienden aus dem Seyn*]" (*GA* 94:388). The growing surface of the desert is the ontic effect of the ontological event whereby beings are cut off from their root, from what hides below the surface, while the self-veiling of being, as the *appearing* of appearance, circulates entirely on the superficies of that which appears. What grows is the cut that insinuates itself into the place of the root it has severed.

Faced with the event of nihilistic growth, we should not jump over (the) sand too quickly. Other than mineral wear and tear and the calcified slivers of long-dead marine life-forms, sand signifies dispersion, the falling apart of dead matter from which even the traces of past perishing, of decay that could nourish a future growth, have been wiped out. Just as sand cannot be gathered into an articulated whole, so the desert precludes the gathering hypostatized in the mediations—for example, of the vegetal kind—between the earth and the sky. The elements are torn from one another and each from itself, and, in this discombobulation, they reflect the fate of beings uprooted from being and scattered across the vastness that lingers in their wake. The space of separation is vital to any relation, but when that space expands beyond measure, the related terms lose touch with one another, two particles of sand on the shore of a vanished sea. With the in-between devastated and ontico-ontological difference imploded, every relation is disarticulated, both in the physical and the discursive registers of disarticulation.

"And what is not all wounded and torn apart in us [*alles wund und zerrissen in uns*]," wonders the older interlocutor in Heidegger's dialogue, when "devastation covers our native soil and its hopelessly perplexed [*ratlose*] humans?" (*CPC* 133/206). The question assumes that devastation has propagated the desert not only outside—on our "native soil," *Heimaterde*, irrespective of its national confines: on the earth, elliptically involving all the other elements, as our native home—but also within us, as Nietzsche had already forewarned. The "tearing up within us," the open wound that consumes our entire being and *is* our being as devastation, is the incapacitation of *logos*, of *articulation*, to which philosophers have a posteriori added the connotations of speech, discourse, or logic. Hopeless perplexity stems from disarticulation, the unthinkable expansion of the vast in us surpassing the limits of comprehension and of receptivity toward existence. Not because we, who are "all wounded and torn apart," are too self-enclosed but because we are too open, too distended, too abstractly possible, too vacant and vacuous to be capacious and hospitable. It is not that, in devastation, there is no clearing in the density of matter/the woods/*hulē* in the midst of which we stand, but that the clearing melts like a lonely cloud on a sunny day in the cleared expanses of what only yesterday was densely material, vegetal, wooden, so that being "in the midst of" winds up in the middle of nowhere.

In Freudian psychoanalysis, "melancholia behaves like an open wound, drawing to itself cathectic energies" and "emptying the ego."[4] With Heidegger, we could say that melancholia is devastating, its "open wound" fatally inflicted on the body of speech. Devastation is unspeakable above and beyond the "decision not to talk any more [*nicht mehr zu reden*] about this devastation for a long time" (*CPC* 133/207), since there is no place in *logos* to accommodate the unconditional undermining of articulations and the very articulateness of *legein* (Freud sees in these articulations the success of cathexis). Devastation transmits a scorching desert silence, which, in lieu of future speech, avers that a permanent exile of the devastated from *logos* is imminent. Comparable to the *existentiale* of being-toward-death, it empties the world of the things found there. But, outstripping death itself, devastation does not stop at the lucid discovery of the horizon for meaning unoccluded by meaningful things; it voids the world itself, annihilating the world's worldhood. "This devastation concerns, after all, our own essence and its world [*unser eigenes Wesen und seine Welt*]" (*CPC* 135/210); it goes to the heart and enucleates "our own essence" (which is, already for Aristotle, a speaking existence) and "*its* world" strung together from spoken articulations that sublimate the spatial articulations of things, the "totality-of-significations" (*SZ* 161). Offsetting phenomenological world-creation, or the de-distancing (*Ent-fernung*) that brings beings near to Dasein in speech (*SZ* 105), devastation unworlds the world, introducing an immense distance, a vast silence that cuts into Dasein and severs it from its world.

In addition to being unspeakable, devastation does not present itself in the form of a phenomenon, which can only emerge with the worldly horizon for a backdrop. "Unknowable in itself," *in sich unkennbaren* (*TE* 85/101), its vastness stays completely hidden to the extent that it surpasses and, in the course of surpassing, razes the determinate (closed) openness of experience. There can be no phenomeno-logy of devastation, as it is incompatible with phenomena and with *logos,* with that which shows itself and the *how* of the showing. "How we encounter devastation [*wie wir der Verwüstung begegnen können*]" signifies "how we can in no way encounter it [*wie wir ihr keineswegs begegnen dürfen*]" (*CPC* 134/208).

Unfeasible as speaking about devastation might be, Heidegger avows the necessity of doing so. The older interlocutor confesses: "Therefore I also feel that it is again and again necessary for me to bring this devastation to speech [*die Sprache darauf zu bringen*]" (*CPC* 135/210, translation modified). Note that he does not feel the necessity to "speak of this devastation," as the English translator of the text Bret Davis renders the German, but to bring the unspeakable and expanding vastness to speech (how close to speech can one bring devastation before its heat scorches discursivity as such?). It is to permit *logos,* or what is left of it, to graze and to be grazed by the unthinkable and the unspeakable, assuming that this mutual grazing can happen between a finite assemblage and the un-de-limited. Heidegger himself brings devastation to speech by means of the category of evil: "devastation is eventuated [*sich ereignet*] as evil" (*CPC* 139/215, translation modified); "the devastation of the earth [*Verwüstung der Erde*] and the annihilation of the human essence [*Vernichtung des Menschenwesens*] that goes along with it are somehow evil itself [*das Böse selbst*]" (*CPC* 133/207). Why this uncertainty of expression: "somehow," "in some way," *irgendwie*? How are devastation and annihilation "evil itself"?

"Somehow" is a cautious word, or a word of caution to those who think they are in a position to categorize, to impose limits, or, in their idealist fervor, to detain the expanding, uncontainable, unconditional vastness in thought alone. More to the point, "somehow" loosens the nexus of moral philosophy and evil, which is, as a result of this normative destabilization, ontologized. Ontological evil, following Meister Eckhart, whose reflections are congruent with the Jewish Kabbalistic tradition,[5] is absolute separateness or the drive to absolutize separation. The signature act of evil is to disarticulate, to dismember, and, most of all, to absolutize the desolate vastness gaping in disarticulation, welcoming no beings and undermining being. Ontological evil is, therefore, the other of being—the other which, inconceivable from the vantage point of formal logic, is not nothing. It forecloses the non-transcendental conditions of possibility for existence, the existential-phenomenological preconditions for being, the possibility of possibility itself. Such evil is defined, if definition is what is at stake, not by the intention behind it but by its activity, with devastation for its content, form, and primary effect. "The devastation we have in mind . . . is not evil in the sense of moral badness. . . . Rather, evil itself, as malice, is devastating [*Vielmehr ist das Böse selbst als das Bösartige verwüstend*]" (*CPC* 134/209).

Taken ontologically, evil is the opposite of *logos*: a disarticulation that creates the vastness of decreation and forbids its own overcoming through healing, rebuilding, or replanting. Reconstruction and reforestation can mend whatever has been affected by destruction. But they are powerless in the face of devastation that, striking at the possible, at the frame or at the framing, dismembers time itself—the time of existence, which is not exactly a continuous chain and which, in its fragility, teeters on the edge of dismemberment. Devastation seeps into the future, indefinitely, and it is by no means evident that the "self-veiling of the beginning" is exempt from the absolute temporal separation (including *from* time), spearheaded by devastation and evil.

When the power of devastation corrals the beginning into nonphenomenality and obscurity, the safekeeping of the beginning, its being "completely untouched in pure inceptuality [*vollends unberührt in reiner Anfängnis*]" (*TE* 86/102), testifies, counter to what Heidegger wants to believe, to its secret allegiance with evil. Furthermore, the machinations of metaphysics, according to which certain entities (ideas, substance, God . . .) are unaffected by accidents here-below, participate in the nonparticipable, alogical logic of evil insofar as the metaphysicians keep these entities in a state of absolute separation. That is why the devastation of being might be as old as Western metaphysics: so long as being, whatever its historically embedded name or misnomer, is sustained apart from beings, immune to what befalls them, and, in its immutable reality, oblivious to the destitution of the world, that being will be synonymous with devastation.

DEVASTATING ENERGY

To recap the argument thus far: A place for dwelling must be sufficiently capacious to contain the dwellers who both articulate and are articulated by it, but its openness must endure within certain limits. De-vastation

(*Ver-wüstung*) is the increase in the vastness of the capacious, steered toward globality and abstract spatiality that distend the interval definitive of Dasein and cause it to implode. To devastate is to remove the vastness of the world's existential spatiality and to trade it for the immensity of the desert (*Wüste*) or wasteland. It is to purify the clearing in a push to eliminate the opacity surrounding it and to obviate speech, among other instantiations of *logos*. Yet, devastation also has a perversely positive side. Undercutting the future of growth and edification (i.e., of dwelling), it grows in a dark parody of *phusis* and beckons with unlimited possibility culled from the world of finitude. At the apex of the absolutely possible (and, therefore, impossible) possibility, existence dissolves in globalized hubs scattered throughout a planet-wide desert, on the flat grid of abstract space.

The positive aspect of devastation is a trace of its energy, of how it puts itself to work (*en ergon*), of its diabolical workings, and of the works it produces. Heidegger brings up the energetic activity of devastation in his asseveration: "it was already at work [*am Werk*] before the destruction began" (*CPC* 142/220). "At work," *am Werk*, is the active dimension of energy, which goes along with its substantive dimension, "in the work." So long as the desert grows, devastation is at work, dimming the worldhood of the world. The destruction that menaces the world's contents is logically, if not temporally, posterior to that process.

It seems, at first glance, that devastation is no less derivative than destruction: it runs on borrowed energy, the potentiality to grow it adopts from *phusis* and a floating standard of vastness it educes from the interval of finite existence wedged in the difference between being and beings. Very quickly, however, it becomes obvious that this borrowed energy does not obey the law of entropy, for it is not subject to gradual depletion on the model of the wear and tear of things in the world. If anything, and quite remarkably, the power of devastation increases in the measure that it presses on toward its only goal, the increase of power, the will to willing: "The devastation, under an errant star [*irrsternliche Verwüstung*], has its unified ground in the codetermination of all powers [*Zusammenstimmung aller Mächte*] in the same will. . . . [It] is guided by the principle of the fastest imitating and quantitative surpassing [*Überholen*]. Nowhere is there transformation, meditation, reconfiguration, but only the single overreaching [*Übervorteilung*]" (*TE* 76/91).

Devastation surpasses and overreaches as a consequence of the work it performs on the limit, the work of decommissioning the limit, putting it out of work. And the delicate limits of the "open yet veiled expanse," of the finite interval of existence and ontico-ontological difference, suffer the most from its onslaught. Negating the veiled and the finite, time and again, devastation endeavors to do away with the actual, with actuality in general and with delimited possibilities. It procures its energy from a contentless and abstract possibility and, in effect, reconfigures energy as this possibility—something we dare not question, given our inveterate preunderstanding (which does not rise to interpretation) of energy in everyday, political, and scientific discourses. For us, moderns or hypermoderns, energy is potency, power (*Macht, potentia*), and, at its most essential, the power to have power, which, in a variation on Nietzsche's "will to power," Heidegger terms "the will to willing [*Wille zum Willen*]." That is why our conception and relevant practices of energy are so devastating: they are the aftereffects of the lethal work devastation has already done on actuality and on existential possibility, with which it aims to dispense altogether.

The energy of devastation resorts to the destruction of actuality as its tool of choice in order to arrive at pure possibility disentangled from the impossible, power per se. When "the last restraints to devastation are overcome," "'destructions' ["*Zerstörungen*"] are recognized as mere temporary passageways [*Durchgänge*]" (*TE* 85/101). At the prompting of devastation, destruction, too, becomes facilitating; its goings-through, leading in every sense nowhere, are permutations of the in-between, void of difference and inhospitable to existence. Awaiting at the end of its passageways is not another actuality but more of the same deactualization: deracination, deforestation, desertification, the expanding vastness, burning up the material-vegetal-wooden frame of life for the sake of "storing up the 'potentiality' of powers [*ein "Potential" von Kräften*]" (*TE* 85/101). It is in keeping with devastation's paradigm that matter is conceived as temporarily detained energy, or in William Rankine's expression, *potential energy* to be "released" at any moment from the prison-house of actuality.

Despite unsealing temporary passageways, destruction confirms that "devastation devastates the in-between." In the service of an accumulating potentiality, extracted from the limits wherein it was "contained," energy is the in-between lodged between everywhere and nowhere. It is the actualization of vastness in a de-vastation averse to actuality. Instead of a site of ontico-ontological difference replete with factical possibilities, the human, more than anything or anyone else in existence, becomes a destructive passageway for devastation tending toward the unconditionally possible. "Human individuals and gangs," the younger interlocutor observes regarding World War II in 1945, "indeed must instigate and sustain such consequences of the devastation, though never the devastation itself. . . . They are the angry functionaries of their own mediocrity [*die wütenden Funktionäre ihrer eigenen Mittelmäßigkeit*]" (*CPC* 136/211, translation modified). Far from an apology for the crimes of the Nazi regime, which would suggest that the supposed instigators of devastation were "just" its mediators or representatives of "the banality of evil" (Arendt), Heidegger's statement locates the functionaries smack in the passageway of destruction. What has been translated as their "mediocrity," *Mittelmäßigkeit*, is their "middleness," their being in the middle (*Mitte*) of and serving as the means (*Mittel*) for devastation, as the passage for the passageways destruction has spilled into. The true function of the middling functionaries is not to be the cogs in the devastation machine but to make sure that it does operate as a gigantic machine for unworlding the world, with the vastness of desolation for its end product.

The energies of devastation need not converge on an event, be it as harrowing as a global war. Mundane and dispersed, devastation permeates our lives, organizing them on the basis of economic rules. That is what Heidegger means when he writes that "devastation reaches its extreme when it settles into the appearance of a secure state of the world, in order to hold out to the human a satisfactory standard of living as the highest goal of existence [*Ziel des Daseins*] and to guarantee its realization" (*CPC* 138/214). A "secure state of the world" is the facade masking sheer worldlessness, and "the highest goal of existence" is held out before a being barred from the delimited opening of being (existence). While a devastated world is no longer de-distanced, Dasein itself suffers de-distancing (and that is the enigma of de-vastation, negating and affirming the vast), becoming ready-to-hand, a means in the vast network of energy supplies that go into "human resources." Again, this development is nothing new; every class society without exception is predicated on the de-distancing of the oppressed. The novel element is not substantial but existential: the acceptance of the economic order as the pinnacle of existence at odds with its existential construal.

The ascendency of economism is hardly surprising given the thorough devastation of dwelling (*oikos*) and *logos* that jointly constitute ecology, the articulated and articulating finite opening of the world. In the ensuing global desolation, ontology reverts to the desert of being, where beings are exposed and disarticulated. Economy, consequently, presents itself as the only solution, slipping *nomos* (law or order; the title of the American police drama *Law and Order* really only says *nomos* twice over) into the vacant spot of *logos*. In this compensatory role, it passes over into economism.

The energy of gathering beings in *logos* is entrusted to the economic *nomos,* which goads humans "to think that the ordering of beings and the instituting of order would bring about the substantive fullness of beings [*bestandhafte Fülle des Seienden*], whereas indeed what is assured everywhere is only the endlessly self-expanding emptiness of devastation [*die endlos sich ausdehnende Leere der Verwüstung*]" (*TE* 141/166). Illusory on the flat and arid grounds of an instituted order, the "substantive fullness of beings" describes a state of actuality, the energy of rest and completion reviving the Aristotelian *energeia*. That fullness and the energy that goes with it are, nonetheless, unreachable. With the actual out of the picture, *nomos* sustains abstract possibilities reduced to "the endlessly self-expanding emptiness of devastation," which, in economic jargon, means "the business of devastation [*das Geschäft der Verwüstung*]" or "work for the sake of increased possibilities for work [*Arbeitsmöglichkeit*]" (*CPC* 154/236). Devastation is in the business of a massive energy conversion, the conceptual and practical transfer of energy from the actual to the indeterminately possible. In parallel, the business of working (the *ergon* of energy) grows more and more devastating as it nears the ideal of nonactualizability, calamitous for actuality as a whole. The vastness of devastation warrants the frenzy of incomplete and unaccomplishable activity bent on depriving the world of its worldhood.

Working without works is the model of energy devastation rechannels from ecology to economy, the energy fixated on the merely possible and palatable to those who crave the potency of power. Economism, which partly overlaps with the logic of capitalism it simultaneously precedes and succeeds, is the pinnacle of devastation's creativity, celebrating a depersonalized subject bereft of substance, perpetually at work and never in the work, isolated from its world. But what exactly is put to work in economism? What does its energy consist in? Certainly, possibility unencumbered with actuality, though, in and of itself, that devastating prospect is inadequate. The energy of economism is, congruent with the logic or logistics of working without works, the "unconditional will to order [*der unbedingte Wille zur Ordnung*]," "the goal of planetary devastation [*das Ziel der planetarischen Verwüstung*]" (*TE* 98/115).

The unconditional nature of the will to order is telling: it nourishes itself on the unconditionality of devastation, indebted, in turn, to the overcoming of limits, leveling everything delimited, actually existing. Its energetic charge is explosive, and it is not content with anything less than the practical possibility of blowing up the entire planet, as Heidegger mournfully quips (*TE* 85–86). So much, then, for a devastating destitution. In the capacity of a will *and* the order it institutes, however, the unconditional is conditioning: it spawns a deactualized actuality, assigning to beings their respective ranks regardless of their *logoi*-articulations. Examined closely, economism is but a *nomism*, an order shorn of dwelling places and devastating the residual possibilities of dwelling (the *oikos* of *oikonomia*) on behalf of the absolute, unconditioned, mere possibility from which it procures its energy.

A linchpin of economism, the unconditionally conditioning order is the mirror image of devastation that, in the same stroke, negates and affirms vastness, or, in a word, de-vastates. The unbearable vastness of pure possibility is in sync with an intolerable stricture of the possible serving the exigencies of "planning and calculating," *Planung und Rechnung* (*TE* 85/101). Just as evil for Heidegger is not a moral but an ontological category, so these operations are not mathematical, or at least not only so. The computation of risks, the assessment of efficaciousness in the language of productivity, the entire apparatus of informatics as the ultimate means of control in private, cultural, professional, and political life are all responses to the economistic (i.e., *nomistic*) directive to shackle possibility divorced from actuality to what is calculable, what can be processed as so many computer data, what is orderable based on a ranking activity in an arrangement where the in-between is an empty slot between two already designated ranks. That which is put to work with the approval of unconditional calculation is strictly that which is thought (i.e., quantitatively determined) to be consistent with the coordinates of the system of calculation and, especially, that which is deemed to hold the potential to augment the substance-free potentialities of that system. Together with the articulations of *logos*, the richness of *nomos*—at the beginning, the divisions of pasturage; later on, the thick fabric of cultural existence, interwoven with customs and different kinds of law—is sacrificed to its single, abstractly universal instantiation in the law of numbers, of data. The world of data evinces the devastation of the world: of Dasein, of countless lifeworlds, of the earth as the elemental fourfold, of the planet . . .

WHAT IS TO BE DONE—ABOUT DOING?

As we try to pick up the shards of our devastated actuality, Heidegger urges us to fight "the obvious temptation to get over it [*mit ihr fertig zu werden*]" (*CPC* 140/216). Kindred to the speculative reversals of de-vastation, the expression *mit etwas fertig zu werden* can have two discordant significations: to come to terms with something and to overcome something, to get over it. Most likely, Heidegger counsels his readers not to overcome the disaster that is our being by coming to terms with it, in the ideological sense of seeing the vestiges of existence through devastation's invisible lens or feeling at home in its generalized and widespread homelessness. Devastation, after all, brings into its fold the movement that aims to overcome it. But, harking back to the phenomenology of failure, the clean cut of negation will not do, either. In a condensed form, devastation evokes all the aporias and hesitancies that clog the project of overcoming nihilism; if nihilism is the overarching title for the metaphysical epoch we are a part of, and if being *is* devastation, then we cannot skip over it without, in this leap, sparking still more devastation or deepening nihilism. So, what is to be done other than patiently accept or rebelliously reject devastation?

In *Black Notebooks* we stumble upon another recommendation: "This devastation must then be endured [*ausgestanden werden*], even if it consumes our powers [*Kräfte*]" (*GA* 94:292). It ought to be lived through, suffered through, borne, albeit without the complicity of having gotten over what is to be endured. Much as it represents the potency of power, or even a super-power standing over and against actuality, devastation "consumes our powers," its energy transformed into an anti-power. In this depletion of "our powers," too, we may sight a hidden promise mixed with the greatest menace. The devastation to be endured may wind up in a final exhaustion, absorbing the powers we still have at our disposal. But the weakening of power as such (rather than of our powers) portends a recovery of actuality, of the energy of the actual, as well as of the actual *qua* energy, after we have sobered up from our inebriation with potency and pure possibility. When the last shred of our powers has been consumed, will we be able (except that this is no longer a matter of ability, capacity, *potestas*) to regain the meaning of being on the hither side of power and powerlessness?

Perfunctory as the above observations might be, they reveal the misguided character of the question, "What is to be done about devastation?" Questions such as this, regarding action, "agency," doing, or "empowerment," ineluctably partake of and contribute to devastation fueled by the endless activity of working without work, the hyperactive will to willing, the creation of an order heedless to the articulations of beings, and the noxious equation of *actualitas* (the Latin translation of the Greek *energeia*) with *actus purus* (*TE* 98). To do something (to do anything, no matter what) about devastation is to help it expand, to see to it that the desert grows vaster yet. At the same time, this critique of doing does not plunge the critic into the sort of resignation that swells from the feeling of impotence, an indefinite lapse into inaction, for which active doing is the default. A properly Heideggerian desideratum, formally reminiscent of the Hegelian negation of the negation to which the dynamics of *Nichtvorhandensein* and *aversio* of *aversio* are also traceable, would be to devastate devastation, to moderate the absoluteness of the vast so that it could revert back to the roomy and the capacious.

Have we not just expressed the issue in the most active terms conceivable? Does "to devastate devastation" not bank on a meta-possibility, exacerbating the tendency already under way?

If we are to avoid "getting over" devastation, our experience of it must be deepened. But deepening the otherwise flat and vast growing desert is not consenting to its spread; to devastate devastation is to endure it with a (phenomenological) difference, to receive the abandonment of beings by being differently, to *actually* receive it in the first place *via* the repetition of a desertion (responsible for desertification, as well) that has been occurring unbeknownst to us. Without as yet letting iterative difference out of our theoretical sight, we might recall Heidegger's complaint that "the being of an age of devastation would . . . consist precisely in the abandonment of being [*Seinsverlassenheit*]." As I cited that complaint, I wrote that the abandonment "comprises the being we abandon and the being that leaves us behind," the being that throws us, exposed and unprotected from the scorching heat of the absence of *logos*, into devastation's desert. In the state of ontological abandonment, we are left on our own, our "own" being not spared. Are these dire straits not promising a new positivity? Provided that we know how to welcome it, from *Seinsverlassenheit* we receive the gift of freedom, hitherto interpreted as unlimited possibility. Freedom (the freedom from being, above all) nestles in the problematic of letting (*lassen*) with all the subtleties aired in the various prefixes that modify this verb.

Heidegger adds to his opprobrium of "the abandonment of being" the lament that devastation "no longer allows for [*läßt*] any beings" (*CPC* 137/213). Buried underneath the division between letting be and not letting be (or letting not be, which is not the same thing) is a letting without the ontological plus or minus sign. It is to a letting antecedent to the question "To be or not to be?" that devastation pushes us. The abandonment, *Verlassenheit*, of or by being is convertible into the energetic quietude of releasement, *Gelassenheit*—letting being in, being let into being, or, more radically still, letting being slip away. In "The Evening Conversation," the forest is the conduit for *Gelassenheit* in the midst of devastation, a conduit that is emphatically not a passage, a means or an instrument for acting-through; "the healing expanse is not that of the forest, but, rather, the forest's own expanse is let into [*eingelassen*] what heals" (*CPC* 133/206). The healing is an expanse that is not so vast as to hand every place over to the desert of spatiality and not so overwhelming as to dwarf every in-between, the site where existence happens. A clearing in the forest fits in without filling this expanse. It lets in and is, itself, let into what heals.

To those who crave "pragmatic" solutions at all costs it might appear that Heidegger's way of dealing with devastation is to send us back to the forest. Ontically as well as ontologically, the forest (the woods and wood, *hulē* and its density, the matrix of *materia-mater-madera*) is the prime target of devastation: at its expense deserts spread and the vastness of space eats into the capaciousness of places. But, insofar as Heidegger emphasizes that the forest's self-veiling opening is embedded in another roomy "healing expanse," he lets us think beyond a retreat—which, frankly, he personally embraced—to the wooded areas, euphemistically known as "natural reserves" or "national parks" still spared the fate of all the other woods that the encroaching desert has swallowed up.

De-vastation breathes with the scorching heat of desert silence and, unexpectedly, with opportunities for self-negation and dedesertification, undoing the vastness it spreads. As an alternative to challenging it from the outside, in a series of actions likely to have devastating effects (if only by virtue of asserting their potency, the power to "change the situation" conditioned by the unconditional oversaturation of powers-possibilities), it is advisable to let devastation de-vastate itself, from within. This does not boil down to waiting, impassively, until nothing remains in the global desert the earth is rapidly turning into. The challenge is to let in (and to be let into) the letting suspended between abandonment and releasement, *Verlassenheit* and *Gelassenheit*. Perhaps only this in-between within devastation can still save us. If not, the next forty years of wandering in the desert will stretch to an eternity already without "us."

6. An Ecology of Property

ECOPROPERTY

Upon hearing the word *property,* immediate associations with the bedrock of the economy flood the mind. In the bipolar universe of value, neither use nor exchange holds any significance without something to be used or exchanged, the notion of ownership supplying a secure substratum for every economic operation. With Marx, we stipulate that such a foundation belongs fundamentally not to economics per se but to *political* economy, where both property and the subject of legitimate appropriation are the foci of struggle: private or public, individual or communal. But, as I argued in chapter 4, that is not the end of story: the abyssal foundation for economic and political economic foundations is ecological. Consequently, the concept of property needs to be rethought in keeping with its noneconomic underpinnings.

Before the legal enshrining of property and the right to possess it, the first word must be uttered, articulating the claim to ownership (think of John Locke's or Jean-Jacques Rousseau's theories of appropriation) and, in a performative gesture, the very being of the owner. That first articulating word, that *logos* establishing economy's law, may be "mine," "ours," or a still more basic semantic unit in the statements "This is mine," "That is ours": "this" or "that," chopping off and individuating a piece of the world into a manageable possession, let alone "is," the copula articulating the articulation, relating me or us to and separating me or us from "that" which is appropriated (and to or from myself/ourselves). Be this as it may, the proprietors are articulated by their own articulation of the claim to property, put together or drawn apart by what they wish to draw toward themselves.

When aggressive acts of seizing, parceling out, and fencing in portions of the world as property muffle *logos* and deride the eco-logical orientation it underwrites, they contribute to the forgetting of being, the two-way abandonment that sees the humans, who consign being to oblivion, themselves consigned to ontological oblivion. Violent silence, a silence that forfends the word, rules the day or the night here. What Marx knew as "primitive accumulation" is a far cry from the civilizing affair Locke had depicted; rather than articulation (say, of the proprietors and their property), the economy that has thrown off the last vestiges of *logos* sets in motion multiple disarticulations (Rousseau's and Marx's "alienation") over which an arbitrary *nomos*-law presides. In this way, the ontology of economism contravenes ontology.

For Plato and Heidegger (the two bookends of metaphysics), there is no more important role reserved for the philosopher than to recover if not the material word itself then the other, fruitful silence and to un-forget being in the midst of a profound ontological amnesia. In their eyes, that is the true philosophical task and the "definition" of truth as *alētheia*. The Platonic-Heideggerian desideratum is not so different from the ancient conception of *oikonomia*, present among others places in the writings of Xenophon and Aristotle, according to which the proprietor was supposed to preserve and indeed augment ontology by taking care of the goods. Conversely, the modern institution of economy unglues property from any ends it might serve and, with nihilistic indifference, hands it over to the work of environmental, social, or other kinds of destruction. The task of the philosopher becomes knottier yet: the un-forgetting of being must engage in a painstaking analysis of economism and its corollary modes of appropriation that endanger planetary existence.

What makes even possessive individualism possible is the appropriation of the human into the Heideggerian "event of being"—our unchosen and mostly preconscious fascination with the world, with the things it contains, and with the human and nonhuman others we share it with. To examine how the ecologico-phenomenological attitude subtends an economico-political approach to "property" I propose to put Heidegger in dialogue with his Russian translator, and an original thinker in his own right, Vladimir Bibikhin. This move will reflect the ontologically fundamental concepts or incepts of the proper and appropriation through the prisms of Heidegger's "event" and Bibikhin's "non-economic thinking," and, in doing so, illuminate the underside of property in the ecology of a human dwelling gathered, organized, captured, and captivated by *logos* before and beneath our struggle to gather, organize, and capture beings in the nets of *nomos*.

A RUSSIAN MOMENT: THE EVENT OF PRIVATIZATION

In an effort to salvage the ecology of property in the era of rampant economism, Russian philosopher Vladimir Bibikhin heeds the call that has echoed from the dawn to the dusk of metaphysics. Heidegger, he relates in a lecture course *Собственность: философия* своего (Property: The philosophy of *what is one's own*), "insists on standing on guard by being, for being [*стоянии настороже при бытии для бытия*]."[1] Asking rhetorically whether what is guarded is the property of the other or one's own, Bibikhin responds: "it is the property that is close, albeit on the hither side of what is one's own and what is other [*при близкой собственности, но по сю сторону своего и чужого*]."[2] The ecology of property could not be closer to us than this proximity outstripping the ultimately economic opposition between the self and *its* other, the proximity we cannot gauge through the categories of physical spatiality or the measurements of metaphysics.

In the same series of lectures, Bibikhin concentrates on the disavowed preconditions for the appropriative drive, namely, the unconscious receptivity of the appropriator-to-be, intensely interested in, absorbed, and captivated by the world and by the prospect of its capture. "People are captivated by capture [*люди захвачены захватом*]," he says, putting an accent on "the captivating might of capture [*захватывающая мощь захвата*]."[3] Rather than a thing—*a* being, in the substantive—to be transformed into property, the act of appropriation itself is what we are addicted to; irrespective of its intended content, the formal actualization of this act is the (unattainable) goal, so much so that it replaces the lost verbal signification of being. We are taken hold of by the unlimited desire to take hold of everything.

Granted: the world does not disappear *in toto* from the panorama of the appropriative view, something that can happen exclusively in being-toward-death. Bibikhin knows this full well, and he discerns in the world "the captivating goal of every capture [*мир как захватывающая цель всякого захвата*]."[4] Aiming at an object, consciousness (i.e., voracious intentionality) invariably overshoots the mark and sets its sights on the entire world. The limit, however, lies within: the act of appropriation is unable to appropriate itself, since it cannot master its beginning in a fascination that, before any decision, has entrusted it with its mission. The "captivating might of capture" is both powerless and exceeds all power exercised in capturing something or someone. It fascinates, and so is uncontrollable, ungraspable. A non-economic proximity intervenes, referring to the untamable beginning that had already begun before I became aware of it: above (or below) all, the proximity to "me" of a life I call "my own." It is this beginning before or without beginning that delineates the ecology of property, that is to say, the overarching context wherein the economic text is rooted and, at the same time, a catalyst for this text's uprooting, investing with meaning and invalidating the basic sense of property as a collection of discrete individual objects receptive to the will of the master-subject.

That Bibikhin's course spanned the years 1993 and 1994 is highly significant. The period immediately following the collapse of the Soviet Union was one of rapid and unregulated privatization, leading to the astronomic enrichment of the few, the worsening of socioeconomic inequities, and a dramatic rise in murders for hire as a way of resolving property disputes. With these bleak circumstances in mind, the philosopher implores his audience (which consists of the present and future Russian intellectual elite and, hence, of those who have already made a decision to quit without ever entering the race after obscene wealth, something that puts the effectiveness of his intervention in question) to stop and think not only about the meaning of property but also about the event of appropriation that appropriates the appropriators to itself, thereby expropriating them *in advance of* the appropriative act. Be the desired property philosophical understanding or be it a previously state-owned company, "the goal, the whole, the world [of which these potential properties are a part] eludes every cunning skill and cannot be captured by any ruse or stratagem [*цель, целое, мир остается ни для какой ловкости неуловимым, никакой хитростью не схваченным*]."[5] The limits of appropriation are its "own" enabling factors: (1) the unchosen spark of interest, prodding us (to say it in Hegelese) to commend our abstractly free will to a determinate thing (with this, the will itself becomes objectively determined), and (2) the horizon of the totality, whence the appropriated chunk is snatched. For Bibikhin, the name for this horizon is *the world*; Heidegger is more specific: it is not the world as a conjunction of interrelated things, but worldhood (*Weltlichkeit*) as Dasein's ontologico-existential a priori (*SZ* 65).

Bibikhin perspicuously construes the process of post-Soviet privatization as "the capture of the world," *захват мира*.[6] It is as though the insatiable drive toward appropriation targets not this or that piece of property but the whole world, along with the world's worldhood, becomes its unarticulated goal. Of course, consistent with Bibikhin's earlier statements in the *Property* course, the fulfillment of this dream is actually impossible. All the world might be a stage for capture, but it cannot be, itself, captured. More than an isolated historical occurrence, the congenitally frustrated desire for world-capture is the crux of the human condition, which is why Bibikhin concludes that "on a steep turn, at a breaking point, Russia has clearly demonstrated the essence of a human being's customary relation to the world [*на крутом повороте, на разломе, Россия отчетливо показала суть всегдашних отношений человека с миром*]."[7] The "customary" relation is that of the always-already-appropriated appropriators, who are, nevertheless, unaware of their captivation by and reception into the world they futilely endeavor to lay hold of as a whole. Their repressed passivity is a remnant of the ecological infrastructure for property, kept in ontological spatiality—the *oikos* of both economy and ecology—before it accumulates in physical space.

Heidegger's "ownmost," that which is most proper to Dasein, is finitude, never to be appropriated: "death is Dasein's *ownmost* possibility [*der Tod ist* eigenste *Möglichkeit des Daseins*]" (*SZ* 263). Whatever we do, we are articulated and disarticulated by this unactualizable possibility complementing the ecology of property with finite time, or with being *as* finite time. We are, in other words, ultimately privatized by death. Bibikhin does not go so far, but a question that surfaces in relation to Russia in the 1990s is whether, in the heat of privatization, captivation by capture was so all-absorbing that it had to be undersigned with the appropriators' deaths, executed by contract killers. Is dying a literal way in which "we mysteriously depart, go deeper into *what is our own,* drown in it [*мы загадочным образом уходим, углубляемся в* свое, *тонем в нем*]"?[8] There is always a risk in radical individuation (e.g., in the course of frantic privatization, or in the death it seems to run into at every corner) that the individuated would be lost nowhere else but in the midst of the individuating element, dissolve into anonymity within that which is most proper. And the Russian "case" is a singular-universal instantiation of this possibility.

Privatization, Bibikhin shows in the footsteps of Heidegger, is imperceptibly under way whenever we relate to the world by refusing to relate to it *as world* and reduce it to a bunch of objects, grasped together. To privatize is to cloister, to set apart, to cast away: the Russian "private property [*частная собственность*] speaks of a part [*о части*]," while the Latin-derived "*private, privatization* emanates from the same word (*privus, privo*) as our *away* [прочь] or *special guard* [опричник]."[9] Grabbing the world chunk by chunk, through appropriable objects "chopped off . . . from the common [*отрубленные . . . от общины*],"[10] I cannot reconstruct the whole from its privatized parts. The capture of the world and its flight from me are mutually reinforcing phenomena: the more private properties or parts severed from the whole I amass, the further away the world (which is ineluctably common) is from me. The event of privatization distances me from being in the measure that I bring beings close to myself; the price for the crystal-clear legal, epistemic, and so forth correlations between an individual subject and the objects under its control is the expulsion of both from the world and from the purview of *logos,* it, too, necessarily shared with the other even in a monologue.

In this event, the economy of property muscles out its ecology and, in this very move, enervates itself. Without the ecological infrastructure for property, imprisoned in mute violence devoid of *logos,* we are ontologically homeless, without the world, as good as dead albeit still biologically alive. The horrors of Russian privatization merely exacerbate the overall tendency to world-devastation and the obviation of *logos* inherent in the economic or economicist attitude. Bibikhin's message, to which Heidegger would undoubtedly give his assent, is that "we"—East and West, global North and South—are all the Russia of the 1990s, to a greater or lesser degree.

ALTERNATIVES TO THE ECOLOGY OF PROPERTY: FASCISM AND LIBERALISM

Somewhat more relevant to the second half of this century's second decade, the retreating ecology of property leaves in its wake the two options that have come to dominate electoral politics worldwide: technocratic liberalism and fascism. On the underside of the appropriative drive, we might remember, the ecology of property articulates our capture of the world with an earlier and largely immemorial captivation by it. In the economicist universe of liberalism, and in line with "calculative thinking," the dogma is that the passivity of captivation is an anachronistic relic of our irrational past. What is demanded of thinking is the activity of "grip [*Zugriff*], grasp [*Griff*], and concept [*Begriff*]," understood "on the basis of grasping" (*TE* 33). Bibikhin's *захват* sends the Russian reader back to the German *Zugriff*, with a bonus, according to which this word "in the history of Russian language not by chance points toward *cunning* [хитрость], *theft* [хищение], *ravishment* [восхищение]."[11] A trace of passivity survives in this semantic kinship, intimating that one's capture of the world is a consequence of having been already cunningly captured, stolen away, ravished by it. As for the concept, Bibikhin reiterates Heidegger's insight: "*Begriff* is from *greifen*—to capture. Understanding is capturing. Conception comes from *capio*, I capture; probably, it is the same word as our 'to grab' or 'to swipe,' *хапать*."[12] Here, the activity of activity is predominant; I grab, grasp, clasp, appropriate things within the economic property paradigm. My ravishment, my being stolen away (especially from myself), does not enter the purview of such conduct.

The mechanics of conceptuality are those of a grasp that precludes being-grasped. That is the logic of global manipulability and calculability, with political ramifications in possessive liberalism and in technocracy. Sooner or later, the repressed, nonetheless, returns: fascism betokens the fascination, captivation, and ravishment of being-grasped without grasping. After the ecology of property that articulated the active and passive voices of *grasp, Griff, хват,* or *capere* is defeated, nothing can prevent a totally irrational, illogical, *logos*-free fascination from setting the existential and political moods. Fascism slips the option of being-grasped without grasping in response to the hegemony of grasping without being-grasped;

hence, it is an immediate and thought-free consequence of conceptual excess, to which it also overreacts by delivering humans to a totality wherein they will be appropriated. We cannot straightforwardly repudiate it, least of all by appealing to the modern and technocratic paradigm of dispassionate rationality, itself the hidden source of fascism, as Theodor Adorno and Max Horkheimer have convincingly argued. Instead of moping for an active capture that would further repress the *pathos* of the proper, we need to work through both conceptual excess and the still darker reaction it triggers.

So, when Heidegger underscores ontological captivation in noting that "the human being exists as captivated by 'being' [*als genommen vom "Sein"*]" (*TE* 56) or when Bibikhin writes that the forest, which as we have already seen is roughly synonymous with matter, "captivates [*захватывает*] and leads us out of metric space,"[13] they do not veer toward fascism; rather, they broach the subject of restoring the ecology of property, devastated by economism, liberalism, technocracy, and calculative rationality. Heidegger, for one, situates fanaticism on the side of "the will to willing [*der Wille zum Willen*]," bent on pure activity, on "activism," *Aktivismus* (*TE* 48). The active will to appropriation and self-appropriation has divested itself of ecology: as we have seen, in it, in this will, there is no more space for the gathering *gatheredness* of *logos* and, as a result, no space for that which makes space or gives room, granting every *oikos* its receptive mark. The real fanaticism is passing being-grasped (by being) for fanatical irrationality, a state that is out of control, unmasterable, dangerous.

Take the example of ecstasy, the I standing outside or beside itself, generally evocative of fascist irrationality. Far from Dionysian self-abandon, the "ecstatic" constitution of Dasein is its finite temporality and noncoincidence with itself prior to the moment of death. Even the rational virtue of self-control presupposes this noncoincidence of the self with itself, a difference to be subsequently brought into line and continually reined in through the correct use of reason. That which is most proper to the I is its essential impropriety, also known as existence; reflecting on Heidegger's *Beiträge*, Bibikhin corroborates the German thinker's insight that "the thought about *what is one's own* conducts outside the *I* [*мысль о* своем *выводит из я*]."[14] A tacit reference to Max Stirner's *Der Einzige und sein Eigenthum*, this pithy statement ties in a single knot of thought, existence, and ownness. Allied to the essential impropriety of existence, the thought of ownness pulsating at the rhythm of finitude escorts the I beyond the sphere that is its own. Fascist ecstasy, in turn, is self-abandon oblivious to the three threads (thought, existence, ownness) Heidegger and Bibikhin weave together. It is a parody of the existential drama we have been following and a knee-jerk response to the overwhelmingly active grasp that has muted the experience of being-grasped.

We are duped by the demand to make a choice between two alternatives: the indifferent grasp of beings and the ecstatic surrender to them, as represented by a group or its leader. With the gathering gatheredness of *logos* shattered into unequal and disjunctive halves, and with captivation taken to be incompatible with capture, the quest for freedom hits a dead end. This dead end is an end of history different from that Francis Fukuyama prematurely celebrated after the fall of the USSR and the instauration of a global liberal hegemony. If history (*Geschichte*) flows from our predisposition "to be constitutively exposed to beings out of belongingness to being [*die schaffende Ausgesetztheit in das Seiende aus der Zugehörigkeit zum Sein*],"[15] then the refusal of exposure to, or captivation by, beings coupled with the non-belonging to being cuts history short. Just as an ecologico-phenomenological attitude subtends an economico-political approach to "property," so ontological propriation into the history of being undergirds our fascination with and our appropriative grasp of beings.

Analogous to the proper that remains fundamentally improper and unappropriable, history sways in the doubling of each event revealing and erasing itself, the event of ecology grounding and destabilizing that of economy. This is a deconstructive double bind, the work of *différance* that transcribes, after its own fashion, Heidegger's ontico-ontological difference. In sharp contrast to history's sway stands the one-dimensionality of liberal technocracy and fascism, which irrevocably, if also inarticulately, decide on gathering *or* gatheredness, capture *or* captivation. (I cannot help but comment that, for Heidegger, the history of being is inconceivable without the oblivion of being, without forgetting our admittedly immemorial ontological exposure, the impropriety of the proper. That is to say, by and large, ontological history proceeds by way of ending, its "process" twisting into the ends, a pair of them—fascism and technocratic liberalism—now looming before us as the only destiny.)

Neither liberal-technocratic nor fascist mutations of the proper, of what is one's own, affect freedom, which, following Heidegger, is an ontological (and, we might add, an ecological) affair. Under the heading "properness," *Die Eigentlichheit,* he remarks: "As appropriated into the truth of beyng, humans are now themselves [*Ereignet in die Wahrheit des Seyns ist der Mensch jetzt der Mensch selbst*]" (*TE* 133). Heidegger appends this remark to his testimony to the effect that "humans come to themselves, come into their own [*kommt zu sich, in sein Eigenes*], because they must now be themselves out of the arrogation into the event" (*TE* 133). Freedom is being ontologically appropriated by being, and, in this way, coming into one's own (which never belongs only to one, nor truly belongs to anyone), becoming an articulated articulator, an eco-logist of the proper, eager to oscillate between the different edges of the event. Bibikhin says something similar, in his own way: "Freedom is, prior to all else, captivation by what is one's own [*свобода есть прежде всего захваченность своим*]."[16] To equate freedom with autonomy is to be seduced by a liberal daydream, while to negate it and embrace its opposite (heteronomy, submission to the other) is to fall into the snares of fascism. Freedom, however, is not a matter of -nomy, of *nomos* that economizes on it, submitting it to a law, whether of the self or of the other. The ecology of freedom is dwelling in, being articulated by, and articulating the proper, that is, the finite "truth of beyng."

THINKING, THE OTHER PROPERTY

Within the economy of liberalism and fascism, thinking is moribund and the attempts to resuscitate it are mercilessly suppressed, as the ongoing treatment of Heidegger by the denizens of liberal ideology demonstrates. Besides the apparatus for thought, inexistent in fascism and superseded by calculation in liberalism, the space where thinking could take place has shrunk almost to zero. Between the Scylla of calculative rationality and the Charybdis of thoughtlessness, between the concept and its total rejection, Heidegger senses the need to free up another in-between, propitious to thought. His preferred syntagm for this undertaking in *Contributions to Philosophy* is "inceptual thinking," *das anfängliche Denken.* "Concept," he writes there, "is here originally the '*in-con-cept,*' and this is first and always related to the accompanying co-concept of the turn in the event [*Begriff* *ist hier ursprüglich "*Inbegriff,*" und dieser zuerst und immer bezogen auf den mitgehenden Zusammengriff der Kehre im Ereignis*]."[17]

Grasping-with, co-concept (*Zusammengriff*) sends a memento of the articulating articulatedness inherent to *logos*; in-grasping, in-con-cept (*Inbegriff*) bespeaks the receptiveness of the dwelling, of *oikos*'s interiority that admits everything and everyone into itself. Combined, they amount to an ecology of thought, the scaffolding of inceptual thinking. Inside and out, in and with, such thinking is the most proper and the most improper, immune to sharing and utterly common. It thematizes relationality, understood ontologically as the coincidence of separation and attachment, a disarticulated articulation preceding differentiation into passive and active postures, rather than the amorphous mesh of things that "relation" and, even more so, "ecology" usually connote. "The turn in the event" is this twisting of the proper into the improper in the in-between of the absolutely singular and the generic that suffuses every relation with meaning.

Bibikhin is alive to the ecological configuration of thinking in Heidegger, who inspires him to write, in a quasi-transcendental vein, that to think is "to free up the place where something new could happen [*освободить место, где могло бы произойти новое*]."[18] At one extreme of the event that place is already freed by death, by the absolutely singular "property" that is both my ownmost and completely other. At the other extreme, being itself makes room as that which is common to all that is "in" being, yet is unique to each and not locatable among beings. "*What is one's own* and *what is one's own* are fissured here to the point of polarity, intimating that we are approaching the real and, hence, risky things [свое *и* свое *раскалываются здесь до полярности, показывая, что мы приближаемся к настоящим и, стало быть, рискованным вещам*]."[19] And that is the turn of the event in Heidegger: the proper slipping into the improper and back again within the spasmodic movement of thought, whose twists neither preexist nor are preexisted by existential roominess.

In the ecology of thinking, freedom no longer contra-dicts captivation, because the task of thought is not the capture of the world but dwelling with and in the world, all the while articulating and being articulated by this difference between "with" and "in." It lets us sample a relation to the world prior to the branching of *capt-* into "capture" and "captivation," later on simplified into activity and passivity (and, therefore, prior to the divergence of anteriority from posteriority). The ecology of thinking, straining toward the *oikos* before its modifications by *logos* and *nomos*, is an ecology inclusive of itself and of its other, which is incidentally why the economy of thought can lean on *and* abnegate ecological articulations. In its ecological modality, thinking whispers—Bibikhin concurs with Derrida's reading of Heidegger—its *yes* to the world antecedent to formal affirmation or negation. Such "concurrence with the world" (or else, a peaceful concurrence: *согласие с миром*) is "the affair proper to thought [*собственное дело мысли*]."[20] The core property of thought is to divest itself of its claim to the proper vis-à-vis the world, to which it delivers itself, just as thought and world, the rational and the actual, lose their original, impenetrable and unmediated, identities in Hegelian dialectics. Inceptual thinking does not sit in judgment of actuality, does not impose its laws-*nomoi* onto *what is*; it does its own job, minds its own business (*собственное дело*), which is, however, not limited in scope but is interested in everything insofar as it is. A world affair, or else an affair with the world, of the world.

Another vector of inceptual thought, namely, its preoccupation with death, likewise moves below the distinction between capture and captivation, activity and passivity. Supplementing and bringing to naught Dasein's properly improper dispersion—my dispersed interest in the world—being-toward-death is a concentration on the improperly proper, on a singularity never to be mastered or appropriated. "Death is to be thought inceptually, i.e. out of the event and with respect to Da-sein [*Der Tod ist anfänglich und d. h. aus dem Ereignis da-seinshaft zu denken*]," Heidegger announces in *The Event* (65). The inceptual prescription is for the end to be thought from the beginning, without being conceived, cograsped, or exchanged with the other. Aneconomically *and* anecologically? As Heidegger explains, "in inceptual thinking, beginning is thought 'intransitively'; not to begin (tackle, take hold of, undertake) something but *to be taken hold of* by something [*an etwas* angreifen] (*in-cipere*)" (*TE* 154). It follows that the inception I get in touch with in my exposure to the thought of death is inclined toward captivation ("to be taken hold of by something"). But, this time around, that by which I am captivated is the future of my own worldlessness, my own absolute expropriation. Whereas the "agreement with the world" provided articulations for the *logos* that went into the ecology of thinking, the inceptual consideration of death disarticulates the I, abstracting what is proper to it from the world. Any relation is an articulated disarticulation or a disarticulated articulation, the concurrence of "with" and "in" investing eco-logy with meaning. It requires both the continuity of an agreement between its terms and a radical disruption of their bond. (The relation *oikos-logos* is not an exception to this rule.)

Bibikhin underwrites Heidegger's appeal to inceptual thinking: "It is not we who should order thought; we should be rather ordered by thought, to the extent that it gives a word to the world [*Не мы должны распоряжаться мыслью, скорее мы должны быть в ее распоряжении, насколько она дает слово миру*]."[21] Here, as well, the contours of the ecology of thought come through. Inherited from Plotinus, the word of the world itself is a pre- or nonhuman instance of *logos*, which thought can only welcome, lending itself to use as a dwelling, or, better still, as a resonance chamber for a discourse that does not begin with or in it. Between "us" and the world, thought articulates us with the world and with ourselves, orders us in consonance with the word that is not, to begin with, ours. But, at the behest of that thought, we must have already experienced the disarticulation (e.g., by death; in Levinas, by the other, etc.) that has handed us over to a new rearticulation.

Nothing could be further than this ordering independent of *nomos* and its conventional arrangements from the economy, where thought serves as a tool in the management of world-property. Economic or economicist thinking, like ethics in chapter 4, stays in the intermediate position—itself degraded and reduced to pure means—but the vector of appropriation now tends toward the opposite side, putting us in charge of being that is "utterly weightless [*schlechthin Gewichtslose*]," "empty of weight [*Gewichtsleere*]," evacuated due to the "unconditionality of power" (*TE* 94). Being without weight is certainly not without mass, which is an ontic quality, the property of beings; rather, it is deprived of the weight of the word, of the world's own *logos*. The moment we order thought with unconditional, self-referential authority and make being unbearably light, the word of the world falls silent, the dwelling wherein it could have been articulated shut closed.

Aspiring to transfer the weight of being to thought and word in his Heidegger-inspired *Язык философии (The Language of Philosophy),* Bibikhin writes: "A philosophical thought weighs exactly the same as a philosophical word. . . . What kind of an ecology should we expect of the human, who creates dirt upon the first contact with things? The first touch of this kind—thought and word [*Какой экологии ждать от человека, делающего грязь при первом прикосновении к вещам? Первое такое прикосновение—мысль и слово*]."[22] Much like the weight of being unrelated to mass, the "dirt" generated upon contact with things is not of a physical but of a metaphysical variety. In fact, from the perspective of existence with all its visceral messiness, metaphysics *is* the dirt, fancying itself as the utmost purity, that overlays things and imputes to them that which is not their own. To anticipate a deconstructive critique, the ecology of thinking would not idolize things as untouchable under the assumption of their original cleanliness (Derrida often plays with the French *propre,* which unites the senses of "own" and "clean"). It would only respect and remark the articulations of the things themselves—the mystery proper to them, "the elusiveness of that which captivates [*неуловимость захватывающего*]"[23]—obeying the phenomenological injunction and realizing that the first touch, the first contact, is never first.

Should it succeed, the ecology of thought and word would gradually merge with that of thing and world until the possessive form of its genitive would dispossess the thinker, expropriate the proper name attached to a body of thought, and hand it back to the world. To Bibikhin's mind, Heidegger has achieved just that (Derrida's "biodegradability"): "The affair that captivated Heidegger was not at all Heidegger's personal affair. . . . There is, strictly speaking, no such thing as 'the Heidegger affair.' In its place is the affair of the world [*дела Хайдеггера в строгом смысле нет. На его месте дело мира*]."[24] Forget what the French dub *l'affaire Heidegger,* to which Bibikhin is undoubtedly alluding with the locution *дело Хайдеггера*! At the level of thinking, a dis- or expropriation of the proper is the moment of releasement, or *Gelassenheit,* inconceivable when it comes to the concept and its economy. Bibikhin's Heidegger has lived up to the precepts of the ecology of the proper and has given his life and thought to it without giving up on anything—not by way of self-abnegation or some other form of a regrettable sacrifice but in the manner of a primordial *yes* that locates the word of the world in the place of the word of a thinker. The thought and the word cede their place to that wherein they take place, what is proper to them expropriated in favor of the material possibility for the proper.

One may be under the impression that what is on the line in the quarrel of economy and ecology over thought are two diametrically opposed, because symmetrically inverted, images of appropriation. But that impression is a misconception attributable to the undiminished power of the concept in thinking the proper. Whenever we order thought, we obfuscate our being-ordered by thought; whenever we capture, we downplay our captivation by the captured; whenever "the allegation that the human being 'has' language [*daß der Mensch die Sprache "hat"*]" is made, those who make it are generally "unaware that this 'having' of language derives from the fact that the word of beyng 'has' the human being [*daß das Wort des Seyns den Menschen "hat"*]" (*TE* 137). The weighty word of the world, the *logos* that participates in the ecology of thinking, is the language that appropriates the human and, once we are or have become its own objects or targets, withdraws, its withdrawal ontologically, rather than physiologically, authorizing us to exercise our capacity to speak and to order our surroundings as our essential properties. That is why economic and ecological attitudes are not on the same footing in the making of the human and why, to live well, it is not enough to procure just a little more balance between our activity and receptiveness to the environment. *Logos* is so generous as to open the door even to its own closure: to consent—silently, or in words we either do not hear or do not know how to interpret—to its expropriation. It motivates us to think the same and the other in a simultaneity that is nonsynthetic, nondialectical. The economy of thinking is an ecology expropriated in the full confidence of having appropriated the world and oneself.

THE HEIDEGGER EVENT (ACCORDING TO BIBIKHIN)

Ever a translator, Bibikhin specializes in making his own what is of the other and, conversely, in making other what is his own. More than a translator's duty, this twofold procedure is the "formula" of thinking. Translating Heidegger is trickier still, to the extent that his translators must render their own that of which the author has expropriated himself, turned over to the world. It is pointless to ask what is proper to Heidegger and what to Bibikhin in the thinking of the proper or of anything else, for that matter. Received by the Russian, the German stands for the event of thought, for how to think properly, say, by ceding one's proper name and the identity of one's thinking to the world. Such an event is antithetical to privatization impinging on the economic sphere and on thinking, which Descartes and Kant portray as a strictly private matter. The question is how to achieve the sort of poverty, the sort of total expropriation "necessary for ontological wealth,"[25] which may permit us to think again or perhaps for the first time. And, if we are to trust Bibikhin, the germ of an answer lies hidden in Heidegger's little-known text "Poverty" ("Die Armut").

One peculiarity of the short essay on poverty is that, despite circling around Hölderlin's dictum on the spiritual need to "become poor in order to become rich," Heidegger singles out Eastern Orthodox spirituality, with the figure of Holy Sophia central to Russian mysticism, as the embodiment of spirit's efficaciousness.[26] At odds with the Western idea of spirit as subject, substance, or both, this figuration approximates Heidegger's ontological reading of spirit; after all, in Orthodox Christianity, Holy Sophia is the hypostasis of divine *logos,* which delves below the economy of spiritual subject and substance. A little heretically, then, Sophia might be said to be eco-logical.

Where there is a subject, there are of necessity objects (at minimum, the subject is an object to itself), and ontic wealth is made up of the objects peppering our environs. In his interpretation of Hölderlin, Heidegger is satisfied with nothing less than a paradigm shift in the meaning of our "surroundings" vacated of objects. We must, he thinks, become ontically poor to become ontologically rich: to transition from the economy of beings to the ecology of being: to see past the world as an aggregate of objects. That is what the figuration of spirit in Sophia, or in *logos,* presages. "The human," Heidegger writes, "abides in a relation to that which surrounds him. . . . What surrounds us normally, what individually stands over against us (=the objects), we also call a being that is. . . . But the exalted relation wherein the human abides is the relation of beyng to the human, namely so that beyng itself is this relation that draws to itself the ownmost of the human as the ownmost that abides in this relation and preserves and inhabits this relation by abiding within it."[27] In an ecological circle, the human abode (*oikos*) is a relation (an articulation, *logos*) to being, which is itself a relation that captivates the human drawn into it. The ownmost, the most proper to the human, is this other-than-human ecology, in and with which we abide—the ecology disengaged from the objective surroundings, on which the economicist attitude preys and in which the inversion of intentionality (our being targeted, captivated, drawn in . . .) is diluted to fascination with the unlimited possibility of acquiring more material possessions.

Impending mortality was the event vacating the world of objects and confronting Dasein with worldhood. Death impoverished ontic reality to impart ontological richness to the one to whom it singularly "belonged." But its workings, indeed its energy, inflated disarticulation and, consequently, incapacitated *logos* itself. Death leaves no room for the word, for speech, for an address. Quite simply, there can be no ecology of death, even if it beckons with a complete expropriation most proper to Dasein. For this reason, Heidegger consults the poetic word, itself secretly vibrating with theosophic mysticism, as he moves to reconcile ontic poverty with the wealth of ontological or ecological dwelling.

In order for thought *qua* thought to achieve ontic poverty, it must throw off the customary vocabulary, where concepts are the mental objects, or the habitual tools, surrounding the thinker. According to Bibikhin, Nietzsche and Heidegger manage to do just that, dropping the formalities of philosophical lexicon with ease. In Nietzsche and Heidegger, he writes, "this untethering to the lexicon has for its obverse the unprecedented attention to the word."[28] The vocabulary of philosophy is a collection of weightless words that, generating metaphysical dirt, are light on being and fit to double as coins in the economy of thought. That vocabulary needs to be aired, ontically impoverished so as to make our thinking ontologically rich. The same is true for our unresolved relation to Heidegger, who, to repeat, stands for the event of thought, as far as Bibikhin is concerned: we, who are still too accustomed to conceptual cogitation, are not yet poor enough to receive him. Not to appropriate, but exactly to receive in the liberated and liberating place prepared for the event of thought. Until that moment, Heidegger, in the words of Bibikhin, is "yet to come in the same way in which Plato is still yet to come [*Хайдеггер пока еще предстоит, как Платон до сих пор еще предстоит*]."[29] And what is more proper to Bibikhin himself, what is more his "own," than a series of blueprints portraying Heidegger's to-come without representing it, without making it present, or predigesting it for the conceptual apparatus of understanding?

Part III
Politics

7. The Question of Political Existence

ONTICO-ONTOLOGICAL DIFFERENCE POLITICIZED

What to make of the seminar on Hegel's *Philosophy of Right* that Heidegger gave in the winter semester of 1934–35 at the University of Freiburg? Considering the array of subjects covered in the lecture notes and overflowing Hegel's text at hand, not to mention the versions transcribed by Wilhelm Hallwachs and Siegfried Bröse, who attended the sessions, the seminar lends itself to a number of thematic interpretations. It also furnishes ample evidence for Heidegger's Nazi-inspired rhetoric (above all, a certain endorsement of the *Führerprinzip*, or "the Leader principle") after his resignation from the post of rector at the same university on April 23, 1934.

Without dispensing with the insights of other readings and, especially, without eschewing the many well-deserved criticisms of the Hegel seminar, I intend to tease out from its compressed propositions Heidegger's unique *being-historical* take on the political philosophy of his illustrious predecessor in that fateful period in German and European history. The self-evident, if precipitous, hermeneutical option is that Heidegger credits Hegelian dialectics with totalitarian, authoritarian, and organicist tendencies. Shamelessly, the argument continues, he puts Hegel in the service of Nazism, supplying a philosophical justification for the theories of state, power, and leadership redolent of this deplorable ideology. The state, for instance, is treated as a spiritual, rather than biological, organism and, in this capacity, expresses the "being of the people [*Staat als Sein des Volkes*]" (§158; *GA* 86:139).[1] To a naked eye, Heidegger's foray into political philosophy seems suspiciously like Nazism dressed in an ontological discourse.

It is feasible, however, to examine the 1934–35 seminar in light of Heidegger's own philosophy, which slots Hegel into the vast project of the destruction (*Destruktion*) of Western metaphysics in a privileged way. Chapter 3 of the present study has provided a synopsis of the logic behind Heidegger's interpretation of Hegel's *Phenomenology* in a lecture course he had given in Freiburg four years earlier. The subtext of that engagement was a confrontation with Husserl, accused of working out a relative phenomenology of beings, while Hegel's phenomenology of spirit stood for the absolute phenomenology of being. Heidegger did not endorse either an exclusive focus on beings or a purely metaphysical philosophy of being, opting instead for the in-between phenomenology of ontico-ontological difference.

He resorts to a similar strategy in political philosophy. In the 1934–35 seminar, Heidegger blames Hegel for dealing with the notion of truth "*ontologically*—but idealistically" [ontologisch—*aber idealistisch*]" (§246, *GA* 86:178). Who is it, then, that plays the role of the political Husserl to the Hegel of *Philosophy of Right*? None other than Schmitt, guilty of being "far too extrinsic [*viel zu äußerlich*]" compared to Hegel's grasp of "originary essence [*ursprüngliche Wesen*]" (§38; *GA* 86:73–74). Whereas political existence in Hegel is under the sway of the totality of spirit freely willing itself, Heidegger diagnoses in Schmitt the opposite conception, contingent upon a relativizing struggle with the enemy other. For his part, the ex-rector defends ontico-ontological difference, slotted between spirit's ontological totality (Hegel) and the ontic, haphazard formation of mutually opposed political groupings (Schmitt). In this intermediate space, Heidegger carves a niche for political existence through a sustained transfer of the philosophical categories from his Dasein-analysis. Adhering to the existential notion of existence, he submits that political being is the work of collective care, a far-reaching thesis worth extricating from the historical and philosophical situation wherein it was first elaborated.

THE PROBLEM OF POLITICAL ONTOLOGY: BETWEEN HEGEL AND SCHMITT

Despite Hegel's purported disinterest in the ontic stratum of beings themselves, Heidegger is amenable to dialectics, so long as it buttresses his critique of metaphysics. For instance, on the subject of the "speculative definition of the state" as the "actuality of the ethical idea," Heidegger scribbles: "*Actuality* ≠ the present-at-hand [Wirklichkeit ≠ *das Vorhandene*]" (§42; *GA* 86:79). The actual might be lower than the possible on the ladder of existence, but political actuality is the actuality or the efficacy of the possible. In other words, the categorial analytic of Dasein, appropriate for human dealings with the world of things, does not apply to the embodiment of the ethical idea in the state. This idea, instead, attains effective existence in the manner of Dasein itself, namely, as a finite being-in-the-world of a people. With Hegel's assistance, Heidegger brings the personification of the state in a Platonic *makros anthropos* and a Hobbesian *magnus homo* to its logical extreme:[2] the state's purchase on being is not akin to that of a chair but to that of someone who sits upon and generally relates to the chair in the mode of everyday concern; or, with regard to another physical position, the state—the status—is standing. Through the body of the state, spirit gives itself existential actuality, political facticity, and freedom.

Thinking with Hegel, one must assert that the state is not identical to governmental institutions, let alone to a set of laws, no matter how constitutionally basic; indeed, the state is not even identical to itself. The excess of the political over its objective accoutrements is existential, and it is in this vein that we ought to read Heidegger's notation, "The state 'is'—as *historical* being [*Sein*]" (§56; *GA* 86:85). The meaning of the word "is" differs from the copula used to characterize a state as, say, democratic or authoritarian. To ascribe particular qualities to a political entity prior to asking "What is a state?" is to run head-on into a fruitless nominalism. In the same way, the being of the state, with its wealth of historical and existential qualities, is not an abstract category but, phenomenologically appreciated, the fulfillment of political intentionality in intuition. The question regarding the being of a state is inseparable from the political beings who realize it in history, whether of the usual chronological variety or in the history of being.

Heidegger credits Hegel with having at least raised the question of the being of the state based on its "*location in the system*" where it is the apogee of spirit's "absolute actuality [*absolute Wirklichkeit*]" (§71; *GA* 86:99), or, in other words, absolute energy. But the author of *Being and Time* refuses to implant "actuality" into the framework of the present-at-hand, allying it instead to existence and its possibilities. In this scheme of things (that are not really *things*), the state is the efficacy (actuality) of spirit's highest possibility, and it keeps its vitality so long that it expresses, without depleting, this possibility. Only in a crowd, where the unity of collective existence has already dissipated, do present-at-hand and occurrent, *Vorkommen*, modalities of being prevail (§220; *GA* 86:168). Formally, if not semantically, the two statements "the crowd is" and "the state 'is'" are just as incommensurate as the assertions "the cup is" and "the child 'is.'"

Hegel's response to the ontopolitical question "What is a state?" is: the state is the existence of the idea that is absolute because, free from external determinations, it corresponds to a fulfilled possible-actual spirit and prevails over the ontic or institutional milieu of politics. The theoretical work still to be carried out consists in considering its existence in existential terms. That is why one should, under no circumstances, view Hegel's political philosophy as "a metaphysics of the bureaucratic state" (§57; *GA* 86:85), its ontic realities dictating the ontology of the political. Nonetheless, Heidegger lays out two fundamental problems with Hegel's philosophy of right. The first is relevant to Hegelian philosophy as a whole; the second pertains to the political aspects of dialectics.

1. The emphasis on the absolute befits a religious outlook, which calls for a "renunciation of being in knowledge and turning to the Absolute" (§215; *GA* 86:164). Heidegger passed exactly the same judgment on Hegel in the course on *Phenomenology of Spirit*, where the worst surfeits of metaphysics are said to annul the thinking of finitude and time itself: "*the pure concept annuls time*. Hegelian philosophy expresses this disappearance of time by conceiving philosophy as *the* science or as absolute knowledge" (*HPS* 12). Beings succumb to the ideality of being, in tandem with the transformation of ontopolitics into an ontotheology. Ideality takes "precedence over the *events* [Geschehenen]" (§217; *GA* 86:164) covering over the interpretation of political existence as historical (*geschichtliche*) being. In doing so, it annuls time.
2. A de-historicizing metaphysics, enamored of the idea's absolute existence in and as the state, precludes not only time but also being. In the section on "Configuration of the State and Concept of the State," Heidegger seems to chide Hegel with these words: "*State* as *being* of the people; being of care [*as* Sein *des Volkes; Sein der Sorge*]"

> (§49; *GA* 86:82). The idea is not the people, regardless of how firmly rooted it might be in something like the "national consciousness." With respect to the being of an idea (or of the absolute), it is absurd to seek the "being of care." An idea does not exist as historical Dasein does, even if *its* mode of being is also different from that of a cup or of a chair. In sum, Hegel lets inner essence overwhelm the existence that makes it manifest, and so deprives existence of what is properly existential in it. Along with time, he undermines finite being, first and foremost as it bears upon the political unfolding of spirit.

In the case of Schmitt, the problem, as Heidegger sees it, is the opposite of Hegel's metaphysical immoderation, so much so that the 1934–35 seminar includes references to Schmitt *either* in order to offset the ontological excesses of dialectical philosophy with the equally (if not more) unacceptable ontic exaggerations, *or* as part of Heidegger's long-standing engagement in a polemic with Schmitt on the primacy of the political or the ontological. (Schmitt calls the "ontological-existential method of interpretation" *Kitschig-banal* and "ethical-characteristic." And in the same set of notes collected in *Glossarium,* he refers to Heidegger as "my dear friend and my honored enemy.")[3] This latter hypothesis holds for the 1930–31 course that studies Hegel's phenomenology as a subterfuge for the critique of "current phenomenology," practiced by Husserl and his disciples (*HPS* 23–24, 28). So, what are the grievances Heidegger files against Schmitt at the close of the seminar on Hegel's *Philosophy of Right*?

Unlike Hegel, Schmitt does not interrogate the meaning of the political under the auspices of the question concerning the meaning of being. "'Political' falls from the sky [*fällt vom Himmel*]" (§228; *GA* 86:171)—not the sky symbolizing the rarified atmosphere of metaphysics, but, to the contrary, the unexamined field of ontic premises. Resorting to the apparatus of phenomenology retrofitted and adjusted for *ontological reduction* (i.e., the reduction of beings to being, which does not dispense altogether with the actual beings), Heidegger insinuates that, when he postulated the friend-enemy distinction as fundamental to the political, Schmitt did not carry the questioning impulse far enough. In spite of having reduced the enemy to "a *being-other* [Anderssein]" (§235; *GA* 86:174), Schmitt did not acknowledge that a preoccupation with the threatening other emanates from the same ontological source as the solidarity pivotal for assembling a community of "friends." The common ground of being-other and being-same is care, *Sorge*, opening onto the existential-ontological stratum of the political, which remained hidden from Schmitt's theorizing. Even relations of opposition can be further reduced to the "*historical being-in-the-world*—as *self-willing*— . . . a willing-*with* and -*against* [*Mit-* und *Widerwollen*]" (§235; *GA* 86: 174). The friend and the enemy turn out to be two modalities in the existential orientation of Dasein's being-in-the-world. The main lines of the critique Heidegger launches against Schmitt are, therefore, as follows:

1. Diametrically opposed to Hegel's absolutizing tendency, Schmitt relativizes "the political." Based on the friend-enemy opposition, the political is essentially a relation, a *relatum*, whose terms are insufficiently clarified. The ontological designation of the enemy as being-other has not been reduced to the structure of care, embracing the willing-with and the willing-against others at the deepest source of political fundamental ontology. The being-same of friends, for its part, has not been sublimated in "their *ownmost* being [*ihres* Eigensten *Seins*]," their sharing the spirit of "self-determining historical Dasein" (§231; *GA* 86:172). A community of friends, as much as contention with enemies, are not primarily factual but spiritual-existential: "*State*—spirit and *not* 'society'—no *factual commonality*" (§176; *GA* 86:148). That, in Heidegger's opinion, is what Schmitt has overlooked in his deduction of a quasi-metaphysical principle from empirical politics.
2. As a consequence of his faulty method, Schmitt turns a blind eye to the being of the political, this time not thanks to an idealist posture (*à la* Hegel) but due to his inattention to the "'*being*' of the people ["Sein" *des Volkes*]—*in and for itself*—i.e. *historical Dasein*" (§243; *GA* 86:177). His "extrinsic" (*äußerlich*) bias causes him to think that a community of friends is all the more united in the face of a shared threat emanating from the enemy other. Stated differently, Schmitt does not cultivate the conditions for a people to grow affirmatively out of its innermost being, without recourse to the oppositional (and, hence, reactive) determination by a threatening other. "The political" in Schmitt does not account for the experience of historical Dasein, other than that inflicted by the enemies who do not belong to (yet, who constitute, from the outside) the history of that Dasein. Driven by a pragmatic and defensive logic of self-preservation, the friend-enemy relation is unrelated to "that of true-false" (§243; *GA*

> 86:177). The truth and falsity Heidegger has in mind here are neither propositional nor formal-logical but existential: the truth of experience as an undergoing, a passion, or an alteration of the experiencing with that which is experienced. Together with the positive and active "self-developing *self-assertion*" (the term Heidegger used in his "Rectorship Address" less than two years prior to giving the Hegel seminar) (§232; *GA* 86:173), the truth as a truth of historical being, or of experience, is nowhere to be found in Schmitt.

The criticisms Heidegger hurls at Hegel and Schmitt converge around both thinkers' disregard to existential political ontology, their ontological and ontic orientations notwithstanding. Heidegger, no doubt, oversimplifies their positions in order to cement his alternative vision of political existence. When it comes to the critique of Hegel, were the absolute limited to a religious outlook, such a limitation would have contradicted its encompassing nature. Religion in Hegel's *Phenomenology* is itself spiritual-ontological, that is, not im-mediate but self-negated and already transfigured by the absolute. The true absolute does not elevate being at the expense of beings; it reconstructs the ontic world from an ontologically all-sided standpoint. I have already pointed out how, reflecting on Hegel's method, Heidegger admits that spirit's journey commences from an absolute beginning, starting absolutely with the absolute, which "*is* not yet absolute" (*HPS* 33). This "not yet" restores dialectical temporality, if on the basis of spirit's ideality. Rather than rejecting actual (political) existence, Hegel bestows upon it a rigorously ontological meaning, in line with the life of spirit wherein beings are reborn.

The thesis that dialectical ontology is idealist is, itself, a humdrum parody of Hegel, as Heidegger knew full well, and the opening paragraphs of the seminar on *Philosophy of Right* offer the best testimony to the unfair nature of the charge. There, state-*qua*-will is listed in the same lineup as spirit, world, and history that occupy the (Aristotelian) middle ground between (and against: *Wogegen*) "natural growth and divine arrangement" (§6; *GA* 86:60). In the manner in which Heidegger inherits Aristotle, however, the systemic place of spirit, world, history, and the state coincides with the in-between character of existence, political or otherwise. The entire discussion of "state as organism" and of the "organic" in §§17–18 hinges on an existential comprehension of truth as being (in) "a *middle*." The static ideality of truth, in effect, precludes the coming into being of an organism's "emergent constitution [*werdende Verfassung*]" (§17; *GA* 86:64). Political existence, not yet formalized in state structures and legal documents, is this unstable emergence of a collectivity Heidegger rushes to label "the people."

Also unfair is the short shrift Schmitt gets from Heidegger. His monumental *Verfassungslehre* (1928), translated into English under the title *Constitutional Theory,* develops the "absolute meaning" of the constitution that satisfies all the Heideggerian requirements for an existential truth. The constitution, in the words of the German jurist, is a living form or a "special type of political and social order . . . not detachable from . . . political existence"; moreover, it is "the principle of the *dynamic emergence* of political unity, of the process of constantly renewed *formation* and *emergence* of this *unity* from a fundamental or ultimately effective *power* and *energy.*"[4] Not a tinge of relativity is evident in this *absolute* conception. The constitution dynamically evolves from the political existence of a group, whose unity is the product of its ownmost energy. (With the locution "effective *power* and *energy,*" Schmitt is reworking—should we say, "reenergizing"?—Hegel's state as the absolute actuality of the idea; "actuality," *Wirklichkeit,* is nothing but the German rendition of the Greek *energeia.*) In this kind of constitution, political existence puts itself to work, energizes or actualizes itself without compromising on the possibilities driving its existence. And, lest existential political energy stagnate in its outcomes, it must be "constantly renewed" by returning to the middle that is existential truth-in-the-making.

Far from abjuring the being of the political, Schmitt creates an existential-phenomenological tableau of political ontology.[5] For him, the state *is* the constitution in the absolute sense of the word. Compare this intuition, together with the citation from *Verfassungslehre,* to Heidegger's commentary on Hegel, where "the state only '*has*' power because it 'is' power—and it 'is' power—because it 'is' spirit" (§251; *GA* 86:180). The only difference between the two assertions is that, for Schmitt, the power and energy of the political emanate from the vicissitudes of existence itself, while, in Heidegger's reading of Hegel, their ground is the metaphysical reality of spirit. Schmitt's nonmetaphysical political ontology, which has all the trappings of a "self-developing self-assertion," is as attuned to existential realities and possibilities as that of Heidegger himself. If one conceives of "the political" in terms of "the *Dasein of the state*—that unity allowing the original constitution and disposition to arise" (§241; *GA* 86:176), then the absolute sense of a constitution as a "living form," or an order that is of a piece with political existence, is a perfect expression of this original unity.

TOWARD A PHENOMENOLOGICAL ONTOLOGY OF POLITICAL EXISTENCE

Heidegger seeks to avoid what he perceives as the pitfalls of the Hegelian absolutization of spirit (as the highest self-relation) and the Schmittian relativization of the political (as a relation to the enemy other). Whereas Hegel will have been the founder of *the ontology of political existence,* in which metaphysical being subsumes beings, Schmitt will have been a proponent of *existential political ontology,* with political beings taking precedence over the being of the political. Faulting each of these positions for its hopeless partiality, Heidegger professes that political existence transpires in the difference between being and beings that Hegel and Schmitt all but effaced.

As he paints his phenomenological approach to political existence in broad brushstrokes, Heidegger tends to regard the state as Dasein, dispersed in the mode of concern (*Besorge*) that marks its attitude toward friends and enemies (§158; *GA* 86:139); thrown (*geworfen*) into a historical epoch (§159; *GA* 86:139); and projecting itself in a "*knowing will—as freedom*" (§150; *GA* 86:136). Accepting that the state is Dasein, with its distinctive way of being-in-the-world, it is at the same time relative and absolute, in that each Dasein is the center of its world, not of *the* world as such. In addition to introducing a virtually unsurpassable contradiction between domestic and international politics (the politics of world*s* and of the world), the principle of fundamental political ontology nestles in the state's being-in-the-world: the positive finitude of the state lies "in a Dasein-based struggle with the beyng and beings of the fissure as tension [*der Zerklüftung als Spannung*]" (§173; *GA* 86:146). The fissure between being and beings is another name for ontico-ontological difference that discloses its political dimension as soon as it is thought of as a tension, its space or spacing subjacent to the friend-enemy distinction and to spirit's self-negation alike.

The essence of the political is its existence. More concretely—and here Heidegger makes several inexcusable slippages—it is the existence of the state as a historical being-in-the-world personified in the singular existence of its leader: "*The essence of 'the state.' What or who? 'Leader state'* ["Führerstaat"]" (§81; *GA* 86:103). "What or who?" restates the so-called question of competence Schmitt addressed in his work on sovereignty.[6] Schmitt's definition of the sovereign as the one who decides on the exception is a response to "Who decides?" and, simultaneously, a rebuke to those who raise the question in its what-modality, as a ruse for disguising the source of sovereignty. In Heidegger's *Führerstaat,* however, it is not the exceptional moment that matters but the entire structure of political Dasein articulated as care. Thrownness and projection come to signify being-led and leading, respectively: "Bearing—(Thrownness)—and leading (understanding) [*Tragend—(Geworfenheit)—und Führend (Verstehen)*]" describe the organization (*Einrichtung*) of political existence (§206; *GA* 86:161). As a thrown projection, the Dasein of or in a state is the relation (thus, an articulated difference) between the leading and the led *within a single existential-political unit.*

Where the phenomenological ontology of political existence parts ways with fundamental ontology is in regard to the possibility of unity. As a rule, finite existence does not tolerate unification, seeing that Dasein fully coincides with itself only in the moment of its death. But "the essence of the state" is precisely "unification [*Einigung*]" (§43; *GA* 86:79–80), and the Dasein of the leader effects "the unification [*Vereinigung*] of powers," which, over and above their "heaping up," denotes their confluence in the essential source of investiture (§36; *GA* 86:73). Were Heidegger asked, he would have rebuffed this objection: unification, *Einigung* or *Vereinigung,* is not unity, *Einheit,* since it presupposes a certain degree of dispersion in whatever (or whomever) it aims to unify. In the same spirit, the final sentence in paragraph 36 reads: "This unification [*Vereinigung*] as return to the origin does not exclude a 'separation' ["*Teilung*"]—in the sense of an articulation—whereby the members also emerge in a new essence." Thrown projection is the very articulated separation that strives toward, without ever attaining, the unity of existence.

Less burdened with allusions to the Nazi construction of the state is another instance of unification Heidegger educes from Hegel's *Philosophy of Right.* The Hegelian state is a dialectical unity of substance and subject, of objective institutions and the political organism, or, in other words, of "the strictly political state and its constitution."[7] Heidegger incorporates these disparate moments into the structure of "care as being in the world [*die Sorge als In der Welt sein*]," arguing that "constitution and disposition" are "each a distinct manner of appearing of the same *one* [*desselben Einen*]—of unification [*Vereinigung*]" (§220; *GA* 86:166–68).[8] An analysis of the unity of care is presented on the heels of this avowal of unification. Care is "a) world-being—*letting world, worlding;* b) being-in—steadfastness [*Inständigkeit*]" (§220; *GA* 86:168). The project of worlding is that of constitution, while the thrownness of being-in is the disposition, steadfastness, or the state as such ("the strictly political state" in Hegel's text). The state, *Staat,* as an objective "disposition," is this status, a manner of standing, steadfastness, *Inständigkeit,* that literally says "standing-in-ness." Its passive appearance in the world has no future unless it develops an active self- and world-constituting disposition that renews (or refuses to renew) the status quo. The dyad of the leading and the led is secondary in comparison to the unification of the constitution and disposition in political care.

The manner of standing, in Heidegger's philosophy, is equivalent to the manner of being: "*How it stands* [Wie es steht um]—the people—with the kind and manner of this being [*Seienden*]—how it is [*Wie es ist*]" (§53; *GA* 86:84). The state is an ontic replica of the ontological standing as a ramification of the "worlding" decision to assume this or that stance ontically made apparent in the constitution. Its political existence is unthinkable outside a phenomenological orientation regulating its manner of standing throughout its lifetime. Schmitt has chanced upon the orientation toward friends and against enemies, Heidegger hints, without identifying it as "an essential *consequence* [*Wesens*folge] of the political" (§235; *GA* 86:173), thus without reducing a key ontic feature of actual politics to its source in the phenomenological ontology of political existence.

Even so, translating the vocabulary of *Being and Time* into political categories proves impossible. In Heidegger's *magnum opus,* the meaning of being was time, the infinite finitude of existence. Is that also the meaning of political being? Not exactly. "*State* as beyng of the people. Certainly—but what does *beyng* mean? Beyng and fissure [*Zerklüftung*] (conflict [*Widerstreit*] and *polemos*)" (§114; *GA* 86:115). The word "fissure," *Zerklüftung,* will resurface later on in the seminar (cf. §173; *GA* 86:146–47), a symptom of ontico-ontological difference in politics. It will remain associated with the "Dasein-based" struggle. But in paragraph 114, "fissure" elucidates the meaning of being no longer as a mere tension but as "conflict and *polemos*," and hence as the political division par excellence. As a result, there is no such thing as the universal meaning of being, given that the difference between being and beings is on some occasions called "time," on others overlaps with Dasein, and in still other instances implicates *polemos*, itself intimately linked (*via* Heraclitus) to the Hegelian negativity and the Schmittian friend-enemy relation. Is ontology fundamental, or is the political? Or, is the political (i.e., ontological difference as *polemos*) the fundamental aspect of fundamental ontology? Schmitt might have had good reasons for writing in *Glossarium*, "*Macht ist Sein; Sein ist Macht* [power is being; being is power]."[9]

Once we scrutinize Heidegger's perspective on the political against the precepts of fundamental ontology, everything that is promising and everything that is pernicious, if not downright appalling, in the 1934–35 outlines of political existence comes to the fore. Especially scandalous is the incarnation of the political in the leader, with all its repercussion for the "applications" of thrownness, projection, and the structure of care. But the good news is that the *Führerprinzip* and the *Führerstaat* are not essential to the phenomenological ontology of political existence. If the state, as a dynamic unity of constitution and disposition, is an example of political Dasein, then the emergent existential framework does not in the least require that power be personified. Under the dark but in my view relatively thin veneer of Nazi-sounding rhetoric, Heidegger readies for us the theoretical tools indispensable to the analysis of collective existence, of being-in and "worlding" the world. Extending the appellation "historical Dasein" even to such entities as the state and the people, he reperforms the philosophical gesture of Hobbes, who described his Leviathan as a "mortal god." Highlighting the fissure of existence at the heart of political ontology, Heidegger forestalls—perhaps despite himself—the absolute closure of totalitarianism. We are yet to gauge the depth of ontico-ontological difference and other aspects of Dasein-analysis in the question of political existence. The work is cut out for us, and if it is to come to fruition in a robust postmetaphysical thinking of the political, we must be exceptionally patient as we separate the wheat from the chaff in the course of reading the seminars Heidegger gave in the 1930s.

8. The Other "Jewish Question"

A QUESTION UNRAISED

As readers will have surmised, the title of this chapter harkens back to Marx's 1843 essay "On the Jewish Question." Before I align that text with the comments Heidegger made about the Jews in the already published volumes of *Black Notebooks*, separated from Marx's essay by roughly one century, I'd like to highlight the word that, despite being uttered, is seldom heard in this context: "question." How can the existence of a group or a people become a question? For whom are they a question; to whom is it addressed? What of self-questioning, putting oneself into question as (or by) the other, well in advance of making a momentous decision on one's own being, which presumably defines the human? And how does it stand with what Heidegger himself reveres as "the question-worthy": "that question that alone opens up the worthiness of the question-worthy: the question of the truth of being" (*GA* 65:52)?

My hunch is that the root of the problem with Heidegger's anti-Semitism is his reluctance (1) to turn the figure of the Jew, let alone "international Jewry," which he parades on the pages of *Black Notebooks*, into a question, and, worse still, (2) to interrogate the very logic and necessity of coming up with a concrete figuration, a clandestine "agency," if you will, for the nihilistic completion of metaphysics. Much more than a temporary drop in critical vigilance is at issue in this failure, which is more profound than the 1930s' rhetorical surface and which is *of* Heidegger in the two senses explored in chapter 2: by slotting a raw, concrete figure into his grand history of being (particularly when the latter comes detached from beings), Heidegger conjugates the most question-worthy and what he treats as the least question-worthy. Peter Trawny has recently coined a helpful term—"being-historical anti-Semitism,"[1] condensing in itself this very a- or pre-logical contradiction, this hidden clash of the least and the most question-worthy in Heidegger's philosophy. For no matter how "world Jewry" is metaphysically deployed and loaded with the dirty work of world-destruction or devastation,[2] absent the questioning impulse, its interpolation into the "being-historical" narrative will not rise to the thought of being.

There are, undeniably, different ways of refusing the question. On the one hand, a deficit of reflection and critique may be responsible for cooling the questioning impulse down. In *Überlegungen* [Considerations] *IX* of the *Notebooks,* Heidegger appeals to the courage (*der Mut*) needed for fundamental reflections, "the courage to track one's own presuppositions back to their ground and to interrogate the necessity of the goals one has set." This, for him, is the essential task of self-reflection (*Selbst-besinnung*), understood not in a crass "psychological," "characterological," or "biological-typological" way but ontologically, as asking about "being and its truth and its grounding and lack of grounds [*das Sein und seine Wahrheit und deren Gründung und Grundlosigkeit*]" (*GA* 95:258).[3] Needless to say, Heidegger did not track his own presuppositions about the Jews "to their ground" (did he lack the courage to do so?), but fell back on characterological and typological crudities encased in a facade of ontological significance. He flirted with disaster whenever he deviated from his own phenomenological commitments and resorted to actual stereotypes, instead of following through the primacy of the possible, throbbing in the power of the question.

On the other hand, the refusal of the question may resort to *ultra-questioning,* as it does in Derrida's *Of Spirit.* While Heidegger "*almost* never stops identifying what is highest and best in thought with the question, with the decision, the call or guarding of the question," the possibility or the privilege of the question is itself unquestioned.[4] Questioning the question is subverting the sovereignty of critique and, vicariously, of the subjects who avail themselves of it. More than that, it is a precondition for radical hospitality, where the other is not put to the question, in the inquisitorial or Inquisitional mode, but maintains the right to interrogate the I.

Rather than contemplating a conscious refusal of the question, Heidegger forges out of it a polemical weapon, an implement in an "attack" (*Angriff*) meant to outstrip the power of critique: "The attack on Descartes, that is, the counter-questioning [*Entgegenfragen*] that is *appropriate* to his basic metaphysical position on the basis of a fundamental overcoming of metaphysics, can be carried out only by *asking the question of being*" (*GA* 95:168). Along the same lines, he confesses: "My 'attack' on Husserl is not directed against him alone, and in general is inessential—the attack is against the neglect of the question of being" (*GA* 96:47). For all its phenomenological insight, its "rejection of psychological explanations and historiological reckoning of opinions," Husserl's philosophy "never reaches into the domain of essential decisions [*die Bezirke wesentlicher Entscheidungen*]." Why? Because, as Heidegger declares in the same paragraph of *Black Notebooks*, "the power of Jewry [*die Machtsteigerung des Judentums*]," which hinges on "the spread of an otherwise empty rationality and calculative skills," is powerless to make essential decisions. What this declaration purports to say is that, despite coming nearer to the ontological domain than "the Jew 'Freud'" did, the Jew Husserl could not dislodge the power blocking his access to the question of being. Right before he opens the brackets, where he ponders his attack on Husserl, Heidegger writes, emphatically: "The more original and inceptive the coming decisions and questions [*die künftigen Entscheidungen und Fragen*] become, the more inaccessible will they remain to this 'race' ["*Rasse*": i.e., the Jews–MM]." The limits of Husserl's philosophy, to which crucial decisions and questions remain opaque, are thus presumably demarcated by his Jewishness.

I am reminded, in this regard, of a bitterly ironic episode from my biography. While I was attending primary school in Moscow in the 1980s, my mother inquired during parents' night as to why, among all the other subjects, "Russian Language" was the only one that did not merit the maximum grade of 5 on my transcript. The teacher's response was brutally honest: "Well, of course, because a Jew cannot master Russian for a 5!" On the surface of it, Heidegger seems to say the same about Husserl's philosophy: "Well, of course, it fell short of the highest ontological question, the phenomenological rejection of psychologism, biologism, and historicism notwithstanding! How could it not, seeing that Husserl belongs to the 'race' of those, to whom fundamental decisions and questions are foreclosed?"

Truth be told, Heidegger does not isolate the Jews from other groups he deems similarly oblivious to being, notably the Cartesians, but also the Bolsheviks, the English, the Americans . . . He showcases them as though they were different specimens of an indifferent metaphysical nihilism. But, in and of itself, the nondifferentiation among political orientations, nationalities, philosophical positions, and so forth—the nondifferentiation mirroring the at-times-oversimplified story about the forgetting of being in the West that makes wildly dissimilar philosophies appear interchangeable—is an index for the persistence of the unquestioned in the thick of the essential question and of the thoughtless (which is not the same as the unthought) in the midst of rigorous thought.

In light of these divergent methods of rebuffing the question—call them the unreflecting and the hospitable—we can reframe the *Jewish question*. If a certain critical deficit needs to be remedied, then we must intensify the questioning impulse, keeping fast to the ground rules of fundamental ontology. Rather than multiply the cast of caricaturesque protagonists in a thoroughly predictable drama of Western metaphysics, we would then allow the *who* of the questioner or the self-questioner to flourish. The existential freedom of this flourishing is in sync with the other way of dealing with the Jewish question: resolving it as a question not with a view to providing a definitive answer or a solution (we have had enough horror unleashed by "final solutions") but for the sake of emancipating the questioned and the questioning as they commingle in a single—and singular—being.

EMANCIPATION

"Emancipation" (*Emanzipation*) is one of the first words in Marx's "On the Jewish Question," and the subsequent development of the entire essay rides on its political, civic, religious, and humanist uptakes. To complete this list, we must let Heidegger enter the fray, since it was he, not Marx, who called for existential emancipation, which takes its cues from the query as to who—not what—a human being is. What does one free oneself from when one declines the what-modality of the question? Among other things, from the "predetermination" of humanity by animality (*Tierheit, animalitas*), "the modern *anthropological* determination [*Bestimmung*] of man, and with it, all previous anthropology—Christian, Hellenistic-Jewish and Socratic-Platonic" (*GA* 95:322). Like Bruno Bauer, whose reflections on the Jewish question Marx probes in his text, Heidegger thinks that the Jew cannot be emancipated as Jew, any more than a Christian can be emancipated as Christian or a Platonist as Platonist; within the confines of Judaic, Christian, Hellenistic, and modern metaphysics, existential emancipation is inconceivable, as it would go against the grain of these systems. Philosophical and religious anthropology is yet to arrive at the meaning of *anthrōpos* beyond its zoo-logical (*zōé*-logical) and divine overtones, that is, beyond the subhuman and the superhuman.

The anthropological way of posing the Jewish question, within and beyond Judaism, is bound to be "*What* is a Jew?" Were fundamental ontology to process this question, its form would have been "*Who* is a Jew?"—the "who" irreducible to blood, ethnic belonging, or religious affiliation, all of which boil down to yet another "what." Heidegger did not give the question a fundamental-ontological form, let alone raise the "Jewish question" as a question. In this he behaved worse than the philosophical anthropology he berated, one where oppositions, such as Jew/Christian and Jew/Greek, are negligible because epiphenomenal compared to the all-encompassing animalization of the human.

Marx, for his part, conjectures that the opposition Jew/Christian will be resolved not on a deeper ideational ground they share as a vestige of the same anthropological prejudice, but by means of meticulous historico-political work. The first stage in this work engenders a critique of religion *as such*, rather than of Judaism, unable or unwilling to drop the attitude of "a foreigner [*Fremdling*] towards the state. . . . The stubbornest form of the opposition between Jew and Christian is the *religious* opposition. How is an opposition resolved? By making it impossible. And how is *religious* opposition made impossible? By abolishing religion [*Dadurch, daß man die Religion aufhebt*]."[5]

The second stage passes through a critique of the state *as such*, rather than of the Christian state, unable or unwilling to extend recognition to the Jews: "We criticize the religious failings of the political state by criticizing the political state in its secular form, disregarding its religious failings. . . . [But p]olitical emancipation is not the final and absolute form of *human* emancipation."[6] As is the case in Heidegger, albeit for different reasons altogether, Marx's "Jewish question" is neither a question nor one about the Jews *proper* but a convenient pretext for a much broader meditation about modernity.

The third stage of emancipation, coded as communism, will be announced at the end of Marx's influential essay. But how do the first two resonate with what Heidegger has to say about the Jews in *Black Notebooks*? Marx formulates the question more or less conventionally with regard to Jewish particularity, non-participation in, and subtraction from the universality of the political sphere, be it filled with Christian content or rendered formal and abstract in a secular state. Heidegger turns this formulation upside down, so that "empty rationality" and "the tenacious skillfulness of calculating [*die zähe Geschicklichkeit des Rechnens*]," disseminating the "worldlessness," *Weltlosigkeit*, of abstraction worldwide (*GA* 95:97), find their embodiment in the Jews. For Marx, the Jewish question rests upon the stubborn exceptionalism of the Jews combined with the dream of a universal emancipation from religious differentiations and from the bourgeois political form. For Heidegger, "Jewry" (*Judentum*) is not the exception but the rule, which, in his peculiar vernacular, is given the designation "the *gigantic*" (*Riesige*) (*GA* 95:97), seeing that it propagates its worldlessness around the world. Appalling as this accusation might be, his recasting of the question does not leave much space for genocidal fantasies of purification that invariably proceed along the lines of wishing, "*if only* the exception were eliminated . . ." Evidently, where the prevailing rule is defective, nothing short of a total overhaul of nihilistic worldlessness would do; hence, the stress on the need for a new inception (*Anfang*) of the West.

From Heidegger's perspective, Marx's proposal—to abolish religion as a form of life or thought and to promote scientific principles in its stead—is itself culpable for the growing worldlessness of the world. An appropriate discipline for studying leveled-down social phenomena in such a world would be sociology, which, as Heidegger quips, is "gladly pursued by Jews and Catholics [*mit Vorliebe von Juden und Katholiken betrieben*]" (*GA* 95:161). Most likely, the remark itself is a jab at Marx. Be this as it may, in the catalog of disciplines or paradigms to which Heidegger voices his aversion (anthropology, psychoanalysis, biologism, psychologism, historicism, and so forth), sociology occupies a special place because it systematizes the breakdown of the world and unconsciously gives it scientific expression.

When all is said and done, Heidegger would reckon the opposition between religious and secular outlooks (subject to overcoming at the first stage of Marxist emancipation) to be meaningless in view of their common metaphysical heritage. Anticipating the thesis of secularization as a movement *within* Christianity, Marx himself admits that pitting the one outlook against the other is not a sound tactic. He argues that "the perfected Christian state is not the so-called *Christian* state which acknowledges Christianity as its basis, as the state religion, and thus adopts an exclusive attitude towards other religions; it is, rather, the *atheistic* state, the democratic state, the state which relegates religion among the other elements of civil society."[7] Following Marx, an atheistic state is the "perfected" fulfillment of a doctrinal Christian state; consistent with Heidegger, uprooted cosmopolitan Jewry is the purest culmination of Judaism. On the heights of metaphysics, the differences between religious and secular Jews (but also, in a certain sense, between Jews and non-Jews) dwindle: "The question of the role of *world Jewry* [Weltjudentum] is not a racial [*keine rassische*] question, but the metaphysical question about the kind of humanity that, *without any restraints* [*die* schlechthin ungebunden], can take over the uprooting [*Entwurzelung*] of all beings from being as its world-historical task" (*GA* 96:243). This phrase, however, demands scrupulous analysis, expanding from *Black Notebooks* to Heidegger's predecessors and to his other texts from the dark period of the 1930s.

Heidegger's 1933–34 seminar "On the Essence and Concepts of Nature, History, and State" labels the Jews "Semitic nomads," who are not privy to the German experience of space (as a fixed place of shared existence): "We heard that people and space mutually belong to each other. . . . For a Slavic people the nature of German space would definitely be revealed differently from the way it is revealed to us; to Semitic nomads, it will perhaps never be revealed at all [*den semitischen Nomaden wird sie vielleicht überhaupt nie offenbar*]."[8] And what is the nomad's experience of space, as Heidegger envisages it? "History teaches us that nomads have not only been made nomadic by the desolation of wastelands and steppes, but they have also often left wastelands behind them where they found fruitful and cultivated land—and that humans who are rooted in the soil have known how to make a home for themselves even in the wilderness."[9] Thus, the difference between the original "Semitic nomads," that is, religious Jews, and their modern counterparts, that is, secular cosmopolitan Jews, is one of scale. With modern uprootedness, nomadism ceased to be an exception and has infiltrated existence on a planetary scale, with deserts growing and forests diminishing at an alarming rate. In Heidegger's account, the lack of "any restraints" in the "world-historical task" of "*world Jewry*" is explicable with regard to the Jews' nonbelonging in a lived, political-phenomenological space of settlement and dwelling. Further, the nomads' ruthless exploitation of and destructive passage through the places they encounter on their errant itineraries parallel the unrestrained "uprooting of all beings from being." The ontic displacement of traditional Jews, sublimated in the secular version of Jewish cosmopolitanism, has mutated, on Heidegger's reading, into the ontological deracination of the world and of being itself. The "world-historical task" of "world Jewry" is, therefore, to deny the world its worldhood and habitability.

I have no doubts concerning the correctness of Heidegger's environmental views on world-destruction and on how our planet is becoming a dump, which is reaching truly cosmic proportions given the increasing orbital debris rotating around the Earth. What is obnoxious is the faulting of "Semitic nomads" for this state of affairs. Nevertheless, Heidegger's argument, including its ontological dimension, is not original. In "The Spirit of Christianity and Its Fate," Hegel foregrounds the revolt of Jewish Law, a force of deadly ideality, against life itself: "And since life was so maltreated in them [*das Leben in ihnen mißhandelt*], since nothing in them was left un-dominated, nothing sacrosanct, their action [*ihr Handeln*] became the most impious fury, the wildest fanaticism. . . . The great tragedy of the Jewish people is no Greek tragedy; it can rouse neither terror nor pity . . . ; it can rouse horror alone. The fate of the Jewish people is the fate of Macbeth who *stepped out of nature itself* [aus der Natur sebst trat], clung to alien Beings, and so in their service had to trample and slay everything holy in human nature, had at last to be forsaken by his gods (since these were objects and he their slave) and be dashed to pieces on his faith itself."[10] How can one fail to see the connections between this passage and Heidegger's argument that uprooting is a rebellion against nature and, *ultima ratio*, against being, wherein beings are primordially rooted? Doesn't the qualification "*without any restraints*" apply to that uprooting which is stamped with the lethal force of the ideal, looming large over and against nature and life?

If I have switched, for the time being, from Marx back to Hegel, that is because the emancipation from religion required by the author of "On the Jewish Question" does not accomplish anything within the Heideggerian scheme. The only effect it might have is that of generalizing the destructiveness of pure ideality, with which Judaism is charged, initially to the entire planet and then to being as such. What to the young Hegel looks as the Jewish "maltreatment" (*Mißhandlung*) of life in their inner existence and outward relation to nature, under Heidegger's pen becomes "the overpowering [*Übermächtigung*] of life" in "machination" (*Machenschaft*) (*GA* 96:56). Alleged Jewish nihilism percolates from its religious core to secular modernity, where it assumes a full-fledged metaphysical character in the guise of a scientific ontotheology. But how is it possible to square nihilistic hostility to life with the anthropological predetermination of the human as an animal, the predetermination that—Heidegger is adamant about this—Judaism shares with Hellenism and with Christianity?

Despite disowning the racial nature of the Jewish question, it is in living "according to the principle of race [*Rasseprinzip*]" that Heidegger locates the power of overpowering life itself: "Through the concept of race, 'life' is brought into the form of what can be bred, which constitutes a kind of calculation. The Jews, *with their marked gift for calculation*, have already been 'living' for the longest time according to the principle of race. . . . The establishment of racial breeding does not stem from 'life' itself, but from the overpowering of life by machination. What machination is bringing about with such planning is a *complete deracialization* [vollständige Entrassung] of peoples, by fastening them into the equally constructed, equally divided arrangement of all beings" (*GA* 96:56). The formalization of life in the principle of race—the act of making life breedable—at the same time animalizes it and drains its vitality. Bred like the animals that they are in light of their anthropological predetermination, humans hand their lives over to a contentless calculative rationality. Nihilism and animality merge in the form of racial breeding, and Heidegger again puts the Jews at the center of this strange fusion, based on the characterological conjecture of "*their marked gift for calculation.*"

Despite the intellectual contortions evident in everything Heidegger has to say about the Jews, it is glaringly obvious that, having temporarily deafened himself to the call of thinking (and of being), he indulges in stereotyping, as he imputes mutually contradictory traits to the same stereotyped subject: the subhuman and the superhuman; an animal and a calculating machine; a racializing and a deracializing agent . . . (The tally will only keep growing in what is to come next.)

"SEMITIC NOMADS," ROOTS, AND RACE

Our interrogation of the Jewish question is suspended, and has been for some time now, on the verge of the second (political) stage of Marxist emancipation. Marx made this kind of emancipation contingent on a critical appraisal of the state form and, specifically, on a critique of the bourgeois state. In a nutshell, the modern state "solves" the Jewish question, along with every other problem of the sort, by driving a wedge between the abstract equality of political citizenship and universal participation, on the one hand, and the pursuit of private interests and protection of "basic liberties," such as the freedom of religion, in civil society, on the other. As Marx puts it: "[The] consummation of the idealism of the state was at the same time the consummation of the materialism of civil society *[D]ie Vollendung des Idealismus des Staats war zugleich die Vollendung des Materialismus der bürgerlichen Gesellschaft*]. The bonds, which had restrained the egoistic spirit of civil society, were removed along with the political yoke. Political emancipation was at the same time an emancipation of civil society from politics and from even the *semblance* of a general content."[11]

Just as Heidegger would regard as immaterial the distinction between the religious and the secular manifestations of "Semitic nomadism," so he would discard the difference between political idealism and the materialism of civil society. Both essentially pertain, as two sides of the same coin, to the completion (*Vollendung*) of Western metaphysics, irrespective of the efforts Marx pours into their dialectical reconciliation in communism. Political evil lurks, Heidegger holds, in the common foundation of the abstract state and the concrete civil society: "the equally constructed, equally divided arrangement of all beings [*die gleichgebaute und gleichschnittige Einrichtung alles Seienden*]." Whether separated by private, egoistic interests or united by shared abstract citizenship, we are under an implicit obligation to enter such an arrangement, which is as much ontological as it is political. How is this order constructed? Through rampant calculation, deracialization, and the untethering of beings from being—the three powers of "machination" Heidegger correlates with the Jews. Contrary to Marx, then, he does not espy in the Jewish question one of many analogous emancipatory projects of modernity, but ferrets out of it a synecdoche for the end of metaphysics. Heidegger does not refute, to be sure, that the Jewish people had existed well before the latest phase in the history of being has commenced. But he asserts that the three powers of "machination," with which he stigmatizes the distended figure of the Jew, have gained extraordinary prominence in this epoch.

While Heidegger's philosophy endeavors to invert the first and the third of "machinational" powers at the close of metaphysics, things get complicated when it comes to deracialization. It would be fairly uncontroversial to say that Heidegger wishes to recover thinking beyond planning and calculation and that he wants to recommit to the relation between being and beings in the shape of ontological difference. Both this difference and non-calculative thinking resist the abstract equality of "the arrangement of all beings," reminiscent of the abstract equality which the bourgeois state Marx attacks in his writings espouses. Does the race principle stand out from this arrangement? It is, by far, not a panacea from the sameness that installs itself at the heart of a deracialized humanity. Clumsily and objectionably, Heidegger presents the race thesis *and* its antithesis with reference to the Jews: they overpower life by planning its form, breeding it, racializing it, and, by the same token, dissolving its qualitative difference in an indifferent calculative mold. So, if not the race principle, then what is meant to unseat the second "power of machination"? The succinct response would have to be: a lived sense of history.

Immediately after venting his ontopolitical discontent with the creation of a homogenized arrangement for all beings, Heidegger writes: "Deracialization goes hand-in-hand with a self-alienation of peoples [*eine Selbstentfremdung der Völker*]—the loss of history [*der Verlust der Geschichte*]—that is, of the domains of decision for be-ing" (*GA* 96:56). Between the lines of this verdict, one can read another charge against "Semitic nomads": the Jews have been the most self-alienated of peoples because their history has not unfolded in a "Jewish space," in the manner that German history has taken place in a "German space." For Heidegger, only in an ecological and phenomenological unity of the place and time of a people's existence can a political "decision for being" be made. Without such unity, history is but an abstraction, such as World History that is, at bottom, historyless. The uprooting from a place entails uprooting from history, marking the end of metaphysics as much as the nature of Jewish experience, as Heidegger construes or misconstrues it. Along these lines, in an earlier notebook he writes: "*What is happening now* is the *end* of history [Was jetzt geschieht *ist das* Ende *der Geschichte*] of the great inception. . . . To know what is now happening as this end hence remains denied, from start to finish, to *those* who are appointed to begin this end in its most final forms (i.e., the gigantic [*das Riesigen*]) and to put forward the historyless in the mask of the historiological as "History" itself [*und das Geschichtlose in der Maske des Historischen als* die *Geschichte auszugeben*]" (*GA* 95:96). We have already witnessed Heidegger reckoning "worldless" "world Jewry" to be "the gigantic" and his generalization of its condition to modern uprooting. The historyless is the temporal supplement to spatial deracination, so that, jointly, these two qualifiers amount to the state of worldlessness.

As I speculated in my 2014 *New York Times* piece, Heidegger has—willfully, most likely—overlooked the uniqueness of Jewish attachment to tradition. I wrote then that the "Jewish mode of rootedness was temporal, rather than spatial; before the Zionist project undertook to change this state of affairs, the Jews were grounded only in the tradition, instead of a national territory. Such grounding is anathema to modern uprooting, with which Heidegger hurriedly identified Jewish life and thought and which is expressed, precisely, in the destruction of tradition."[12] Were he to have paid attention to a lived sense of history unfastened from physical space, he would have thought twice before lumping together religious and secular Jews under the same heading of "Semitic nomads." Cosmopolitan, secular, and largely assimilated Jewry might have still corresponded to aspects of the unflattering portrait of uprooting Heidegger sketched, but so would, also, all atheists, be they from formerly Christian or other backgrounds.

Regarding Marx's view of history, Heidegger acknowledges that it "is superior to that of other historical accounts," insofar as it recognizes the estrangement indicative of "the homelessness of modern man" (*GA* 9:340).

Likewise, in the conclusion of "On the Jewish Question," the fulfillment of history in a truly human emancipation (communism is still unnamed here) might resemble the expectations Heidegger harbored for the other inception, germinating in the completion of Western metaphysics. "*Every* emancipation," Marx writes, "is a *restoration* of the human world and of human relationships to *man himself* [Alle *Emanzipation ist* Zurückführung *der menschlichen Welt, der Verhältnisse, auf den* Menschen selbst]."[13] It is possible, for instance, to hear the words "the human world" (*menschliche Welt*) in a Heideggerian tonality, as heralding a decisive victory in the struggle against worldlessness, historylessness, and the powers of machination. What speaks against such an interpretation, however, is the kind of reconciliation Marx has in mind for emancipatory world-restoration.

In the narrative structure of Marx's essay, "feudal society was dissolved into its basic element, *men*; but into *egoistic* men [egoistischen *Menschen*] who were its real foundation."[14] The utility-maximizing members of civil society are the passive, apolitical, sensuous subjects of need, who have nothing to do with the "*political* man," the "abstract, artificial man, man as an *allegorical, moral* person."[15] The advent of communism, or "human emancipation," alone will sublate the confrontation of an actually existing member of civil society and an abstract political agent, "when the real, individual man has absorbed into himself the abstract citizen [*wenn der wirkliche individuelle Mensch den abstrakten Staatsbürger in sich zurücknimmt*]; when as an individual man, in his everyday life, in his work, and in his relationships, he has become a *species-being*; and when he has recognized and organized his own powers (*forces propres*) as social powers so that he no longer separates this social power from himself as *political* power."[16]

Heidegger's assertions in *Black Notebooks* would make of Marx's reconciliation nothing more than a Jewish solution to the Jewish question. Whereas Marx detects an intense contradiction between the political and the economic, Heidegger pinpoints diverse manifestations of the Jewish "powers of machination" on both sides of what is, for him, a fake divide. Private egoistic members of civil society represent the power of calculation; abstract citizenship and public, artificial, allegorical personhood stand for a deracializing homogenization and the divorce of beings from being. If anything, Heidegger would take the "absorption" of the one in the other, the reconciliation of the ideal political actor with the real egoistic individual, as proof for the consolidation and the coming into its own of the Jewish essence, the amalgamation of its three "powers."

Evidence for Heidegger's proclivity to convert the figure of the Jew into a *complexio oppositorum* (i.e., the complex of opposites, where otherwise antithetical traits coexist without the work of dialectical mediation) abounds. Besides the religious and the secular, the private and the public, racialization and deracialization, he pins pacifism and militarism on "international Jewry": "The imperialistic-warlike way of thinking and the humanistic-pacifist way of thinking are only 'dispositions' that belong to each other . . . because they are just offshoots of 'metaphysics.' Thus, 'international Jewry' [*das "internationale Judentum"*] can also make use of both, can proclaim and bring about one as the means for the other—this machinational concocting of 'history' catches all players equally [*gleichermaßen*] in its nets" (*GA* 96:133). There is more than a grain of truth in the allegation that war and peace are more and more indistinguishable, from "the war to end all wars"—which is probably the implied referent here—to the permanent states of exception (Agamben) or the humanitarian wars (Zolo) of the late twentieth and early twenty-first centuries. But, since Heidegger endows his cartoonish representation of the Jews with the capacity to serve as the vanguard of the completion of metaphysics, he concentrates this tendency in their hands. Insofar as "all players are equally" caught in the nets of this machination, "the equally constructed, equally divided arrangement of all beings" at the social level of deracialization replicates itself at the political level of a meaningless divisions between the right and the left, as well as war and peace. The non-separation of social and political powers, which Marx lauded, reveals itself here in the form of a metaphysical cobelonging of different parts in the same homogenized order.

It's time to take stock of this exegetical exercise. First, however, I cannot neglect to mention that Marx deals with the "Jewish question" better to the extent that he is more attuned to the singular historical situations, wherein the question crops up: "The Jewish question presents itself differently according to the state in which the Jew resides. In Germany, where there is no political state, no state as such, the Jewish question is purely theological. . . . In France, which is a *constitutional* state, the Jewish question is a question of constitutionalism, of the incompleteness of *political emancipation*. . . . It is only in the free states of North America, or at least in some of them, that the Jewish question loses its *theological* significance and becomes a truly *secular* question."[17] Heidegger, on the contrary, focuses on "international Jewry," a theoretical fiction and an abstraction that is on the par with the "intangible" (*unfaßbar*) power he invests in it (*GA* 96:262). He does not feel that he ought to qualify his statements depending on the varied national contexts of the Jewish people, because, in his view, the "historyless" and landless existence of "Semitic nomads"—in a word, their worldlessness—exceeds all such contexts, and so justifies a sweepingly generalizing modus operandi of interpreting it. In the spirit of immanent critique, it behooves us to ask: Isn't this modus operandi itself "Jewish," in the sense Heidegger deposits into "Jewishness"? Where are the rigors and precautions of the phenomenological method, fundamental ontology, and the hermeneutics of facticity in relation to an "intangible" presence, swathed in other negations (of the world, of history, of the decision, etc)? What kind of *logos* makes it tangible and visible? Is thought absolved of *its* limits, responsibilities, and fidelity to being when it tackles an object it perceives to be devoid of inherent limits, responsibilities, and ontological bonds?

A NON-FIGURE

To reiterate the beginning of this chapter, Heidegger's botched treatment of the Jewish question puts in the spotlight a much wider lacuna in his thinking about the figuration of metaphysics at the time of its completion. However valid, the rejoinder that the Jew is a wrong figure for this epoch in the history of being is insufficient, unless we add that *no* figuration at all suits the age of impersonal technologism and technocracy *per definitionem*. At the same time, the reasons behind the choice of the Jewish figuration in *Black Notebooks* are as clear as they are clearly indefensible: in the Jew, Heidegger spots a figureless figure, rid of racial connotations (albeit linked to the *Rasseprinzip*) and encompassing the cosmopolitan (largely secularized) Jewish diaspora at the leading edge of globalizing uprootedness. With this unpardonable choice, he approximates the notion of an absent presence or a representation without presentation, matching the current stage of metaphysics. To put it differently still, he describes the Jews in terms of what we now dub "a trace."

In a slim but important volume *Heidegger and "the jews,"* Lyotard repeats Heidegger's gesture of dissociating "the jews," spelled with the lowercase "j" and placed between quotation marks, from prefabricated identitarian categories. "I write 'the jews' this way," Lyotard explains, "neither out of prudence nor lack of something better. I use lower case to indicate that I am not thinking of a nation. I make it plural to signify that it is neither a figure nor a political (Zionism), religious (Judaism), or philosophical (Jewish philosophy) subject. . . . I use quotation marks to avoid confusing these 'jews' with the real Jews. . . . 'The jews' are the object of a dismissal with which Jews, in particular, are afflicted in reality."[18] He, too, inscribes "the jews" into the morphology of the trace, and, at this point, in this inscription, the other "Jewish question," as the question of the other, effectively originates. Outside biologist, nationalist, and religious parameters, the singular-universal question "*Who* are the Jews or 'the jews'?" spearheads existential emancipation. Heidegger inadvertently stood at the genesis of the question insofar as he (1) refused to reduce it to the issue of race, (2) outlined the placeless place of the Jews or "the jews" in the history of being, and (3) distinguished anthropological whatness from existential whoness. But he also churned up a careless answer when he made the Jews or "the jews" into a faceless face, the obscure and distended figuration, if not the "intangible" incarnation, of the end of metaphysics.

In Lyotard's book and in the philosophy of Levinas, the Jews or "the jews" are, in sharp contrast to Heidegger, the others of metaphysics, uncontainable within its totality. As such, they cannot be understood as the representatives of calculation or computation—the hegemonic metaphysical framework for the age of technological rationality—even though ontological homelessness remains central to the thinking of their non-identity. "'The jews,' never at home wherever they are," writes Lyotard, "cannot be integrated, converted, or expelled. They are also always away from home when they are at home, in their so-called own tradition, because it includes exodus as its beginning, excision, impropriety, and respect for the forgotten."[19]

Lyotard's exemplary strategy is one of inversion and intensification: the inversion of the meaning and value of homelessness and the intensification of the process whereby identity undergoes denaturalization, first, by being stripped of the biologicist trappings it had borrowed from the conventional concept of race, and second, by giving up all stable ontic markers and flipping into a non-identity. Not by accident, Lyotard's strategy looks like a carbon copy of repeating metaphysics after its completion: underlying the Jewish question is the question of metaphysics itself—of its current state or status, possible representation, and figuration. To no avail will we negate, point-blank, "metaphysical prejudices" replicated in every such negation. And our vehement rejection of Heidegger's own prejudices, or, worse yet, of his entire philosophy "tainted" by them, will be also in vain. If *Black Notebooks* have anything to teach us, it is the art of saying "yes-no" to Heidegger, and, by implication, to the legacy of metaphysics.

9. Philosophy without Right?

On Heidegger's Notes for the 1934–35 "Hegel Seminar"

with Marcia Sá Cavalcante-Schuback

HOW TO READ HEIDEGGER'S *GEDANKENSTRICHE*

To return to Heidegger's seminar on Hegel's *Philosophy of Right*, the tremendous difficulties we come across in reading its manuscript are not restricted to the fragmentary character of the notes, a text of half-sentences and incomplete paragraphs.[1] In and of itself, the excess of hyphens, of *Gedankenstriche*, and ellipses already imposes a certain pace and discontinuous rhythm on the act of reading. It forces us to jump from one thought, one comment on Hegel, one piece of evidence for Heidegger's residual Nazism to another. More problematically still, in order to accompany Heidegger on this rough journey, we must stop following another philosophical rhythm, namely, the systematic and smooth-paced unfolding of Hegel's dialectical argument. And, vice versa, if we are to remain faithful to Hegel's philosophy of right, we cannot allow Heidegger to lead us into the thickets of dialectics. The connection between guidance and following is irreparably disrupted, just as it was in Derrida's interpretation of the "Rectorship Address" in *Of Spirit*.

Although this is not a matter of a simple disjunction, the ambition to join Hegel *and* Heidegger in a linear fashion, procuring in this combination something like the political ontology of right, cannot be carried through. To think *between* Hegel and Heidegger, one must grow accustomed to jumping from one to the other, without the security of "baselines"

(*Grundlinien*) that hem philosophy in from all sides and bestow upon it the gift of right.[2] The right to leading in thought or in exegetical endeavors is irretrievably lost and, lost with it, is the duty to follow. As Hannah Arendt perceptively said in a different context, we must entrust ourselves to a "thinking without banisters," *Denken ohne Geländer*. Could this be a shape of thinking the possible without constantly glancing back at and consulting the actual? Without guidance *and* without a pregiven right? Does such a possibility of thinking (the possible) survive in the interstices between Hegel and Heidegger, the in-between where and upon which one can still dwell? Is rhythmic discontinuity—above all, between dialectical continuity and fundamental-ontological discontinuity—itself a cryptogram of existential temporality liberated from the linear dynamics of actualization?

Faced with the incompleteness of a text, such as Heidegger's seminar notes, the temptation is to fill in the blanks and smoothen the rough edges of its "thought outlines" or *Gedankenstriche.* To act on this desire would be perhaps disrespectful not so much toward Heidegger as toward the ineluctable incompleteness of every philosophical text. In saying what *has not been* said, we disturb the silence that vibrates between the fragmentary lines and that, in any case, *cannot* be said.[3] Yet, the incomplete text of these seminar notes revolves around worries about the completion of philosophy at a moment in history when philosophy's right (to say anything meaningful and effective whatsoever; to interfere in worldly, political affairs; to exist) is put into question. (Nowadays, the questioning of—European—philosophy's right to existence concentrates, in a sort of malicious synecdoche, on the interrogation of Heidegger's right to posthumous existence as a philosopher.) That which comes through between the lines of the Hegel seminar is something other than a curious philosophical aporia or an aporetic mode of thinking; it is a story about how philosophy itself, in the "end," becomes an aporia (*Verlegenheit*) and loses its right to dictate what is right and what isn't.

What Heidegger's seminar notes may divulge is overshadowed by another kind of silence, one that was typical of his attitude to the shameful episode of his Nazi involvement. Latched onto and turning upside down the synecdoche Heidegger-philosophy is our claim that "the case of Heidegger" is the case of philosophy facing the loss of its right. And what are all the controversies surrounding Heidegger's Nazism about if not the right of and to his thought, as well as the right to think further on his path: despite, against, or with his past? The right to a way of thinking as such is at stake in all the noisy controversies unable to hear the multiple silences that have precipitated them.

Does political engagement—fleeting and flirtatious or sustained and enduring—determine the right to a philosophy elaborated by the same "person" who has committed her- or himself politically? Does a given philosophical position (e.g., concern with the completion of metaphysics) lead straight to a practical political program? Expressed in these terms, the queries sound absurd, to say the least; nonetheless, they have served as the guiding threads for the unraveling of *l'affaire Heidegger* for decades, and will likely continue to do so with the publication of more volumes from *Black Notebooks*. As Derrida said in his 1988 talk on Heidegger's silence, these discussions and their penchant for decreeing the end of Heidegger betray, for the most part, "their political irresponsibility" and "their sociological inexperience."[4]

To sidestep the hollow discussions corresponding to the shallowest layer of silence they react to, let us say that the true difficulty in the case of Heidegger is the relation between philosophy and politics, when both politics and philosophy lose their footing and their right. This relation is far more convoluted than the configuration of "theory" and "praxis," than the discussion of how thinking is or is not action, or than the question of how an idea can or cannot be practically actualized in the world. The problem is not really how the universal—philosophical or political; being as a whole (*Sein im Ganzen*) of the whole of beings (*das Ganze des Seienden*)—may or may not coincide with the particular. What this "case" exposes is the historical consonance of politics and philosophy in their mutual divestment and shared approximation to an end, at which both, almost simultaneously, lose their right (or is it "their rights" that they are stripped of?). That is why the case of Heidegger mobilizes a question that is also ours, demanding an "active reading" à la Lacoue-Labarthe, rather than the reading of a historian or a philologist.

COMPLETION AND EMERGENCE

But what is meant by the "end" of philosophy, as well as of politics? How do they come to an end? In having reached their completion, in having grown exhausted, oversaturated, too full of themselves and also, paradoxically, empty of meaning? Heidegger's reading of *Philosophy of Right* reunites philosophy and politics (the latter, in the guise of right) precisely in the common destiny of their end as completion and exhaustion. It asks about the meaning of existence *after* the loss of right—to philosophy and to politics. That loss is not an altogether bad thing, seeing that, at the end of metaphysics, existence becomes meaningful in and of itself, its possibilities emancipated from the tyranny of potentiality and actuality. But let us not rush to hasty conclusions. In line with the seminar's paragraph 70, where Heidegger presents the "plan" for his reading of Hegel and foregrounds the issue of the completion of Western philosophy, the question is: What are we to understand by completion, *Vollendung* (*HPR* 125)?

Heidegger's lifelong critique of dialectical philosophy, laid out, among other places, in the seminar notes, takes issue with the meaning of completion. Given the in-finite character of Hegel's dialectics, *Vollendung* does not stand for the abrupt end of something that has been completely surpassed and overcome. It does not refer to the inexorable teleology of actualization, bringing every potentiality to fruition. The dialectical back-and-forth, return to itself and closure unto itself of metaphysics, spells out a *perpetual ending* that frames the thinking of completion. Completion means an end that doesn't cease to end,[5] so that a "completed" meaning becomes vacuous—an insight gathering together a set of topics (the overcoming of metaphysics, the question of technique, the end of philosophy and the task of thinking, and so forth) that will keep obsessing Heidegger in his later work.

Even if the provisional definition of *Vollendung* goes some way toward clarifying the situation of politics and philosophy, it does not thereby let either of them leave the metaphysical sphere of influence. The existential meaning of existence must wait on the sidelines there where metaphysical ideals have receded and left behind their opaque imprint: nihilism. In the background of existence after the completion of philosophy and politics, there is "the bad infinity . . . of Hegel," "the being of the dangerless calm that sublates everything in itself—where everything and nothing occurs" (§173; *HPR* 163). That is to say: at the close of metaphysics, everything is philosophy and nothing is philosophy; everything is political and nothing is political. In their ceaseless end, philosophy and politics are boundless, shorn of fixed boundaries, the *peras* that used to define what they were and set them over and against their "other." Where nothing is actual, unlimited possibility gains an upper hand. The outcome is the "general confusion of the spiritlessness of the last generation" (§21; *HPR* 106) and the distended "scope of dialectic: Back and forth—going—| Dissolution—confusion" (§92; *HPR* 136).

It is to the dissolution of political and philosophical baselines (in a word: the loss of right), which he perceives all around him, that Heidegger juxtaposes National Socialism, which he romantically conceives in terms of "the *original—letting emerge* and thus a properly *grounding originality*—a *sound* [gediegene] originality—one that *does not just dissipate*" (§261; *HPR* 195). The nondissipation of the original is far from the grandiose delusion of the eternal, transhistorical Nazi polity Faye ascribes to Heidegger.[6] To the extent that the seminar notes still roam some paths of the "Rectorship Address," they indicate that the completion of philosophy and politics spawns a kind of matter without its proper forms. Rather than trying to figure out a new set of forms—let alone the ideal form—for thinking or for action, Heidegger wants to capture the emergent being-historical form of his time, hylomorphically (phenomenologically) proceeding from the political matters themselves.[7] But, if that is so, then he *must* part ways with Hegel's dialectics, where all a philosopher can hope to do is grasp, wistfully and retrospectively, those forms that have passed away or are about to pass away. The Owl of Minerva is a symbol of cautious, albeit powerless, wisdom. Its cautiousness was sadly sparse in Heidegger's thought in the 1930s, probably due to his craving for ontological power.

More audaciously than capturing what is emerging, Heidegger wishes to bring into full view the quasitranscendental "letting emerge." He wants to recommit himself, along with the German University, the German people, and so forth, to the "grounding originality" that he seems to have discerned in the forming, not-yet-formed movement of National Socialism. In it, in this still vague historical form, he appears to have recognized some of his thoughts from the 1920s: Dasein as being-with, the question about the destiny of the people, historicity, and the destiny of Western metaphysics, or, better yet, the destiny of the West as metaphysics and its completion. National Socialism is, for him, not a stage in the overcoming of metaphysics but a field of power where a new possibility is nascent on the horizon of appearing, the power that has the wherewithal to resist the ongoing dissolution of *what is* in that which is limitlessly possible and, hence, impossible.

From Heidegger's standpoint in the 1930s, the political forms of democratic liberalism and socialism have been completed, in tandem with the history of metaphysics, whence they had emanated. As such, they are doomed to a pointless repetition, the back-and-forth of an exhausted dialectics (§198).[8] Contrary to this exhaustion, National Socialism is growing, forming, and, in Heidegger's view, it holds out the possibility of something new at the source of all possibilities: a "letting-emerge" that does not fit within the existing frames of being but, against the ontological horizon, delimits being in its own way. In his treatment of the "Rectorship Address," which he translated and retranslated in the 1970s, Gérard Granel reflected on Heidegger's impressions of this forming force and proposed that "what is at stake is not all of a sudden—and, in a sense, it is never at stake—to give shape to new possibilities; rather, it is a matter of recognizing what has sketched itself anew [or, "something of the new (*de nouveau*) that (again) has sketched itself"] in the possible."[9] Perhaps he was right.

This is one dimension of the problem. The other is that Heidegger actively foments the emergence of new forms, which is why he considers "exercises" and the "*preparation*—for thinking with—interests and actions" (§110; *HPR* 141) necessary. The "Rectorship Address" is unequivocal on the possibilities that could thrive at a reformed university, where science would be brought back to its existential roots, to "all the world-shaping forces of human historical existence."[10] In the seminar notes, which are, as Richard Polt observes, like the "Rectorship Address," concerned with the issue of "self-assertion,"[11] this proposal is plausible on the condition that it is implemented together with the people grounding the state. The existential foundation for "science" and for "the people" would thus replace the metaphysical bases for philosophy and politics after the exhaustion, or the completion, of both. But, without a preestablished right, coexistence is not the only articulation of philosophy and politics at the end of metaphysics. We must also look into the ontologico-didactic notion of "preparation," which is a crucial piece of Heidegger's controversial engagement with Hegel in this seminar.[12]

The existential grounding of the state and of science in the being of the people and in people's lives cannot count on the epistemologico-metaphysical foundations that have been paramount from Plato to Hegel.

Shorn of ready-made supports, the refounding of the university and of the state has an air of an existential revolution, the revolution in and of the singular. Nonetheless, Heidegger suggests to go further: his utopian desire is to "prepare" the situation for this singular and largely unpredictable event, to think ahead (rather than back, as Hegel does) toward it, to affirm (*behaupten*) a mode of thinking, a state, and an era, where and when the modern concepts of knowledge and of private, social, or political existence would surrender their aura of self-evidence and would finally show themselves as what they are, namely, exhausted. This preparatory work is as much philosophical as it is political; it endows both philosophy and politics with their postmetaphysical right. But Heidegger made unpardonable political mistakes when he dared to assert *his independence* from Hegel and to regain the future from the twilight of dialectical past. In addition to seeking the "letting-emerge" of existential possibilities, much of Heidegger's writings from the mid-1930 (and, in particular, from *Beiträge* onward) was a series of exercises and preparations for the active "making-come" of the event, initially misrecognized as National Socialism.

A pure self-assertion, absolutely indifferent to the negation of otherness, is unthinkable within the dialectical scheme. But, if Heidegger admits that self-assertion is unreachable *via* the negation of negation, this does not mean that it requires a pure affirmation, which might explain to some extent his "destructive" readings of Nietzsche in the same period. Although negativity retains its weight, it cannot be of a dialectical kind. Hegel's dialectics, moreover, remains a philosophy of re-active right, and no dialectics of negation and affirmation is in a position to retrieve the meaning of self-affirmation, as far as Heidegger is concerned.

Already in 1923, in the lectures published under the title *Ontology: The Hermeneutics of Facticity*, he contends that "all dialectics lives from the table of others. The shining example: Hegel's logic." "Dialectics," Heidegger continues, "lacks radicality, i.e, is fundamentally unphilosophical, on two sides. It must live from hand in the mouth and develops an impressive eloquence in dealing with this readymade material. If it gains acceptance, the burgeoning Hegelese will once again undermine even the possibility of having a mere sensitivity to philosophy."[13] That self-assertion does not live "from the table of others" is not a hallmark of hubris, but the opposite—the humility of existence grounded on itself alone and, therefore, radically ungrounded, abyssal. The self-assertion of philosophy and politics (institutionally: of the university and the state) at the "end" of metaphysics channels, according to Heidegger, the revolutionary emancipation of existence without right from the misnomers for being that have for too long manipulated it from above or behind the scenes of this world. Does his misidentification of a dreadful historical event as this revolution rule out the possibility of a new beginning in the ceaseless completion, or the endless end, of metaphysical philosophy and politics?

We could say: Heidegger saw in the emergence of National Socialism and in its search for a form of life the hatching of another beginning. That was his biggest *historico-political* blunder. To be more exact, he thought, close to the political foundations of fundamental ontology, that National Socialism represented a qualitative transformation in the essence of power, heralding a transformation in the power and meaning of being. In the notes on Hegel's *Philosophy of Right*, the concept mediating between power and being (conjoined in Schmitt without any mediations) is "work," which works on possibility at the expense of actuality from "the essential will *as* work—*as historical Dasein*" in the seminar's paragraph 13 (*HPR* 104) to governmental power as "*a conducting and keeping-at-work* of the willed decisions of the humans" in paragraph 253 (*HPR* 192). An actual reorientation of power and work toward the possible—that is, toward the fundamental ontology of Dasein, in keeping with the priority of phenomenological possibility over actuality—was Heidegger's *philosophical* blunder.

Heidegger treaded dangerously in believing that a transformation in the essence of being could be effectively instituted by way of rethinking and reorganizing power and work. Already his endorsement of an effective institution and accomplishment of finite being contradicts that which is to be instituted *qua* possible, in excess of its actual instantiation. Worse still, the interpretation of nonmetaphysical being as power, in the hopes of changing political ontotheology, usurps the concept of right in favor of the historical powers that exist (literally, the power that *be*) or are emerging at the time: the *Führer* and the *Volk*. In National Socialism, the meaning of being as power results in a completion that is more totalizing and suffocating than any previous completion of metaphysics. Prepared for its institution, the "other" beginning turns out to be not at all other, but a despicably overwrought version of the same.

POWERLESSNESS

What are the alternatives? Heidegger's mistake does not by any means imply that his diagnosis of the metaphysical impasse, his dissatisfaction with the tired political options of liberal democracy and socialism (nowadays delegated to technocracy and neofascism), or even his critique of the futureless course of Hegel's dialectics is incorrect and deserves to be brushed off without giving it a second thought. A drastically different path opens in Maurice Blanchot's *déclaration d'impuissance*, declining the invitation to think whatever remains of being at the end of metaphysics under the sign of power. If this declaration were made in all seriousness, then, for the first time, philosophy and politics would join in a constellation with powerlessness and a positive absence of right. This is also something Derrida has alluded to in the introductory remarks inaugurating the collection *Who's Afraid of Philosophy? Right to Philosophy I.*[14]

But is dialectics really powerless to teach us about the meaning of powerlessness, which is the core (and power) of finite existence? Isn't its dependence on the other, its "living from the table of others," a good counterweight to the surfeits of self-assertion that run the risk of converting being into power? Doesn't dialectics sketch out, if negatively, the power of powerlessness (the fortitude required for living and thinking without a foreordained right) and the powerlessness of power (the incapacity of the mightiest of all powers to perform the only truly significant act and give itself up)? Heidegger himself would keep this luxury back from dialectics, if we are to judge by the text published on September 21, 1969, in the *Neue Zürcher Zeitung*, where he is adamant that "dialectics is the dictatorship of questionlessness" (*GA* 13:212).

The protocols and "Mitschriften," appended to the seminar notes on Hegel's *Philosophy of Right* in the text's German edition, see Heidegger turn to Plato in an effort to understand the workings of dialectics. According to Hallwachs's notes, Heidegger would have understood that Plato's dialectics differs from Parmenides's through the claim that *non*being is. For instance, when we see a piece of wood (*Stock*) reflected in water as broken in two, the broken piece is still something even if it is also a nothing (*GA* 86:553). What shows itself is something, even if it is not what is being shown; for Plato, even nonbeing is being and, moreover, the concept of being comprehends nonbeing. If "right" is a political variation on metaphysical ontology, then living and thinking without right, in the state of un-right, we are, already or still, under the clout of what has been negated (the broken reflection, so to speak, of right). Inasmuch as it declares anything whatsoever, phenomenologically bringing powerlessness into view and putting it into words, Blanchot's declaration of *impuissance* negates the very thing it declares. Conversely, "our" incomplete dialectics, unfolding within "our" hermeneutical situation, vacillates between philosophy and politics without right, on the one hand, and an endless negotiation of the right to philosophy and to politics, on the other: between finite possibility undocked from the transcendental domain and an indefinite possibility unburdened by any content whatsoever.

While Socratic dialectics, as Heidegger construes it, is peirastic in its questioning search for truth (despite the Platonic reification of being that encompasses its other, nonbeing), Hegel's dialectics does not invent a method for seeking the truth of being but identifies the truth of being itself as a method. Within the same metaphysical tradition, two versions of the infinite present themselves as two dialectical philosophies that open and close this tradition. The Greek ongoing, nonactualizable search, where the thinker's nonarrival at truth is the power of powerlessness that stimulates further philosophical quests, is nowhere to be found in Hegel's system, where thought is infinite because it sublates and incorporates everything into itself, even as it impregnates everything. Or, as Heidegger puts it in the seminar notes: "*Dialectical method—as philosophical—absolute—in-finite thinking*" (§184; *HPR* 166). Hegel's thought operates within the exploded limits of completed incompleteness: everything (including itself, its other, and the way out) is included in it. And so, it, itself, is a spectacular example of the powerlessness of absolute power, the incapacity of this power to abdicate its absolute privilege absolutely, without a hope of recovering itself upon another self-negation.

Heidegger thinks not just in the 1930s but also well into the postwar period that the Hegelian dialectics is, more than a theoretical possibility, the actual state of affairs. Combating Schmitt's view, in the seminar on *Philosophy of Right* he quips "'Hegel died'—no! he had not yet 'lived'!" (§57; *HPR* 119). Years later, in the 1957 seminar on *The Fundamental Principles of Thinking* (*Grundsätze des Denkens*), Hegelian dialectics is declared "the actuality of the world," *Weltwirklichkeit*. Heidegger writes: "Dialectics is today, perhaps, the actuality of the world. Hegel's 'dialectics' is one of the thoughts that has been widely considered to 'guide the world,' and it remains equally powerful there where dialectical materialism—in a slightly different style of thought—is believed to have refuted it."[15] As such, dialectics marshals its absolute right over *what is*, trumping a wide array of other phenomenological possibilities. It does not engender the fruitlessness of a method for thinking the reality of the world, but the reality of the world as fruitless, hollowed out, virtual, abstract. Bracketing the Cold War that is lurking behind Heidegger's assertion, the evidence for the dialectical "completion" of metaphysics is neither ideal nor real but phenomenological. The reality of appearing, in Hegel, is the actualization of the rational, or, as Heidegger writes in §193: "*Rational*—the *appearing unconditioned universal, speculatively thought—absolute spirit*—will" (*HPR* 169). The common end of philosophy and politics becomes apparent in a singular phenomenalization of *logos* that shows itself from itself in a total and totalizing nightmare, without regard to the phenomena themselves.

In the 1957 seminar, Heidegger characterized dialectics as "a uniform thought that has achieved world-historical domination [*Herrschaft*]."[16] He will endorse this view in his discussions on "the essence of technique"[17] and his thoughts on the planetary as "unconditional anthropomorphy."[18] It is, then, the sovereignty, mastery, or dominance (*Herrschaft*) of thought and action (in a word, everything designated by the old concept of "right") that is at issue in the ends of philosophy and of politics, more labyrinthine than ever before and less prone to being overcome. Another set of commentaries would need to be written on Heidegger's concept of *Herrschaft* in the 1934–35 seminar on Hegel and in other writings from this and later periods. We limit ourselves to reading a fragment of paragraph 250 that locates the meaning of power "in *ideality* as mastery [*Herrschaft*] over every finitude" (*HPR* 192). In retrospect, it is obvious that the darkest excesses of metaphysics tend to be repeated and magnified in every attempt to master and idealize finitude, putting it at power's disposal. Do living and thinking "without right" provide a sufficient insurance against this possible repetition, drifting toward the impossible? Our wager in this chapter has been on the incomplete dialectics of the *without* and an enduring search it instigates for the right to philosophy and to politics *with* others. Whether or not it could work, only being as time would tell.

Notes

INTRODUCTION

1. Michael Marder, "A Fight for the Right to Read Heidegger," *New York Times* ("The Stone" column), July 20, 2014, https://opinionator.blogs.nytimes.com/2014/07/20/a-fight-for-the-right-to-read-heidegger/.

2. Some of the volumes have already been translated into English, e.g., Martin Heidegger, *Ponderings II–VI, Black Notebooks, 1931–1938*, trans. Richard Rojcewicz (Bloomington: Indiana University Press, 2016).

3. Victor Farias, *Heidegger and Nazism*, ed. Joseph Margolis and Tom Rockmore (1987; Philadelphia: Temple University Press, 1989).

4. *The Heidegger Controversy: A Critical Reader*, ed. Richard Wolin (Cambridge: MIT Press, 1992).

5. See Jacques Derrida, Didier Eribon, and Richard Wolin, "'L'affaire Derrida': Another Exchange," *New York Review of Books*, March 25, 1993, http://www.nybooks.com/articles/1993/03/25/laffaire-derrida-another-exchange/.

6. Emmanuel Faye, *Heidegger: The Introduction of Nazism into Philosophy*, trans. Michael B. Smith (2005; New Haven: Yale University Press, 2009).

7. Martin Heidegger, *Gesamtausgabe*, 102 vols. to date (Frankfurt am Main: Vittorio Klostermann, 1976–), 95:97. Hereafter cited as *GA* with volume number followed by a colon and page number.

1. "HIGHER THAN ACTUALITY"

1. Martin Heidegger, *Sein und Zeit* (1927; Tübingen: Max Niemeyer Verlag, 1993), 38; *Being and Time*, trans. John Macquarrie and Edward Robinson (San Francisco: Harper Collins, 1962), 62–63. Hereafter cited as *SZ* using the pagination of the original German work.

2. See *SZ* 255, 262, 265.

3. Samuel Beckett, *Three Novels: Molloy, Malone Dies, The Unnamable* (New York: Grove Press, 1958), 414.

4. Jacques Derrida, *The Politics of Friendship*, trans. George Collins (London: Verso, 1997), 29.

5. Jacques Derrida, *Given Time: I. Counterfeit Money*, trans. Peggy Kamuf (Chicago: University of Chicago Press, 1992), 14.

6. Jacques Derrida, *Rogues: Two Essays on Reason*, trans. Michael Naas and Pascale-Anne Brault (Stanford: Stanford University Press, 2005), 33.

7. Martin Heidegger, *Introduction to Metaphysics*, trans. Gregory Fried and Richard Polt (New Haven: Yale University Press, 2000), 27.

8. Martin Heidegger, *History of the Concept of Time: Prolegomena*, trans. Theodore Kisiel (Bloomington: Indiana University Press, 1985), 70. Hereafter cited as *HCT*.

9. In *Of Spirit*, Derrida contends that "*the experience of the question*, the possibility of the *Fragen*," stands "at the beginning of the existential analytic." Derrida, *Of Spirit*, trans. Geoffrey Bennington and Rachel Bowlby (Chicago: University of Chicago Press, 1989), 17.

10. Jean-François Courtine, "Phénoménologie et/ou tautologie," in *Heidegger et la phénoménologie* (Paris: Vrin, 1990), 390.

11. Robert Bernasconi's comprehensive essay "Repetition and Tradition" treats this very topic in the aftermath of destructuring. My focus here is the knot in which repetition and tradition are tied to possibility. Bernasconi, "Repetition and Tradition: Heidegger's Destructuring of the Distinction between Essence and Existence in *Basic Problems of Phenomenology*," in *Reading Heidegger from the Start: Essays in His Earliest Thought*, ed. Theodore Kisiel and John van Buren (Albany: SUNY Press, 1994), 123–36.

12. Miguel de Beistegui, *Thinking with Heidegger: Displacements* (Bloomington: Indiana University Press, 2003), 58.

13. "Hearing constitutes the primary and authentic way in which Dasein is open for its ownmost potentiality-for-being" (*SZ* 163).

14. Paragraph 10 of *History of the Concept of Time*, titled "Elaboration of the thematic field," is followed immediately by a paragraph that bears the title "Immanent critique of phenomenological research."

15. It seems to me that Heidegger agrees with Kant on the need to place "reason" within certain limits. Neither thinks that these limits are to be deduced from tradition, but while the latter stipulates that they are internal to reason itself, the former insists on the limits that coincide with the matters themselves as the guides of *logos*.

16. Emmanuel Levinas, *Otherwise than Being, or Beyond Essence*, trans. Alphonso Lingis (Pittsburgh: Duquesne University Press, 1998), 151. In Levinas's terms, dethematization unsays the said to "reduce" it to the saying it harbors.

17. Recall that, before Kant removed them from his table, Aristotle had included time and space in his list of the categories.

18. Michael Marder, *Energy Dreams: Of Actuality* (New York: Columbia University Press, 2017).

19. This will be crucial to Heidegger's treatment of the question of being. Since the being of an entity is not another entity (another being), one cannot approach thematically, without instantaneously losing from sight, that which is approached in this way.

20. Jean-Luc Marion, *Reduction and Givenness: Investigations of Husserl, Heidegger, and Phenomenology*, trans. Thomas A. Carlson (Evanston: Northwestern University Press, 1998), 76.

21. Martin Heidegger, *Basic Writings*, ed. David Farrell Krell (San Francisco: HarperCollins, 1993), 217.

22. Heidegger, *Basic Writings*, 217.

23. I am bracketing the issues related to the priority of existence over essence in Heidegger. On the conjunction of action, accomplishment, and the "'fundamental' possibility" of being, see Jean-Luc Nancy, "Originary Ethics," in *A Finite Thinking*, ed. Simon Sparks (Stanford: Stanford University Press, 2003), 177.

24. Paul de Man, *The Resistance to Theory* (Minneapolis: University of Minnesota Press, 1986), 80.

2. FAILURE AND NONACTUALIZABLE POSSIBILITY

1. "fail *v.* Probably before 1200 *failen* [meant] cease to exist or function, come to an end, be unsuccessful, in *Ancrene Riwle*; borrowed from Old French *faillir* be lacking, miss, not succeed, from Vulgar Latin *fallire*, corresponding to Latin *fallere* deceive, be lacking, or defective." Robert Barnhart, "Fail," in *The Barnhart Dictionary of Etymology* (Chicago: H.W. Wilson, 1988), 365.

2. Philippe Lacoue-Labarthe, *Heidegger, Art and Politics: The Fiction of the Political*, trans. Chris Turner (Oxford: Basil Blackwell, 1990), 31. Translation modified.

3. Dominique Janicaud, *The Shadow of That Thought: Heidegger and the Question of Politics*, trans. Michael Gendre (Evanston: Northwestern University Press, 1996), 87–88.

4. David Farrell Krell, *Daimon Life: Heidegger and Life-Philosophy* (Bloomington: Indiana University Press, 1992), 138.

5. Krell, *Daimon Life,* 140.

6. The existential background of failure needs to be conceptually uncoupled from the plenitude resulting from the correction of failure in time understood as the succession of "now-times." In this vulgar temporal scheme, failure may be rectified in the present, the way that a lacuna is filled: "what has failed or eluded us '*on that former occasion*' is something that we must '*now*' make up for" (*SZ* 406). What is at stake in this uncoupling is nothing less than the possibility or the impossibility of "redemption."

7. Heidegger, *Ponderings II–VI,* 35.

8. Regarding this upset, see also: "If a lack, such as failure to fulfill some requirement, has been 'caused' in a manner characteristic of Dasein, we cannot simply reckon back to there being something lacking in the 'cause'" (*SZ* 283–84).

9. Marion, *Reduction and Givenness,* 188.

10. Derrida, *Of Spirit,* 44.

11. Derrida, *Of Spirit,* 10. Although *handliche Regel* is still close or ready-to-hand, it diverges from a kind of *Handwerk* or "manual" crafting of law which Heidegger might have approved. Cf. Jacques Derrida, "*Geschlecht* II: Heidegger's Hand," trans. John P. Leavy Jr., in *Deconstruction and Philosophy: The Texts of Jacques Derrida,* ed. John Sallis (Chicago: University of Chicago Press, 1987), 161–96.

12. Bernard Stiegler, *Technics and Time, I: The Fault of Epimetheus,* trans. Richard Beardsworth and George Collins (Stanford: Stanford University Press, 1998), 88.

13. See also chapter 1 of the present study and *HCT,* esp. 135–38.

3. THE PHENOMENOLOGY OF ONTICO-ONTOLOGICAL DIFFERENCE

1. Martin Heidegger, *The Basic Problems of Phenomenology,* trans. Albert Hofstadter, rev. ed. (1927; Bloomington: Indiana University Press, 1982), 328. Hereafter cited as *BPP.*

2. Martin Heidegger, "Hegel's Concept of Experience," in *Off the Beaten Track,* trans. and ed. Julian Young and Kenneth Heynes (Cambridge: Cambridge University Press, 2002), 107. Hereafter cited as "HCE."

3. Qtd. in Thomas Sheehan, "General Introduction: Husserl and Heidegger: The Making and Unmaking of a Relationship," in *Psychological and Transcendental Phenomenology and the Confrontation with Heidegger (1927–1931),* trans. and ed. Thomas Sheehan and Richard E. Palmer (Dordrecht: Kluwer, 1997), 17.

4. Martin Heidegger, *Ontology: The Hermeneutics of Facticity,* trans. John van Buren (Bloomington: Indiana University Press, 1999), 33.

5. Martin Heidegger, *Hegel's Phenomenology of Spirit*, trans. Parvis Emad and Kenneth Maly (Bloomington: Indiana University Press, 1988), 28/40 (page numbers following the slash are from the German edition). Hereafter cited as *HPS*.

6. Edmund Husserl, *Psychological and Transcendental Phenomenology and the Confrontation with Heidegger (1927–1931)*, trans. and ed. Thomas Sheehan and Richard E. Palmer (Dordrecht: Kluwer, 1997), 421.

7. This assumption was not in the background of Heidegger's thought ten years before the course on Hegel, in the already cited 1923 seminar *Ontology*. There, Heidegger took the side of Husserl's phenomenology, accusing dialectics of a reactive work on ready-made materials and hence of a reliance—uncharacteristic of the absolute—on the ontic world (36).

8. Martin Heidegger, "Letter to Karl Jaspers, Freiburg, June 27, 1922," in *The Heidegger–Jaspers Correspondence (1920–1963)*, ed. Walter Biemel and Hans Saner (New York: Humanity Books, 2003), 34.

9. Heidegger, "Letter to Karl Jaspers," 34.

10. See chapter 1 of the present study on the dynamics of this repetition.

11. Dominique Janicaud, "Heidegger-Hegel: An Impossible 'Dialogue'?" in *Endings: Questions of Memory in Hegel and Heidegger*, ed. Rebecca Comay and John McCumber (Evanston: Northwestern University Press), 41.

12. Emmanuel Levinas launches a parallel critique of Husserl, writing that "it is a question of descending from the entity illuminated in self-evidence toward the subject that is extinguished rather than announced in it." *Discovering Existence with Husserl*, trans. R. Cohen and M. B. Smith (Evanston: Northwestern University Press, 1998), 156.

13. On "being called by Being," see Heidegger, *Basic Writings*, 245. On "what is called thinking—and what does call for it?" see Martin Heidegger, *What Is Called Thinking?* trans. J. Glenn Gray and Fred D. Wieck (New York: Harper & Row, 1968), 21.

14. Edmund Husserl, *Experience and Judgment: Investigations in a Genealogy of Logic*, trans. James S. Churchill and Karl Ameriks (Evanston: Northwestern University Press, 1973), 64.

15. "*The pure concept annuls time.* Hegelian philosophy expresses this disappearance of time by conceiving philosophy as *the* science or as absolute knowledge" (*HPS* 12).

16. "We do not learn anything about visual and auditory sensations, about the data of smell and touch (the very least that today's phenomenologies would demand)" (*HPS* 54).

17. Cf. paragraph 85 of Edmund Husserl, *Ideas Pertaining to a Pure Phenomenology and to a Phenomenological Philosophy*, First Book, trans. F. Kersten (Dordrecht:

Kluwer, 1983), as well as Michel Henry, *Material Phenomenology*, trans. Scott Davidson (New York: Fordham University Press, 2008), 7.

18. In addition to the two treated here, consult texts on negativity from 1938–39 and 1941–42 gathered in volume 68 of *GA*, selections from *Being and Truth*, courses on Hegel's *Logic* and on logic in Aristotle and Hegel in volume 21 of *GA*, as well as the recently published engagement with Hegel's *Philosophy of Right* in volume 86 of *GA*.

19. Heidegger, *Ontology*, 37.

4. TO OPEN A SITE

1. Martin Heidegger, *Hölderlin's Hymn "The Ister,"* trans. William McNeill and Julia Davis (Bloomington: Indiana University Press, 1996), 85. Hereafter cited as *HHI*.

2. Martin Heidegger, *Parmenides*, trans. André Schuwer and Richard Rojcewicz (Bloomington: Indiana University Press, 1998), 89. Hereafter cited as *P*.

3. I have written on political geometry as it bears on the exception in the thought of Carl Schmitt in *Groundless Existence: The Political Ontology of Carl Schmitt* (London: Continuum, 2010).

4. "*Das Unheimliche*, however, the uncanny, is not meant to be understood in terms of an impression but to be conceived in terms of *das Un-heimische*, the unhomely, namely, that unhomely that is the fundamental trait of human abode in the midst of beings" (*HHI* 90–91).

5. Martin Heidegger, *Poetry, Language, Thought*, trans. Albert Hofstadter (New York: HarperCollins, 2001), 218. Hereafter cited as *PLT*.

6. Martin Heidegger, *Introduction to Metaphysics*, trans. Gregory Fried and Richard Polt (New Haven: Yale University Press, 2000), 162. Hereafter cited as *IM*.

7. Martin Heidegger, *On Hegel's "Philosophy of Right": The 1934–5 Seminar and Interpretative Essays*, ed. Peter Trawny, Marcia Sá-Cavalcante Schuback, and Michael Marder (London: Bloomsbury, 2014), 156.

8. Martin Heidegger, *Basic Writings*, ed. David Farrell Krell (San Francisco: HarperCollins, 1993), 256. Hereafter cited as *BW*.

9. Martin Heidegger, *Four Seminars*, trans. Andrew Mitchell and François Raffoul (Bloomington: Indiana University Press, 2012), 39. Hereafter cited as *FS*.

10. Martin Heidegger, *Basic Concepts of Aristotelian Philosophy*, trans. Robert D. Metcalf and Mark B. Tanzer (Bloomington: Indiana University Press, 2009), 48.

11. Heidegger, *Basic Concepts of Aristotelian Philosophy*, 73.

12. Heidegger, *Basic Concepts of Aristotelian Philosophy*, 73.

13. Heidegger, *Introduction to Philosophy—Thinking and Poetizing*, trans. Phillip Jacques Braunstein (Bloomington: Indiana University Press, 2011), 24.

14. Heidegger, *Introduction to Philosophy—Thinking and Poetizing*, 3.

15. Probably, the first sense of economy is the one Reiner Schürmann intends in coining the term "economy of presence" to translate "Heidegger's noun *Anwesenheit.*" *Heidegger: On Being and Acting: From Principles to Anarchy*, trans. Christine-Marie Gros (Bloomington: Indiana University Press, 1990), 298ff.

16. Martin Heidegger, *Nietzsche*, vol. 4, ed. David Farrell Krell (San Francisco: HarperCollins, 1987), 177.

17. Heidegger, *Nietzsche*, 4:177.

18. "[T]he Between is Being itself" (*GA* 96:83).

19. Martin Heidegger, *On the Way to Language*, trans. Peter D. Hertz (San Francisco: HarperCollins, 1971), 140.

20. Heidegger, *On the Way to Language*, 88.

21. Martin Heidegger, *Basic Concepts*, trans. Gary E. Aylesworth (Bloomington: Indiana University Press, 1993), 35.

22. Heidegger, *Basic Concepts*, 4.

23. For more on this role of things in Heidegger, consult Andrew Mitchell's excellent study *The Fourfold: Reading the Late Heidegger* (Evanston: Northwestern University Press, 2015), esp. chapter 1, "The Technological Challenge to Things."

5. DEVASTATION

1. Martin Heidegger, *Country Path Conversations*, trans. Bret W. Davis (Bloomington: Indiana University Press, 2010), 138/213 (page numbers following the slash are from the German edition); hereafter cited as *CPC*. In *The Event* (trans. Richard Rojcewicz [Bloomington: Indiana University Press, 2013]), too, Heidegger interprets devastation as "the abandonment of beings by being [*Seinsverlassenheit des Seienden*]," 85/101 (page numbers following the slash are from the German edition); hereafter cited as *TE*.

2. Heidegger, *What Is Called Thinking?* 29–30/11.

3. Friedrich Nietzsche, "Thus Spoke Zarathustra," in *The Portable Nietzsche*, ed. Walter Kaufmann (London: Penguin, 1982), 417, translation modified.

4. "The complex of melancholia behaves like an open wound, drawing to itself cathectic energies—which in the transference neuroses we have called 'anticathexes'—from all directions, and emptying the ego until it is totally impoverished." Sigmund Freud, "Mourning and Melancholia." *The Standard Edition of*

the Complete Psychological Works of Sigmund Freud, Volume XIV (1914–1916): On the History of the Psycho-Analytic Movement, Papers on Metapsychology and Other Works, trans. and ed. James Strachey (London: Vintage, 2001), 253.

5. Gershom Scholem, *Major Trends in Jewish Mysticism* (New York: Schocken Books, 1974), 237–38.

6. AN ECOLOGY OF PROPERTY

1. Vladimir Bibikhin, *Собственность: философия* своего [Property: The philosophy of *what is one's own*] (St. Petersburg: Nauka, 2012), 334. All translations of Bibikhin's texts from the original Russian are mine.

2. Bibikhin, *Собственность,* 334.

3. Bibikhin, *Собственность,* 22–23.

4. Vladimir Bibikhin, *Другое начало* [The other beginning] (St. Petersburg: Nauka, 2003), 372.

5. Bibikhin, *Собственность,* 27.

6. Bibikhin, *Собственность,* 373.

7. Bibikhin, *Собственность,* 374.

8. Bibikhin, *Собственность,* 101.

9. Bibikhin, *Собственность,* 97.

10. Bibikhin, *Собственность,* 98.

11. Bibikhin, *Собственность,* 44.

12. Bibikhin, *Собственность,* 46.

13. Vladimir Bibikhin, *Лес* (*hylé*) [The forest] (St. Petersburg: Nauka, 2011), 58.

14. Bibikhin, *Собственность,* 240.

15. Martin Heidegger, *Contributions to Philosophy (From Enowning),* trans. Parvis Emad and Kenneth Maly (Bloomington: Indiana University Press, 1999), 10.

16. Bibikhin, *Другое начало,* 372.

17. Heidegger, *Contributions to Philosophy,* 45.

18. Bibikhin, *Собственность,* 138.

19. Bibikhin, *Собственность,* 148.

20. Vladimir Bibikhin, "Дело Хайдеггера" [The Heidegger affair], introduction to the Russian translation of *Time and Being* (Moscow: Respublica Publishing, 2003), 10.

21. Bibikhin, "Дело Хайдеггера," 12.

22. Vladimir Bibikhin, *Язык философии* [The language of philosophy] (Moscow: Yazyki Slavyanskoy Kul'tury, 2002), 7.

23. Bibikhin, *Другое начало*, 374.

24. Bibikhin, "Дело Хайдеггера," 12.

25. Bibikhin, *Собственность*, 149.

26. Martin Heidegger, "Poverty," trans. Thomas Kalary and Frank Schalow, in *Heidegger, Translation and the Task of Thinking: Essays in Honor of Parvis Emad* (Dordrecht: Springer, 2011), 4–5.

27. Heidegger, "Poverty," 6, translation modified.

28. Bibikhin, *Собственность*, 39.

29. Bibikhin, *Собственность*, 59.

7. THE QUESTION OF POLITICAL EXISTENCE

1. All references to this seminar are made parenthetically in the text. Martin Heidegger, *Seminare: Hegel—Schelling, GA* 86, ed. Peter Trawny (2011).

2. These conceptions are criticized in Carl Schmitt, *The Leviathan in the State Theory of Thomas Hobbes: Meaning and Failure of a Political Symbol*, trans. George Schwab and Erna Hilfstein (1938; Chicago: University of Chicago Press, 2008), 18ff.

3. Carl Schmitt, *Glossarium: Aufzeichnungen der Jahre 1947–1951*, ed. E. Freiherr von Medem (Berlin: Duncker & Humblot, 1991), 109–10, 263.

4. Carl Schmitt, *Constitutional Theory*, trans. J. Seitzer (1928; Durham: Duke University Press, 2008), 60–61.

5. This is the main line of argument in my *Groundless Existence: The Political Ontology of Carl Schmitt* (New York: Continuum, 2010).

6. Carl Schmitt, *Political Theology: Four Chapters on the Concept of Sovereignty*, trans. George Schwab (1922; London: MIT Press, 1985).

7. G. W. F. Hegel, *Hegel's Philosophy of Right*, trans. T. M. Knox (Oxford: Oxford University Press, 1967), 163.

8. When Faye writes that Heidegger "abandons the properly Hegelian question of the reconciliation of the individual and the universal, retaining only the identification of the state with absolute power and the spirit of the people" (228), we cannot help but wonder whether the author of these lines is commenting on the same materials that are at our disposal. Certainly, "the reconciliation of the individual and the universal" is a part of the philosophical discourse, to which Heidegger does not subscribe, though he does reconcile the "self-willing of the individual" and "the will of the state," willing "the being [*Seins*] of the individual in the people" (§220). But what about his critique of the absolute, not to mention his insistence on the historicity and finitude of the people and of the state? Where is the (admittedly elusive) ontico-ontological difference in this "identification"? And

how is the existential conception of politics squared with trying to ensure "the very long-term durability of the Nazi state" (203)? Faye, *Heidegger: The Introduction of Nazism into Philosophy.*

9. Schmitt, *Glossarium,* 242.

8. THE OTHER "JEWISH QUESTION"

1. Peter Trawny, *Heidegger and the Myth of a Jewish World Conspiracy,* trans. Andrew Mitchell (Chicago: University of Chicago Press, 2015), 6.

2. See chapter 5 of the present study.

3. I am grateful to Richard Polt for his English translation of the key passages related to "the Jewish question" in *GA* 94–96.

4. Derrida, *Of Spirit,* 9–10.

5. Karl Marx, "On the Jewish Question," in *The Marx-Engels Reader,* ed. Robert Tucker (New York: Norton, 1978), 28.

6. Marx, "On the Jewish Question," 31–32.

7. Marx, "On the Jewish Question," 36.

8. Martin Heidegger, *Nature, History, State: 1933–34,* trans. and ed. Gregory Fried and Richard Polt (London: Bloomsbury, 2013), 56.

9. Heidegger, *Nature, History, State,* 55.

10. G. W. F. Hegel, *Hegel on Christianity: Early Theological Writings,* trans. T. M. Knox (New York: Harper Torchbook, 1961), 204–5, emphasis added.

11. Marx, "On the Jewish Question," 45.

12. Marder, "A Fight for the Right to Read Heidegger."

13. Marx, "On the Jewish Question," 46.

14. Marx, "On the Jewish Question," 45, translation lightly modified.

15. Marx, "On the Jewish Question," 46.

16. Marx, "On the Jewish Question," 46.

17. Marx, "On the Jewish Question," 30.

18. Jean-François Lyotard, *Heidegger and "the jews,"* trans. Andreas Michel and Mark Roberts (Minneapolis: University of Minnesota Press, 1990), 3.

19. Lyotard, *Heidegger and "the jews,"* 22.

9. PHILOSOPHY WITHOUT RIGHT?

1. As Andrew Mitchell observed, Heidegger's seminar notes "are a collection of half-phrases, terms and references, only occasionally rising to the form of complete sentences of paragraphs." Mitchell, "Translator's Preface," in Martin Heidegger, *On Hegel's "Philosophy of Right": The 1934–5 Seminar and*

Interpretative Essays, ed. Peter Trawny, Marcia Sá Cavalcante Schuback, and Michael Marder (London: Bloomsbury, 2014), 97. Hereafter cited as *HPR*.

2. See Michael Marder, "Given the Right—Of Giving (in Hegel's *Grundlinien der Philosophie des Rechts*)," *Epoché* 12, no. 1 (Fall 2007): 93–108.

3. On the most recent discussion of the question of silence in Heidegger, see Claudia Baracchi, "A Vibrant Silence: Heidegger and the End of Philosophy," in *Being Shaken: Ontology and the Event*, ed. Michael Marder and Santiago Zabala (Basingstock: Palgrave Macmillan, 2014), 92–121.

4. Jacques Derrida, "Heidegger's Silence," in *Martin Heidegger and National Socialism: Questions and Answers*, ed. Günter Neske and Emil Kettering (New York: Paragon House, 1990), 146.

5. Cf. §84: Dialectical Thinking—Conceives and Is Being Itself. In its completion in itself the development of the content—soul of the same; §85: Dialectic as (Absolute) System, the in-finite Logos; §86: Scope of the Dialectic, Back and forth—going—| Dissolution—confusion; §92: In-finite 1.) the end-less: a) End | simple cessation not πέρας b) -less—the perpetual etc. outside-each-other [*auseinander*]; §93: Something is only then speculatively-dialectically thought—i.e. as "'self' knowing appearing in itself"—this being known [*Gewußtsein*] is the authentic being [*Sein*]—it is the concept—idea—of absolute "idealism"; §95: "Dialectic"—method, not finite—rather in|finite—(closed on itself—turning-back); §146: Its in-finitude; dialectical return into itself—Negation of negation; §169: Dialectical method—as philosophical—absolute—in-finite thinking.

6. Faye, *Heidegger: The Introduction of Nazism into Philosophy*, 203.

7. Martin Heidegger, *Réponses et questions sur l'histoire et la politique: Martin Heidegger interrogé par "Der Spiegel"* (Paris: Mercure de France, 1977), 10–11.

8. The paragraph reads: "Hegel—Philosophy—Completion of the West—back and forth in our age. (The twaddle about the 19th century and liberalism. For twenty years the same phrases)."

9. "Il ne s'agit pas là tout de suite—et en un sens il ne s'agit jamais encore—de donner figure à de nouveaux possibles, mais de reconnaître ce qui s'est dessiné de nouveau dans le possible." Gérard Granel, *"Un singulier phènomène de mirement" in L'époque dénouée* (Paris: Hermann, 2012), 166. Our translation.

10. Martin Heidegger, "The Self-Assertion of the German University," in *The Heidegger Controversy: A Critical Reader*, ed. Richard Wolin (Cambridge: MIT Press, 1992), 33, translation modified.

11. Richard Polt, "Self-Assertion as Founding" (*HPR* 67–81).

12. See Peter Trawny, *Heidegger und das Politische: Zum "Rechtphilosophie-Seminar" in Heidegger Studien* (Berlin: Duncker & Humblot, 2012).

13. Heidegger, *Ontology*, 36.

14. Cf. Jacques Derrida, "Privilege: Justificatory Title and Introductory Remarks," in *Who's Afraid of Philosophy? Right to Philosophy I,* trans. Jan Plug (Stanford: Stanford University Press, 2002), 1–66.

15. "Dialektik ist heute eine, vielleicht sogar die Weltwirklichkeit. Hegels 'Dialektik' ist einer der Gedanken die—von weither angestimmt—'die Welt lenken,' gleichmächtig dort, wo der dialektischen Materialismus geglaubt, wie dort, wo er—nur einem leicht abgewandelten Stil derselben Denkens—wiederlegt wird" (*GA* 11:133–34).

16. "Dialektik . . . ein gleichförmige Denken zur Weltgeschichtlichen Herrschaft gelangen" (*GA* 11:139).

17. See also Heidegger's statement: "Die Methode des dialektischen Vermittelns schleicht sich an den Phänomen vorbei (z. B am Wesen der modernen Technik)" (*GA* 13:212).

18. Martin Heidegger, *Nietzsche,* vol. 4, ed. David Farrell Krell (San Francisco: HarperCollins, 1987), 87.

Index

MICHAEL MARDER is Ikerbasque Research Professor of Philosophy at the University of the Basque Country (UPV/EHU), Vitoria-Gasteiz, Spain. He has written extensively on environmental philosophy, phenomenology, and political thought, and is author of *Grafts: Writings on Plants,* a Univocal book (Minnesota, 2016).

www.ingramcontent.com/pod-product-compliance
Lightning Source LLC
LaVergne TN
LVHW010732020926
846742LV00029B/65

www.ingramcontent.com/pod-product-compliance
Lightning Source LLC
LaVergne TN
LVHW010732020926
846742LV00029B/65